T0271653

THE
HAPPY
NOMAD

Praise for *The Happy Nomad*

'Charlotte Bradman's book about her journey through trauma and adversity to the peace and clarity of blue spaces, provides proof that water in the form of driving rain, wild river, icy lake, or turquoise ocean can build back a body, mend a tattered mind, heal a broken heart, and soothe a weary soul.'

— Dr Wallace J Nichols, marine biologist and author of *Blue Mind*

'Charlotte is a unique individual, but she is also every one of us, doing her best to navigate and understand life and all its trauma, working out where to allow it to take her. The only answer, of course, is to leap into the ocean, ride the waves and bask in the summer sun… The writing is visceral … and the subjects are difficult but Charlotte tackles them with clarity, humour and understanding and takes us past them and into a future of endless possibility and warmth. The conclusion? Get in the van and go go go!!!'

— Martin Dorey, author and travel writer

'Charlotte manages to capture the essence of van life beautifully, portraying the highs and lows of this unique way of life in a way that entices readers into wanting to learn more about alternative living. A truly wonderful read.'

— Sebastian Santabarbara, author of *Road Life* and *Van Life For Dummies*

CHARLOTTE BRADMAN

THE
HAPPY
NOMAD

HOW I LOST MY HOUSE
& FOUND *Freedom*
IN A CAMPERVAN

First published in Great Britain in 2024 by Yellow Kite
An imprint of Hodder & Stoughton
An Hachette UK company

1

A CIP catalogue record for this title is available from the British Library

Hardback ISBN 978 1 399 72055 7
ebook ISBN 978 1 399 72056 4

Typeset in Electra by Hewer Text UK Ltd, Edinburgh
Printed and bound in Great Britain by Clays Ltd, Elcograf S.p.A.

Hodder & Stoughton policy is to use papers that are natural, renewable
and recyclable products and made from wood grown in sustainable
forests. The logging and manufacturing processes are expected to
conform to the environmental regulations of the country of origin.

Yellow Kite
Hodder & Stoughton Ltd
Carmelite House
50 Victoria Embankment
London EC4Y 0DZ

www.yellowkitebooks.co.uk

Contents

Prologue

The rain beats a gentle lullaby on the campervan roof, pitter-pattering on the metal, scattering drops of silver sound in every direction, like I'm sleeping in the heart of a cloud. The soothing melody offers a tranquil path to follow whilst drifting softly to sleep. As I listen to the rain, eyes closed, half in a dream, feelings of safety and contentment rise through my body. I'm so grateful for my tiny, wheeled house.

The heady scent of sandalwood, tempered by the delicate floral of lavender, drifts up from my freshly washed cotton sleeping bag. Nestling deeper into bed, I press my nose against the fabric, inhaling the earthy scents. I'm parked on a quiet backstreet, directly under a street lamp, whose warm glow filters through the edges of the campervan curtains, softening the night-time darkness of my little home with its muted, golden light. Sleep never used to come as easily as it does now, and life was very different not so long ago . . .

Chapter One
The Letter

One of the most profound changes in my life was heralded by nothing more unremarkable than the barking of the dog as the postman neared the house and the subtle nausea that always rose in my stomach at the thought of what he might push through the letterbox that day. As a general rule, it was usually bills, warrants for my arrest or demands for unpaid store cards from when I was twenty years old and shopping sprees at Topshop were the solution to any problem.

A letter duly arrived. It wafted gently on warm currents of dog breath towards the well-worn welcome mat, settling there, face up, the bold red lettering of 'private and confidential' stark and loud on the white background of the envelope.

Picking it up, I tried to determine its contents based on how official the typeset looked and the quality of the envelope. On days when my anxiety was particularly prominent, the letter would have been ripped up and thrown away, denied the opportunity to divulge its frightening contents. It was an avoidance technique that didn't remotely work as the letters just kept on coming. Being now in my early thirties, I'd had enough counselling to understand the unproductive nature of burying my head in the sand (and hiding unopened bills in the bottom of the wheelie bin, under the bags of dog shit).

I sat down on my favourite and largest piece of furniture, a gloriously unique seventies floral settee. The autumnal colours of rich mustards and burnt oranges, combined with the heavily stylised bold print, were hugely offensive to some and adored by others (not many others, I might add). Gently tearing open the envelope, I pulled out the expertly folded, crisp white letter inside.

The letter was from a firm of solicitors instructed by the person I'd bought the house with when I was in my early twenties – an ex-partner who hadn't lived in the house for at least eight years. With the passive-aggressive professionalism synonymous with the legal system, the letter detailed that if I did not sell my home ('our' home, I should say, for legal accuracy), their client would begin court proceedings in order to force me to do so. Hysterical laughter rose up, spilling out of me, fuelled by shock and disbelief.

My ex-partner and I had been through some difficult times in the early days of our relationship. However, that was in the past, and at the time the letter from the solicitors arrived, we were on general speaking terms, enough to exchange pleasantries if we met in the street, which was why I was so surprised by the letter.

My ex-partner hadn't contributed to the mortgage for years. Nor, crucially, had he contributed to the cost and care of *his* dog, an addition to our family of two that I hadn't wanted at the time, but had somehow ended up with, along with the massive mortgage and decaying house. We're not talking about a lovely little teacup Yorkshire terrier here, whose worst behavioural issue would be to occasionally do tiny teacup wees on the floor out of excitement. No. This was a pure-bred American Akita that weighed more than me and had an endearing habit of actively attempting to kill almost all the other dogs she encountered and, indeed, some humans, without rhyme or reason. She was a lovely dog, honestly, once I'd built up enough muscle to handle her and developed eyes in the back of my head. For an animal bred to fight bears, the name 'Peggy' didn't really fit the bill, a name her previous owners had given her which we hadn't changed.

As is the way with all names, it evolved to become 'Pegg-shoe', a nickname that came about for no reason that I can remember or articulate with any coherence. In the fraught moments when I found myself dragging her off another dog that she was attempting to maul, her name evolved to become 'Dickhead' pretty rapidly.

When my ex decided that the responsibility of a massive mortgage and a massive dog were too much for him and left me with both to move back in with his family, my financial and housing options were limited to say the least. It was not financially possible for me to pay the mortgage on my own, despite working full-time as a housing litigation consultant (ironic, I know). I couldn't move back in with either of my parents; my dad didn't have the space and my mum was terrified of dogs. Unable to afford to rent a property on my income alone (can anyone?), I was backed into a corner without an obvious way out. What could I do? How would I manage? Where would I live?

The solution presented itself when a friend suggested that I look into renting out individual rooms in the house. The household bills would increase, but there would be money left over to help me pay the mortgage and council tax. Ultimately it would mean that I could stay in the property and provide a stable home for what was now my dog.

So, at twenty-four years old, I became a live-in landlady.

Renting out rooms to complete strangers was a frightening and risky business, not least because I was a young, single woman who had a trusting naivety when it came to character assessment. Being under the debilitating financial pressure of having a substantial mortgage meant that I didn't necessarily have a choice regarding who I rented out the rooms to. This resulted in some rather terrifying and memorable experiences: a new lodger once used the landing at the top of the stairs as a stage to loudly preach about the Devil's place of residence, which, in his opinion, was on Ilkley Moor (I mean, it's nice there, but I can think of better places to live if I was the personification of evil itself, like maybe Bognor Regis – lovely beaches, sunshine and loads of charity shops in case Beelzebub fancied a cheap new frock). Another lodger, who was a functioning alcoholic, had an interesting habit of sleepwalk weeing, nightly urinating in various areas of the house, namely areas that weren't in or even near the toilet, which was unfortunate to say the least. Let's just say that I learnt early on not to go into the kitchen without shoes on (with multiple lodgers employing varying degrees of hygiene standards and a constantly heavily-shedding dog, the only time you took off your shoes in my house was to get into bed and, even then, that was a gamble). Yet another lodger began hoarding cutlery in his room, mostly teaspoons and spoons, and then my drill went missing, which had been a gift from a family member. Soon after that, the lodger himself went missing, along with all his clothes and possessions (including many that were mine), which is when I discovered, via conversations with his immediate family, that he was a heroin addict – a detail which his mum had conveniently neglected to mention when she had originally approached me about renting the room for him. Having said all this, many of the lodgers I had over the years, from when my ex-partner moved out in my early twenties to when he sent the solicitor's letter in my early thirties, became fantastic friends, and some I consider to be lifelong.

When it became clear that renting out rooms was working, at least on a financial level if not a personal safety level, I decided to put a cheap caravan in the back garden to use as my 'bedroom' so that I could rent out my own room in the house. This presented something of a logistical challenge as my back garden had a reasonably tall wall around it. Thankfully, I had a 'Dave'.

Everyone needs a Dave in their lives. I'm lucky enough to have multiple Daves, but the Dave in this story was born in Papua New Guinea and somehow, from that unlikely destination, his journey brought him to Keighley looking for a room to rent, and subsequently to my door. Dave is the kind of guy who could feasibly build you a flux capacitor. You may not travel back in time, but you'd definitely travel somewhere – or parts of you would anyway. He had the solution to my caravan problem, which featured the use of a flatbed truck, two motorbike ramps, a winch and some friends who needed a laugh that day. Using the winch, the caravan was loaded on to the flatbed truck, which was of a similar height to my wall. The motorbike ramps bridged the gap between the top of the wall and the truck. When everything was in position, the caravan was gently lowered via the winch on to the ramps and then on to the top of the wall. It was at this that point the neighbours started to stream out of their homes, phone cameras at the ready, hoping for the £250 *You've Been Framed* win.

The caravan wheels and, indeed, the entire caravan, were completely balanced on the wall – the only thing holding it there were the four idiots (myself included) standing at each corner, trying to stop it from tipping. From there, it was a case of executing the very delicate manoeuvre of sliding the motorbike ramps out from under the wheels of the caravan while it was precariously balanced on the wall, then repositioning the ramps at the other side of the wall in order to lower the caravan into the garden. We didn't have four ramps, as that would have been too easy. Much to the chagrin of my neighbours, who all went home dejected, feeling like they'd been done out of the prize money, the caravan was lowered successfully, and without major incident or injury, into my back garden, where it became my bedroom for many years.

My house had the most beautiful bathroom suite that I'd ever seen, which was one of the reasons I'd fallen in love with the property when we had initially viewed it. The sink, bath and toilet were a fabulous burnt orange, like mountain heather in autumn. It was a seventies original: the tiles were stylised and colour-coordinated with the bathroom suite and there was a big, round, terracotta retro mirror. Soaking in the bath in that space was like being held in the warm arms of Mother Earth herself.

I adored it. But the beautiful nostalgic bathroom dream would soon come to a devastating, unique and bitter end . . .

It was incredibly old, my home. The fuse box still required the type of fuse where you manually replace the wire if it blows (some of you won't even know what they are, lucky bastards) and the electrics tripped out regularly. At least once a week, I had to don wellies and venture down into the dark depths of the flooded cellar to replace a fuse, the combination of knackered electrics *and* water making the whole operation like a domestic and dangerous version of *The Crystal Maze*. There was a damp issue in nearly every room that no amount of stain block paint could eradicate, the roof leaked every time it rained and the loft had no insulation whatsoever – I could see sky from under the eroding roof tiles. The old plaster was crumbling into dust, so much so that a substantial section of the downstairs ceiling actually fell off and landed on the dog (she was not impressed, but I felt that it served her right for sleeping in such an obstructive place and not in the bed that I had bought for her). And finally, the ancient boiler, which had been chugging away inefficiently since I'd moved in, decided enough was enough and promptly packed in.

Buying a brand-new boiler, even back then, when things were apparently cheaper, was about as feasible as winning the lottery or riding a two-headed unicorn through the streets of Bradford. Thankfully, when the ancient boiler emitted its final clonking death rattle, Papua New Guinea Dave, the man who can, was still renting a room at my house. He did what only a Dave could do and 'fixed' the boiler. This involved a complete bypass of the thermostat. In case you don't know, that's the thingymawotsit that regulates the water temperature. Some people would argue that a thermostat on a boiler system is essential, and they might just be right . . .

On the day of the 'incident', one of my housemates was heading upstairs to his room. I asked him to run the bath for me while he was up there, expressly advising him on pain of, well, pain, that he needed to run both the cold and hot taps at the same time.

That was the highly advanced operational system that we'd put in place after the loss of the thermostat.

That didn't happen.

As I sat reading in the living room, waiting for the bath to fill, the pitter-patter of dripping water reached my ears. I stood up, trying to locate where the sound was coming from. Venturing into the hallway, I glanced into the kitchen. Cascading from the ceiling at various points was a deluge of steaming, molten-hot water. Running upstairs to the bathroom, I burst in to find that my housemate had neglected to switch on the cold tap and had only switched on the hot tap. The water was so hot due to the lack of a thermostat that it had melted clean through my beloved burnt-orange fibreglass bath and was pissing through the kitchen ceiling at alarming rates. I switched off the tap and took in the melted, gaping hole. It was almost unbelievable that the water had been hot enough to melt clean through the bath, but it blooming well had. And that was the end of my beautiful bath. If it's possible to grieve for uniquely coloured fibreglass bathroom fixtures, then I will admit that I absolutely did.

Thankfully, Keighley is a town full of opportunities, if you have an entrepreneurial mind and zero dignity. The bath was replaced within a day. Admittedly the 'new' bath was white and didn't match the bathroom decor in the slightest, but it was completely free, rescued (a term more accessible than 'stolen') from one of the many skips that line the roads and decorate the gardens of the houses in the area. One person's rubbish is someone else's treasure and, when all your money is taken up with a mortgage, bills and vehicle running costs, you never drive past a skip without stopping to take a look. That's the unwritten code of the financially challenged.

The solicitor's letter was placed with due importance on the red-brick mantelpiece above the ancient gas fire that no longer worked. After some deliberation, I decided that phoning my ex-partner was the quickest and cheapest way to come to a resolution (cheaper than instructing more solicitors anyway). He answered the phone and I jumped straight in . . . 'Ey up, you all right? What's this letter all about then?' He told me that he had a new partner and that they wanted to buy a house together, but because his name was still on our property, he would be unable to get a mortgage on another. I explained that the house was in negative equity, alongside being in a state of reasonably severe disrepair, and selling it would leave us both in more debt. I made a suggestion that I would later regret: if he wanted to live with his new girlfriend, why didn't they both live in my house and I would move in with my new partner Lee, who lived in the Lake District. My ex could take on the mortgage payments and bills, which would give me a much-needed break from the worry and stress of trying to make ends meet. We didn't discuss how we would manage the situation in the future; I was simply so relieved to be handing it all over that I didn't want to think that far ahead. He agreed with the proposed solution to our housing problem, so I began planning and sourcing another place to live.

The new home that I would be moving into with my new partner in the Lake District wasn't conventional. Then again, neither was winching a caravan into my back garden and renting out my rooms to satanists. Due to the fact that I had a dog, and the area we were moving to was one of the most affluent places in the UK, alongside the fact that we would both be students, a caravan was our only option.

It took me three weeks to empty my home prior to my ex moving back in. Storing my possessions either in a designated facility or at my mum's house simply wasn't an option for me, not only because of my lack of finances (storage units are expensive), but also because I would feel too fragmented. Parts of me, in the form of the objects from my life, would be strewn about in different places, hidden away in dusty, dark spaces, boxed up and forgotten about, except for the heavy invisible tie that was my ownership of them. Instead, I opted to cut the ties, to release myself from the things and relinquish both the possession that I had of them and the possession that they had of me.

Every knick-knack that I'd ever collected, every piece of art that had moved me enough to buy it (if it was cheap enough, of course), love letters and poetry from previous partners, every item of furniture, every physical manifestation of a memory – from fridge magnets to decorative plates – every kitchen gadget that couldn't be used in a caravan, piles of books, bags of clothes, shoes – indeed anything that would take up valuable space unnecessarily in my new caravan home – it all went to the charity shop or into the bin.

And it felt great.

Better than great. It felt as if a weight had been lifted. All of these anchors had been cut away, cast out into the sea of life, and I was suddenly a ship without a port. No longer ungainly, slow and laden down, heavy with things, I was light, agile and able to manoeuvre. The uncertainty was both anxiety-inducing but also excitingly intoxicating.

All I now had in this world was a rusty old van, some clothes and half shares in an ancient caravan. I was no longer held to ransom by the deteriorating stone prison I called my home, with its leaking roof, broken boiler, decaying electrics, damp and the never-ending bills that were relentlessly pushed through the rusty letter box.

I had no idea when I'd be living in a house again, and I found that I didn't care.

Lee and I paid the fees required for our caravan to be sited on a lovely little campsite in Cumbria. After two or three months of living there, I received a telephone call from my ex-partner. I should have expected it really.

He told me that he didn't realise how expensive the house would be to run and that he couldn't afford it. He'd split up with his girlfriend and he was giving the keys to the house back to the mortgage company, effectively getting my home repossessed. There was nothing I could do; I was working part-time while studying and had no spare income at all. If anything, I had less than I had before. I couldn't save the house, my home for thirteen years. As I took all this in and processed it in the moments after the phone call had ended, I realised that, in some ways, I was glad. Yes, I was upset that I was losing the place that had been my island, my rock, for many years. But I didn't want it anymore. Not just the house, that I'd tried so hard and sacrificed so much to keep running, but the overwhelming and all-consuming stress that came with it. I was done. I didn't want to worry about how I was going to pay the gas bill over winter, I was tired of the electric running out on the key meter, the despondency and despair that was almost constant in the battle to just stay afloat financially. What was it all for? Really? For the privilege of giving the bank all of my hard-earned money? For somewhere to sleep? A roof over my head? Where was my quality of life? More importantly, *what* was my quality of life?

The house was given back to the bank and they auctioned it off, selling it for only half of what it was originally on the market for when we bought it. I've calculated that, over the years, I paid the bank approximately £60,000. Probably more. Most of that was literally just the interest that they charge for the privilege of borrowing. And all I had to show for this experience was poor mental health, an empty bank account and more debt.

Surely there must be another way to live?

And it turns out that, for me, there was . . .

Chapter Two

The Water Fox

In the empty, eerie and derelict space of an industrial park in the twilight hours, I furtively search for a water tap. There is the evening meal still to prepare and I'm hoping to have enough water to wash the sheen of summer sweat and road dust from my skin. I sense movement in the shadows of one of the huge, red-brick buildings; the hairs rise on the back of my neck as I antici-pate a burly security guard, or something more frightening. Instead, out trots a skinny young fox, all head and gangly legs. I exhale the breath that I didn't know I'd been holding. He pauses, only metres away. Bold as only a fox could be, we lock gazes, eyeing each other. The moment passes as he decides I'm not a threat and pads off into the hazy dark.

As I move from building to building, hoping for the tell-tale shape of an outdoor tap on a wall, I think about my life before: the running water, the four stone walls, the 'security'. The old me certainly craved the stability of putting down roots, of having a fixed base in the form of a house; somewhere I could always return to when the sea of life became too rough, an island made of concrete, plaster and stone. The present me has been trans-formed by circumstance and experience. What I need now, with regards to security, is very different.

With my empty water bottles glinting in motion-censored lights that flick on and off as I search, I consider the concept of freedom. Being free means something different to all of us. As a child, it was assumed by my parents that I would follow what could only be described as a preordained pattern: I was born, I was educated in what the establishment deemed appropriate, I was sent out to work and then encouraged to borrow money so that I could buy a stone or brick structure to reside in. My dad set the example for me by constantly being in competition with his peers, always striving for the biggest house, the biggest car, the biggest caravan and the most material possessions. And to stay ahead in this seldom-acknowledged contest, he borrowed money that he didn't have.

Both my dad and my mum worked hard to pay for the second-hand Range Rover, the speedboat, the six-berth caravan, the fishing boat, our four-bedroomed house and all the things in it. As a child, I never understood why we'd moved from the first house that we'd lived in – it had been situated on the edge of rolling green fields that were perfect for playing in, sledging in the winter or making daisy chains in the spring. My mum had wanted to stay there and saw no need to move, but my dad, always feeling the pressure of having less than his friends and being driven by a sense of inadequacy, was adamant that we needed a bigger home.

He was, at this time, a builder by trade. When his friends, who also worked in construction, began to buy plots of land in order to design and build their own homes, my dad, unwilling to be outdone or left out, followed suit. Which involved more borrowing – a lot more.

Out of the seven days in a week, my dad would work six in order to generate enough income to pay the bills, placate the many lenders, pay debts and ensure that there was enough money left over for the other essential costs of living that weren't considered as important as speedboats or fishing trips, like food. As soon as my brother and I were considered old enough to safely get ourselves to school and back (I think I was eleven), my mum switched from working part-time hours, which fitted in with school, to working full-time as a medical secretary for the NHS. The financial pressure that they were both under was immense. It exacted a terrible toll that wasn't worth any amount of second-hand Range Rovers, speedboats or houses of any size.

Working long hours in a physically demanding job, battling the elements and being outdoors in every weather imaginable in order to keep up with the many payments, mortgages and loans that he'd taken out, Dad was struggling. He turned to alcohol as a refuge. This liquid disinhibitor acted as a key, which opened the door to his deep discontentment, insecurity and general rage at the world at large. He communicated his suffering through violence.

Always wanting more and never being content with what he had was the reason that my mum, brother and I (and possibly my dad too) all ended up with post-traumatic stress disorder (PTSD), a mental health issue, which manifests itself in a multitude of challenging ways. As a present-day adult who's had years of counselling and has experienced first-hand the expectations of what it means to be a successful human in our society and the financial pressures of running a household, I can now, if not forgive my dad, at least understand the heavy weight that he was carrying.

It became very clear, early on in my life, that the measure of my success was down to several factors, some of which were shared by all, and some only by specific groups. Being female, my success and value seemed to be determined by how closely I resembled the current beauty ideal and how sexually desirable I was. The apparent gauge to measure this success came down to the amount of people who wanted to sleep with me, which is a concept more toxic and damaging than I could ever accurately describe.

As an adult, my success and status seemed to be measured by my financial position and the various material possessions that

I owned: my car, and how new it was, how big my house was (or whether I owned one at all), how many holidays I took a year, the brand of clothing I could afford to wear and the brand of cosmetics I used on my face. The pressure to be seen as successful, even if that success was 'borrowed' via the use of overdrafts, store cards, mortgages, car finance or credit cards, was immense (and still is, if you subscribe to those measures).

The measure of status and success in working-class northern England, during my upbringing, can be summarised and communicated effectively by the 'Netto' carrier bag phenomenon. You may not recall, but Netto was a supermarket way back in the nineties, before the advent of Aldi or Lidl. It sold cheaper goods than any other leading supermarket. The colours used for the branding were black and bright, primary yellow, which featured heavily on its plastic carrier bag design. If you came from a 'successful' household, you would be sent to school with your gym kit in a Sainsbury's carrier bag (only well-off people could afford to shop at Sainsbury's), which subtly increased your value and status in the eyes of your school peers. Being sent to school with a Morrisons carrier bag was acceptable – the middle-of-the-road supermarket neither increased nor decreased your social status. If you were unlucky enough to be sent to school, however, with your lunch in a bright yellow Netto carrier bag, you were bullied to the point of suicide, cast out from all social circles (apart from the greasy-haired moshers and goths who hung around near the music corridor – they'd accept anyone, there was strength in numbers) and called names like 'scratter' and 'scum bag'. And if your family drove a Lada car *and* shopped at Netto, you were well and truly fucked.

So I understood why my dad had felt compelled beyond reason to take on much more than he could handle, both financially and mentally. Using the simplest explanation, he desperately didn't want to be the kid with the Netto carrier bag or the man driving the Lada when all his peers shopped at Sainsbury's and had Range Rovers.

When I first became a homeowner, it wasn't necessarily out of choice. After my mum finally found the courage to leave my dad (I was fourteen years old), both my brother and I chose to live with her (neither of us wanted to cohabit with a violent, angry, physically and verbally abusive, desperately unhappy man). By the time I was fifteen, hormonal and psychologically unstable due to a childhood of domestic violence, my mum had changed her life completely; from hosting Tupperware parties and potpourri-arranging evenings, she was now wearing black leather jackets, hanging out with rock stars and sourcing cannabis off my brother's dealer for her new boyfriend. It wasn't long before we never saw her as she spent most of her time at her new partner's house in another town. After twenty-five years in a devastatingly abusive and controlling marriage, she was a beautiful bird who had been released from the dark, loveless cage that was her relationship with my dad. You can't blame her for wanting to live her life now that she could, but I did. For a long time.

From the age of fourteen, I started to drink excessively and take drugs. At the time, I considered it preferable to feeling sad, unloved or anxious. My first official boyfriend was a compulsive liar, who was frequently unfaithful (he was also very young and had his own issues to contend with), my so-called 'best friend' bullied me to the point of causing me physical harm, my mum wasn't around and my brother was off doing his own thing. By the time I was sixteen, I was snorting cocaine and dancing in city-centre clubs, hanging out with people older than me, individuals who I deemed to be sophisticated and successful because they could afford class A drugs and frequented stylish bars. It wasn't long before I began to have depressive breakdowns and unmanageable outbursts of violent rage, brought on, I suspect, by PTSD, and fuelled by alcohol and drug abuse. At these times, friends, and sometimes complete strangers, would call my mum. They had no idea how to deal with me in those states and, quite rightly, had no desire to take responsibility for me, or for who I'd upset or what I'd done. My mum would almost always find a way to drive to wherever I was, motivated, I think, by the sense of guilt she had from leaving us and also by her responsibility as a parent.

I am deeply ashamed of my behaviour during those times, behaviour that led to physical fights with my mum, attempting to jump out of moving cars, smashing up the possessions of those I felt had wronged me (which was everyone, after drinking a litre bottle of Mad Dog 20/20), starting fights and generally being out of control and destructive in every sense of the word.

Eventually, when I turned twenty, my mum sat me and my brother down and asked what our thoughts would be on her selling the home she owned that we were living in so that she could move in permanently with her boyfriend. Her plan was to sell the house and, with the money generated from the sale, buy a property in her partner's town, then lend me enough for a deposit so that I could buy my own house. For a twenty-year-old who was perhaps more balanced and world-savvy than I was, this could have been a fantastic opportunity to get on the housing ladder (I detest that phrase, likely invented by estate agents, as it suggests that, by buying a house, you are climbing up, becoming more successful and winning at the game of life, when, for me, it has always been exactly the opposite). For a mentally ill, destructive, dysfunctional, barely functioning substance abuser, entering into a mortgage possibly wasn't the best idea. Still, I didn't have much choice and was excited by the prospect of 'owning' my own home. This was the first house that I would buy.

Mum and I found a tiny back-to-back terrace on the fringes of a council estate which needed updating, but it was reasonable enough to move into straight away. It was marketed at £40,000, one of cheapest houses in the area at the time. My mum lent me

£10,000 as a deposit and ensured that we had a document drawn up by the solicitors so that, if the property was ever sold, she would automatically receive the full amount back into her bank account.

If I'd have kept that house, I would have been mortgage-free by the time I was thirty (although, on a technical level, as I now live in, a van, I am mortgage-free). But, unfortunately, life doesn't work that way. Well, some people's lives might, but not mine.

The sale went through without issue, and I was now officially a homeowner. I was the first out of my young friendship group to 'buy' a house. Moving into my new home, if anything, made my mental health drastically worse. On top of undiagnosed PTSD, anxiety and depression, I now had the added responsibility of paying a mortgage and bills, rather than just handing over money to my mum for her to deal with it all, as I had done when I lived in her house. Sober, I could just about function, but when I was drunk and having psychotic breakdowns, I would need to be restrained by whoever was there and strong enough to hold me down, screaming out demands to be taken to a mental ward – genuine pleas that were always ignored due to my inebriation.

Because I was struggling so much, and I didn't have a name for what I was feeling or a professional diagnosis, I assumed that I was simply broken; that I was worthless, a burden to those around me, a toxic mess, unstable, unfixable and unlovable. The knowledge that it would be easier for those around me if I were no longer there was something I knew, at that time, to be absolutely true (even though it absolutely wasn't). I began to search for other experiences, beyond drug-taking and alcohol, that made me feel, if not better, then at least different to the usual hyperaware, heart-racing, sleep-deprived, hungover, hand-shaking, intrusive-thought-thinking, anxiety-riddled, suicidal norm. And I did. It came in the form of retail therapy.

At this time, shops, banks and other lenders were heavily pushing store cards, credit cards and overdrafts at everyone, and anyone, who was old enough to sign a contract. At school, we were never taught how to manage finances, or how to budget, or how to effectively run a household. Instead, we were taught really useful things like algebra, the population density of Luxembourg and the biology of frogs, which, of course, are skills and knowledge that I use every single day.

A new dress from Topshop was never going to be the cure for any ailment or issue. However, in the moment of acquisition, I felt an elation that put everything else on hold for a very short while. Owning new things made me feel successful, like I had worth and value. Being able to evidence to both myself and my peers that I had enough money to buy these things, and the attention I received from dressing myself in the latest, most daring, fashions, became yet another addiction.

The substance abuse increased and, alongside it, so did my debt. My take on financial management went something like this: when the money stopped coming out of the cash machine, or my card stopped working, it was time to either open another bank account with an overdraft facility or get another credit card. Eventually, because of my debts, I was forced to remortgage the house. I was twenty-two years old at this point.

One evening, I was out drinking in one of my usual haunts with a chap who I had recently entered into a relationship with, one that would (yet again) turn out to be highly volatile. Promiscuity seems to go hand in hand with non-existent self-esteem and self-worth. We were full of ourselves, high on our new romance and drunk on tart, cheap sherry. In a bold statement to the rest of the group that we were out with, we declared that we would be buying a house and moving in together. We hadn't discussed it prior to that night – it was a decision made mostly by the sherry (alcohol has *a lot* to answer for, not just in my life, but since its very conception).

Partly through fear of losing face in front of our friends and partly 'fuck it, why not?', the very next day, still slightly drunk, we had an interview with a mortgage adviser at the bank. Our joint mortgage was set up and I put my substantially remortgaged first house on the market; £3,000 was all that was left after it sold and Mum had reclaimed her £10,000. We found another house to buy, bigger than my first home, and, in no time at all, we were living together.

Of course, it all went wrong, as this sherry-induced poor decision-making was the beginning of the journey that eventually led to the repossession of my home.

But did it go wrong? Really? Or did it only go wrong when measured against the ideology of success that society teaches us?

The shape of a water tap makes itself known in a disjointed shadow on the front of what was possibly a tyre garage on the industrial estate – it's hard to tell in the dark, with the shuttered doors rolled down against the thieves of the night. Furtively looking around to ensure that I am still alone, I head over, hoping that there aren't any movement-sensor security lights to illuminate my watery crime. Thankfully, the dark stays dark. Putting my empty bottles on the ground, I check out the water tap. The handle that turns the tap on or off has been removed – someone is obviously wise to late-night H_2O theft. Fortunately, this is something that I've come across before. Like an expert thief in a film, I pull out the tools of my trade: a set of medium-sized mole grips. Attaching the mole grips to the top of the tap, I am able to turn it on. Happily, the tap has not been completely disconnected and water cascades out. One of my previous jobs was as logistical support for a team of community nurses in the NHS, and part of my role involved turning on the taps every week in the clinics that weren't in use. This needed to be done in order to prevent Legionella bacteria forming, which can happen in stagnant or long-standing water. Running a tap for five minutes will ensure that any bacteria which may have formed is flushed out. This is something I'm always very careful of when 'borrowing' water from unknown sources. Legionnaires' disease, a form of pneumonia, can be fatal. Although it can feel counterproductive when trying to live in a less wasteful, more sustainable way, sometimes a few litres of water wasted to prevent serious illness, or even death, is definitely a good call.

With my water-collecting mission a resounding success, I head back to the van. It's Saturday night and unlikely that the industrial estate will be open the next day, with it being Sunday, so I move the van to a quiet little spot near the entrance. Popping the kettle on, I boil some water for a washing-up bowl strip wash – under tits, pits and bits, in that order (please excuse the crudeness of my description, I chose rhyme over dignity). Tea (or dinner, depending on where you're from) will be chestnut mushrooms and broccoli, lightly fried in salty butter, served with jasmine rice drizzled with soy sauce, cooked on my single gas stove. As I settle in to watch David Attenborough on the laptop, I am clean, fed and happy, far removed from the person I used to be.

Chapter Three

The Downstairs Toilet

I'm sitting on the roof. Below me, lines of winding streetlights look like beads of gold strung out across velvet. The rolling hills beyond are silhouetted against the moonlit sky. The wind pushes and pulls gently at my fleece pyjamas. Soft fabric contacts my skin with a feeling of warmth and simple comfort, before being pulled away again by the wind. The bare soles of my small, ten-year-old feet connect with the cool smoothness of the grey slate roof tiles beneath them.

I can hear shouting from inside the house – the open window behind me allows the sounds to drift out. The discordant melody moves with the wind, louder then quieter, as the vibrations are filtered by the wide expanse of sky. Fear begins in the space between my shoulder blades, prickling like a day-old nettle sting, moving swiftly down the length of my spine. My body shivers in response. Travelling through me, it settles in my stomach, fluttering and churning like a moth caught in a storm.

Glancing down, I take in the sparkling black of the tarmac which lies metres beneath my rooftop perch. I know that if I fall, parts of me will break. I allow my mind to dwell there for a moment, wondering whether I'd scream if I fell or if I would be silent, breaking with no sound at all. Would the shouting stop then? When I lie broken? When red-hot blood pools on the cool, impassive asphalt and shards of shattered bone lay scattered?

I won't fall.

On this tiled and sloping garage roof, I am in control.

The shouting undulates like an ocean edge, two voices entwined: one reaching towering crescendos of high-pitched fear, clear, like the top of a wave in the moment before it breaks; the other, the deep angry bass of a growling squall, foaming, spitting, skin-stripping, sand-grit rough.

Perhaps tonight we will be swiftly bundled into the car. Coats hastily thrown on over pyjamas, feet without the comfort of socks thrust into cold, stiff leather shoes.

Quickly. Quickly now.

Adrenaline courses through me at the thought of escape. I am ignited with heightened awareness. Each quick, staccato beat of my heart fills me with a feeling of aliveness, sharpened by fear. Ink-black pupils dilate to take in every detail. Muscles pulse and flex in anticipation of rapid, exploding movement.

I am ready.

Behind me, the warm, yellow light of the open window spills out across the roof tiles, telling lies of safety and shelter. The space within is cluttered, a spare room used for things that must be kept, but not thrown away: an old computer, dusty on its laminate beech desk, board games, neglected toys and forgotten mechanical relics from the days of my mother's keep-fit promises. A single bed, made up, vies for space among the disorder.

This is not my room, but this is where I sleep.

The space that I call mine lies across the hall. It could be called a bedroom; it has a bed and it is a room, but instead, it serves as my exhibition space, its contents curated and displayed with meticulous attention to detail – swirling, curling seashells of every shape and colour, soft feathers with speckled patterns, smooth pebbles and clear quartz crystals. A cobalt-blue glass bottle with gold flecks reminds me of a faraway galaxy and houses a heady, jasmine perfume that was once my mother's. All of these things, and more, have been given a place in my exhibition, arranged according to symmetry, shape and the level of power I have assigned each one based on its ability to comfort me. An unopened bottle of blue bath foam has centre stage on my dressing table. The label on the tall, plastic bottle presents images of delicate purple lavender flowers and informs me in a gentle, curvaceous font that it will 'soothe the mind and relax tired, aching muscles'.

I hold on so tightly to these words, like a life ring out in the dark, shoreless depths. I need them. My mind anchors on to the feelings they invoke and the promises they make. The bath foam will never be used, except perhaps in what I would consider to be an emergency, a moment when my young mind can no longer cope with the fear. To use it would be to detract from its perfection as a thing, an object of comfort. The simple solace in having ownership of it is enough, reading and rereading the words on the bottle, occasionally opening the lid to allow the synthetic scent to wash over me, hoping that, by doing so, my mind will be soothed and all will be well.

When I am surrounded by my collection, sitting within the space that I have carefully curated, I feel safe, as if the objects themselves could protect me. This room is under my control; it is the only thing that I can control, so its perfection is my obsession. My brother learnt that all he had to do in order to cause me distress was to crease the perfectly made, colour-coordinated, curated object of art that was my bed.

In order not to taint the perfect order, the symmetry and the cleanliness, I sleep surrounded by the clutter and broken things of the spare room: dusty, untidy, imperfect and unloved.

I tug at the collar of my pyjama top, pulling it up to cover the nape of my neck, the tiny hairs there lifting, responding perhaps to the coolness of the breeze or to the tension of the night. Behind, the light from the open window beckons me, demanding that I find the courage to investigate the shouting from inside the house. To the right of where I sit lies my planned escape route; a swift and careful shimmy across and down the steep sloping garage roof, a short drop to the patio beneath, finishing with a sprint across the back garden to the tall, wooden gate which leads to the main road and freedom.

I could do it. I could run. But where would I go? The arguing continues as I deliberate, purposefully putting off the inevitable – the nauseating fear-filled fact that I can't simply be a silent listener; if I am to protect my mum, I must also be a watcher.

I turn and tiptoe my way across the grey slate roof, back into the light and chaos of the spare room. With a practised hand, I close the window without making a sound. Trepidation furrows my brow and fear is a churning sickness in my stomach. I can feel my heartbeat in my throat. With controlled movement, I pad stealthily across the landing to the stairs, the thick carpet warming my slate-cool feet. Lowering my tense body, I sit on the top step, folding my arms around my bent legs, hugging them towards me and resting my chin on my knees. My gaze is focused on the empty hallway at the bottom of the stairs. The decor there assaults my senses, contributing to the feelings of danger and fraught anticipation. Bright, lurid turquoise covers the top half of the walls, the lower half violated by a heavily patterned wallpaper in deep claret, sickly gold and stale-blood burgundy.

Closing my eyes, I try to focus only on sound, extending my hearing as far as my ten-year-old body will allow. Resonance and tone arrive first, before being shaped by my ears into coherent words. My dad's voice, low, deep and menacing; a malevolent tone designed to instil fear and exert control, slurred by heavy intoxication.

'You stupid ugly bitch, all I do is work for you fucking cunts.'

A whimper from my mother. She says his name as a plea, begging him to stop. I know that I should not have heard this. That I cannot unhear it. There is no time to process the words; there is only now, the loaded space in between the menacing voice and the fists that may follow. On the top step of the upstairs landing, I start to unfurl, unwrapping my arms from my knees and sitting up straight, preparing for flight. A familiar thought runs through my hyperaware mind: I wish I was a boy, big, tall and strong. I could stop it then. I could stop him. I would hit him back, so hard, that he could never hurt us again.

And then silence. My child's mind races to determine what the silence might mean. I analyse every detail available, trying frantically to determine my dad's level of inebriation, of rage, of unpredictability and lack of self-control from the nuance and tone of his voice when he spoke. I tune into the shape and feel of the air around me. Has he hit her again? Is she unconscious? A wave of nausea hits me. What if she's dead? What if, this time, he's gone too far? Bile rises from my stomach into my throat; burning, choking acid fear. Without thought, slowly, so slowly, I begin to descend, one silent step at a time.

Wait, there is movement. I pause. My ears pick up sounds that indicate someone has walked into the kitchen. The tip-tapping on the tiled floor announces the identity; still wearing the pointed-toe high heels of her secretary job, it must be my mum. I hear her flick on the kettle and allow the comforting sounds of tea-making to wash over me. It must be okay, she must be okay. Someone who is grievously injured, dead, unconscious or traumatised beyond the ability to function wouldn't make tea. Maybe the danger has passed, but I know it hasn't. It couldn't and it wouldn't until either she left or he was dead.

Tip-toeing on soft, thick carpet, I silently make my way back upstairs, moving across the landing and into the spare room. As I pass my bedroom, I glance in, making sure everything is where it should be, taking strength from the symmetry of my collection and the evidence of my control. Everything is okay. My room is perfect. I am in control. I am okay. Mum is okay.

As the adrenaline begins to leave my body, it feels heavy, the weightlessness of terror giving way to the leaden sensation of being completely spent. Surrounded by clutter, I tuck myself into bed, pulling the blankets over my head so that the monsters can't get me, but so that I can still peek out to see them if, and when, they come. I've left the door open a few inches so that the landing light shines through in a long shard of yellow, just enough to hold the dark at bay. My senses are still alert, listening, feeling for danger, but my eyes refuse to stay open. Sleep arrives and is a welcome relief from feeling anything at all.

The house that my dad borrowed too much money to build had three bathrooms: a family bathroom, an en suite and a downstairs toilet. The downstairs toilet was one of my favourite places; it was small, and warm, with running water that I could drink, a pot that dealt with bodily functions and a lock, to keep the monsters out. As a child, I saw it as a safety capsule. I would take picnics into the downstairs loo, lock the door and camp out, playing with my plastic unicorns, feeling protected and in control of the small, enclosed space.

Angie the hamster also lived in the downstairs loo; she was my soft, warm, little animal friend, named after my cousin as they both had auburn hair, or fur, whichever the case may be. Angie and her cage were relegated to the downstairs toilet as she was constantly running rings on her plastic exercise wheel, which, when she was at top speed, sounded like an aeroplane taking off. Hamsters are nocturnal, so bedrooms aren't the ideal place for them to reside, unless you're a vampire with a love of small mammals. Angie seemed happy enough in her metal and plastic world, with her blue plastic wheel and the orange plastic pretend house that she slept in. When the bathroom door was shut, I would wake her up and let her out, where she'd scamper around on the floor tiles, sniffing indifferently at my treasured plastic horses, no doubt searching for a way to escape from the spinning wheel of infinite tedium.

One rainy Saturday morning, after waking, I went through the usual charade of pretending to brush my teeth, got myself dressed in my favourite red jumper and blue leggings, then packed my current set of plastic horses and unicorns into a little bag, ready to be relocated to my play area for the day. In the kitchen, I made myself a fortifying chocolate spread sandwich (spreading most of the sugary brown gloop on the worktops rather than the bread) and packed it in my unicorn-filled bag ready for later. Everything was set for a few hours of playtime in the lockable, small space of safety that was the downstairs loo.

As I opened the door to my safe place, with my bag clasped tightly in one hand, I was assailed by a waft of stale ale. It was a smell that I recognised instantly, my little body becoming immediately alert, senses switching on, system flooding with adrenaline in response to the alarming olfactory trigger. If there was alcohol, there was danger. I put the bag of toys and squashed sandwich on the floor in the hallway and cautiously opened the door fully. I could see the toilet and the sink – they looked like they did every day, no cause for concern there. Perhaps the smell was coming from the toilet? After all, if beer goes into a body already smelling awful, then surely, it'll come out smelling even worse? I glanced into the toilet, checking the colour of the water to see if that was where the stink was emanating from. The water was clear. Not there then. So where was the smell coming from? I heard a rustling sound behind me. I turned quickly towards the sound and the sight that confronted me took a moment to process . . . Angie, my tiny auburn hamster, was sitting hunched over, shivering uncontrollably, on the roof of her orange pretend plastic house. Beneath her, like a moat around a castle, was a sea of dirty, stinking, stale beer piss. The entire bottom of her cage was filled.

Extreme fear is an arresting experience, especially in a child, yet it doesn't necessarily manifest in ways that might be expected as a result of that fear; screaming, crying or shouting. Even during the most traumatic events of my childhood, like being shaken so hard when I was very small that I inadvertently defecated, an occurrence which I wasn't aware of until the danger had passed, or being knocked unconscious on several occasions, I didn't cry. Instinctively, even when I was very young, I knew that screaming or crying would only enhance the danger that I was in. Instead, I was silent. I learnt to watch with sight that went beyond what I could physically see: I evaluated, analysed, judged and assessed. And then, as I grew, I learnt to please, to manipulate, to communicate, to influence, to choreograph and to control.

I took Angie out of her cage, gently wrapping her in toilet paper to try to increase her body heat. She must have been sitting on her island with her beautiful, soft fur wet through with piss for hours. Was Dad in the house? I wasn't sure, but fear spiked sharply in my tummy as I carried Angie into the living room. If he was, he would know that I knew what he had done, which would make him angry. It wasn't the first time he had used urine as a protest; he'd once pissed all over a set of photographs that my mum had laid out on the dining room table, chosen especially to go into a family album. As I sat down with Angie in front of the lit gas fire, my mum came into the living room and glanced down at my hands in bewilderment at the hamster rolled in toilet paper. 'Is Dad in?' I asked. 'No,' she replied. I told her about the piss-filled cage in the downstairs toilet and lifted my hands to show her the shivering hamster. She didn't say much; what could she say? As usual, she cleaned up the mess with quiet resignation, sorting out the hamster cage and bringing me a soft tea towel to wrap Angie in. I laid the half-drowned hamster in front of the fire, tucked up in the tea towel, stroking her fur to try to stop the shivering. Her usually bulging black eyes were barely open. After an hour, I asked my mum if I could give Angie some brandy. I'd heard at school that if a goldfish was dying, floating on its side in the tank, a drop of brandy in the water would bring it around and save its life. Perhaps it would work for Angie if she drank some? I think Mum must have known that Angie's time was near, so she handed over the booze without question. Using a tiny, pink plastic cup from a doll set that I had, I tried to pour a little bit of brandy into Angie's sharp-toothed mouth. It went in without issue. So I gave her a little bit more. I was willing to try anything. After several millilitres of the finest Morrisons own brand, the poor unconscious animal was involuntarily hiccupping, convulsing gently every few seconds, her paws lifting into the air each time. She was completely drunk.

Full of brandy, rolled in a tea towel and covered in piss, Angie the hamster took her last breath – or hiccup, which would be more accurate. I'm not sure what actually ended her life in the end, whether it was the overnight bath in 10 per cent proof urine or the possible drowning via brandy; either way, sadly, she didn't make it. She was buried without ceremony in a Kellogg's variety cereal box in the back garden. Some people would argue that she died happy because she was drunk, but when did drinking alcohol ever equate to any kind of happiness? At least she was numb, unaware and unconscious when her little soul went off to the big hamster wheel in the sky, the only thing that alcohol is good for. I'd like to say that her final resting place was final, but unfortunately that wasn't the case. A month later, I dug her up to see how she was. She hadn't spontaneously come back to life, which was very disappointing for me, but not for my cat, who saw Angie's exhumed corpse as a better snack than a bowl full of Kitekat. Rest in pieces, dearest Angie.

Chapter Four

A Little Bit of History

The teacher who educated us in the subjects of history and geography at my high school was called Clifford. He looked exactly as you'd expect a geography teacher called Clifford to look: wild, mid-length white hair with a white beard and moustache, glowing skin tanned a healthy yellow gold, beige cotton slacks, white socks with mid-brown leather sandals and a taupe shirt, crisply ironed. Neither tall nor short, and of a medium weight, he wouldn't have looked out of place on a desert safari riding sand-coloured camels or searching for the Ark of the Covenant with Indiana Jones. To his credit, he was passionate about the history of humanity and the geography of our world, and I expect that if I had shared his passion for these subjects, then we may have gotten along rather well.

As it was, my interests were elsewhere, namely focused on boys, smoking, cider, cannabis, Tammy Girl, avoiding my school-based oppressors (I was bullied relentlessly by two girls in my school year; they came as a pair unfortunately) and surviving the alcohol-induced violence of my parental oppressor on the weekends. I was thirteen years old. Lucky for me, as a cherry on top of the bullshit cake, I was one of the first in my year group to officially become a woman. My periods started when I was just eleven, heralded by the worst pain that I have ever experienced, pain so extreme that I genuinely thought I was dying. I hated the fact that I had no control over this messy, painful thing that happened to my body without my consent or choice. How rude of evolution, or God, or aliens, to force me to go through what was essentially the equivalent pain to having a heart attack every month with nothing but paracetamol and Bodyform as a defence.

Understandably, with everything that I was contending with, you might say that I often became distracted in class. But history, as a lesson, was one of my absolute favourites, even though the reason it was had nothing to do with the subject and, instead, had everything to do with who I sat next to in class, which was Joni.

At thirteen years old, Joni knew who she was. Which is why, I think, she was bullied. To be so sure of your identity at such a young age, when so many of your peers are not, is to be singled out, instilling jealousy in those who are yet to find themselves. Joni embraced her lesbian sexuality, and the LGBTQ community, decades before it became the powerful social movement that it is today. She didn't follow the social constructs expected of her: she cut her hair short, had piercings and showcased an edgy, individual style that was way ahead of any Tammy Girl nonsense. I was in thrall to her strength of character and her stoic unwillingness to be affected by those who feared difference and tried to hurt her as a result. Being her friend at school was my privilege, although I'm sure that I could have been a better friend.

Joni's intelligence, coupled with a wit sharper and with more observational clarity than cut glass, was true escapism from the myriad of challenges that both of us faced. Together, we were the bane of Clifford, our teacher, who was frequently provoked by our disruptive behaviour to become a vision of angry beard in furious beige. We were unmanageable, maintaining our own comedic agenda far removed from any interest in learning about the many wives of Henry VIII that, at least once a week, one of us would be sent outside the classroom. I did feel sorry for Clifford, but not enough to give up the endorphins that I deemed more essential to my existence, at that time, than an education in history or geography.

The day came when I finally pushed Clifford beyond what he could professionally handle.

When I was nearly four years old, a relatively new soul on the planet, I was forced to come to terms with the fallibility of humanity, and it wasn't through the domestic violence that I had experienced and witnessed. It was, instead, via a very simple occurrence. I was being pushed along in my buggy by my mum, content with the world as I knew that our destination was the shop, where I might be bought sweets (Choc Nibbles were my favourite – and still are). Trundling down the hill at a sedate pace, my mum misjudged the size of a pavement kerb as we were crossing the road and I was tipped out of the buggy, to land roughly on the tarmac. I don't think I even cried. The shock that this person who I worshipped – my mum, a goddess who could do no wrong, a vision of perfection, an adult – had made a mistake, was overwhelming. She promptly picked me up and plonked me back in the buggy. When the sides of my mouth started to turn down, indicating that I was about to protest loudly, and with tears, she said, with her Yorkshire no-nonsense voice, 'Don't start, there's nowt wrong with you' and carried on down the hill as if the universe hadn't shifted entirely and my little world hadn't changed at all. It was clear, from that point, that adults weren't to be trusted, and that I could only, truly, rely on myself from here on in.

Joni and I sat at a desk by the classroom door, set apart from the rest of the class, not for any particular reason, but simply because we had chosen that desk at the start of term. In retrospect, that choice tells its own story. Perhaps, because we were bullied, we consciously made choices that distanced us from others; rather than allow ostracisation to be an external force that happened to us, we did it to ourselves before anyone else could. I have always sat by the nearest exit in any space, even now. My experience of domestic violence, of being trapped upstairs in a house while horrific events unfolded downstairs, events that I was occasionally involved in, means that I always have an escape route planned. It's probable that these factors have contributed to why I feel more comfortable living in a space that can be moved – residing in a van means that I'm always near the exit, so to speak. Thankfully, these days, I am very rarely in situations that could be considered as genuinely unsafe, unless throwing myself into sub-zero temperature water counts as unsafe.

We were up to our usual antics, Joni and I, dissolving into fits of irrepressible laughter, existing in our own bubble set apart from everyone else while Clifford tried to educate the rest of the class. As he attempted to speak over the disrespectful din that we were creating, I watched his face begin to turn pink, making the white of his hair and beard even brighter in contrast to the rage that was clearly building. Oh shit, we've done it now. Nudging Joni, I urgently indicated that we'd better cease fire immediately, but it was too late . . .

'Charlotte Bradman.' His voice rang out into the class, clear as a school bell and with the same effect. Silence dropped like a stone down a well and all eyes turned to me. 'Let me tell you and the class what Charlotte Bradman's future will be.' His voice wasn't raised; it was flat and fat, matter-of-fact, like a grey breezeblock of sound. There were some sniggers as he made this grand proclamation, holding his arms out wide, clearly in the throes of some sort of vindictive passion. He looked directly at me and I stared back, wide-eyed like a rabbit caught in headlights, terrified of what was coming.

'You will be out on the streets somewhere with your friends drinking cheap cider . . .' he paused as the wave of titters and laughs from the class rolled away, settling quickly back into bated silence. 'You'll meet some young lad, who has no future prospects. You'll drink two halves of cider and, before you know it, you'll open your legs and end up pregnant, living on a council estate surrounded by screaming kids until you die.'

Nobody laughed this time.

For once, I didn't have a witty response or a sarcastically scathing comeback. It was all I could do to process what had just been said, in front of everyone. I bowed my head and stared fixedly at the desk in front of me, not knowing where to look and scared that, if I did, I would find everyone looking back. I tried to sink deeper into my chair, pulling my tatty, black blazer around me like a shield, refusing to allow the stinging tears of shock that were pricking my eyes to fall. No one was going to see me cry; I was the joker, the comedian, the boundary-testing rebel. People like me didn't cry. What he had said was obviously meant to be derogatory, hurtful, insulting, yet what was so wrong with getting pregnant young, if the dreams and goals of an individual were to raise a family? A woman's value or prospects don't decrease because of pregnancy or children, but that's exactly what he was implying – that raising a family is somehow a waste of educational resources and intelligence.

It was clear that Clifford knew he had overstepped a boundary, but, of course, what is said cannot be unsaid (although I have often wished that could be so with some of the alcohol- and trauma-fuelled statements I have made or terrible, hurtful things I have said over the years). He swiftly resumed teaching as if nothing had happened, perhaps hoping that a quick return to normality would suddenly erase his words like they had been written on a blackboard and not carved into the wall of my impressionable, angst-ridden, traumatised young mind.

When the bell rang and the class was over, I leapt out of my chair like it was on fire – I had to get away before the gossiping in the corridors started. I went home; even though home was hardly a place of comfort and safety, it was all I had. School friends advised me to report Clifford for what he had said in class, but I didn't want to prolong the issue – I just wanted it to go away. If anything, I blamed my disruptive behaviour for my teacher's outburst and, at the time, assumed that I probably deserved what he had said. I didn't return to school that day. In fact, I stopped going to school for a large proportion of my last year, except to attend my two favourite subjects, English and art. Both my parents were out at work through the day, which made taking unauthorised time off school easy, always making sure that I snuck in the back door to the house so that the neighbours didn't see.

It was less than two years later when Clifford's dire prediction regarding my life came to pass. I had indeed been partaking of an apple-based alcoholic beverage (although I'm positive that what I was drinking had never even seen an apple) and I'd met a boy.

At fifteen years old, I was pregnant.

Chapter Five

Van, Caravan and Nursing Home Life

He was drunk the first time he told me he loved me, proclaiming his feelings with slurred, barely coherent words over the telephone at the moderately early hour of eight o'clock in the evening. I was at work.

I'd stopped drinking and taking drugs six years prior to meeting him. The counselling I'd finally received had taught me to love myself enough to understand that alcohol only compounded my mental health issues, it didn't offer a solution. Yet, at this point in my life, at thirty-two years old, I still didn't love myself enough to walk away from a relationship which perhaps wasn't right for me at that time, or any time, if I'm honest. From the experience I'd had in my childhood and early adult life, I had learnt to fear the effects of alcohol in the people around me, especially in those who were closest to me. In the past, it had invariably resulted in violence, on their part or mine. People who are drunk are unpredictable, and unpredictability isn't helpful for someone with severe anxiety, clinical insecurity, low self-worth, low self-esteem and a history of alcohol-exacerbated trauma. Lee drank, and I worried. Counselling taught me that I had the capacity to control how I reacted to situations and how I felt, but it was easier said than done.

In order to move forward with the relationship, either I would have to learn to manage my anxiety and change my deep-rooted view that any alcohol intake equates to violence, volatility, infidelity and suffering (it doesn't always, of course, just most of the time, especially if it's me that's doing the intaking) or Lee would have to stop drinking. Even though he had never once displayed any inclination towards being violent, when drunk or sober, his drinking patterns still demonstrated the same behaviours of my dad and previous partners.

He stopped drinking. The relationship was new, he was in love and he feared losing me. It is something that I will always be grateful for. His family and friends couldn't believe it. They told me frequently that I was the best thing that had ever happened to him, although I'm not sure that I was. I think they were unaware of my own issues, which Lee, using great patience and compassion, supported me with.

Regardless of whether Lee and I were ready to cohabit, having given my dilapidated house back to my ex-partner, my housing situation forced a speedier progression of our relationship. We had been together fewer than twelve months and had already dealt with, and continued to deal with, the challenges of his alcohol intake and my severe insecurity and anxiety. I can't say that I felt safe in the relationship at this point, nor did I feel like it was particularly stable, but that was nothing new, going by most of my previous romantic experiences. The main priority for me was my dog, Peggy – her needs came before anything else, and she needed a home. Even though I had a campervan at this time, for holidays, the possibility of living in it permanently didn't cross my mind. Instead, I bought into the dream of a future that depended on being part of a couple.

Lee was already living in the Lake District when I met him, studying for a degree as a mature student. He lived in a flat near one of the main towns. His rent was paid for by his parents (something which was unheard of in my working-class background) and his living costs were covered by a small wage that he received from a part-time job. While we were looking for somewhere to live, it became clear that almost all the rental properties stipulated a 'no pets' policy, and the one Lee was living in was no different. After weeks of searching for a houseshare, a bedsit or a flat that would accept pets, but also be affordable, it became clear that there was nothing.

As a solution to our housing problem, I put forward the idea of buying a caravan to live in and placing it on a campsite in an area that was central to each of our universities.

When I first met Lee, I was in my last year of study for a degree in fine art (I'm incredibly proud to say that I was awarded a first). Having found the confidence and motivation to return to study in my early thirties, I was encouraged and supported by my tutor, the artist Carole Griffiths, to continue to develop my creativity, and the writing aspects of my art, by undertaking a master's in creative writing. I applied to study the masters at a university near the Lake District, and was accepted.

Lee wasn't so sure about living full-time in a caravan – his life had been conventional until he'd met me and he was a big fan of keeping to the rules. The main rule, in this situation, was that using a caravan as a sole residence (your main place of habitation) on a campsite is technically against the law as most campsites are not licensed for residential occupation. Yet people living permanently on campsites, even when they shouldn't, is relatively common, and becoming more so as the cost of living rises. I eventually managed to convince Lee that living in a caravan was a viable option for us, based on how much money we would save by doing so, and he begrudgingly agreed.

A full-season pitch equates to ten months of use as most campsites close for approximately six weeks a year, from early January onwards, in order to avoid any issues with council tax. The cost of a pitch works out at about £300 per month (depending on the campsite), and the fees are required to be paid in full before a caravan is sited. If we decided to move forward with the idea to live in a caravan on a site, there would be the issue of where we would live for the six to eight weeks that the campsite would be closed, but I've never been one for forward planning – I find it takes the excitement out of life – so I figured something would turn up when we needed it. Being open to opportunities and possibilities sometimes requires letting go of plans and expectations. And sanity, letting go of that too.

All we needed now was a caravan.

The caravan that I'd winched over the back wall of my old house and used as a bedroom while renting out the rooms wasn't big enough for two people and a large dog to live in full-time. When I'd handed over the keys of my house to my ex, I'd had to get rid of my little caravan – it wasn't a garden feature that he'd wanted to keep. I put it on eBay with a starting bid of 99p. After the seven-day bidding period was over, it sold. For a tenner . . . not much more than a coffee and a piece of overpriced cake from a Nero café.

The people who had won the caravan on eBay were coming to collect it the next day, but I'd somehow forgotten about the wall, which completely sealed the caravan into the garden – the very same wall that we'd winched it over in the first place. There was only one thing I could do really. In the morning, two hours before the buyers were due to arrive, I simply knocked down the wall. Problem solved. If I remember correctly, I was still wearing my pyjamas while I inexpertly wielded a borrowed sledgehammer. The neighbours had ceased to be shocked by anything that occurred at my house.

I spent hours scouring caravan adverts on all of the available platforms and eventually found something that caught my eye. It was a poorly written advertisement with the straightforward, catchy title of 'big caravan for sale. old. no damp'. Most people wouldn't have clicked on it – the main photo they'd used for the advert was a bit blurry and it wasn't exactly selling itself. From experience though, I knew that it was often these adverts that had the most potential for the least amount of money. I clicked on it to read the full advert and have a look at the rest of the photos. The caravan was a four-berth, fixed double bed, twenty-six-foot-long, seven-and-a-half-foot-wide, twin-axle, Tabbert Comtesse Deluxe. And it was beautiful. The cupboards were made of real veneer and solid wood, rather than plastic laminated MDF, and the floor was a parquet design, giving it the feel of a seventies farmhouse cottage. For fifteen hundred quid, it was a bargain. Unfortunately, it was also in Essex, which was some distance from the Lake District.

The secret weapon of this operation was my friend Viking Andy, who had every towing, driving and motorbiking licence you could think of. He is a regular mead-drinking, axe-throwing, spoon-whittling, metal-drumming, transport legend. He agreed to collect the caravan for us from Essex (for a price, of course) and deliver it to whichever Lake District campsite we decided on. The deal was done, the caravan was paid for and the transport was arranged.

The Camping and Caravanning Club Windermere was the campsite that we had chosen. It was in a great location (despite the name, it was not what anyone would call particularly close to Lake Windermere, but it was closer than, say, Swansea was) and was one of the cheapest campsites in the area. We arranged to meet Andy, who had our new caravan in tow, at the campsite that would be our home. My campervan and Lee's smaller work van were packed to the rafters with all of our belongings, and poor Peggy squashed in amongst it all.

At a certain point on the journey up to the Lake District, the landscape opened out like it was auditioning for a film, filling the windscreen of my van. The rolling, companionable hills of the Yorkshire Dales promptly gave way to the jagged, untamed drama of the mountains. It's a view that will pause an exhale and capture a breath quicker than any meditation practice. The Lake District was now my home and, despite any misgivings I had about my relationship, I was excited at the prospect of being in and part of such an inspiring landscape.

We arrived at the campsite at the same time: Andy, towing our substantial caravan with his huge Mercedes van, me, with my large campervan, and Lee, with his smaller van. Our convoy caused a stir with the staff at the campsite, who came flying out of the reception office with facial expressions that weren't very welcoming. Lee calmly explained that we'd purchased a seasonal pitch and had agreed today as an arrival date with the campsite manager. There was some huffing and puffing among the staff as we clearly didn't fit the usual bill of middle-class retirees with a shiny new thirty-grand caravan in tow. I must admit, with our collective vehicles, together with our old, beige-coloured caravan, it's possible that we did look like individuals from a travelling community of some description, which I think is exactly what the staff at the campsite thought.

They argued that the length of our caravan was longer than the campsite had stipulated they would accept, but we knew that it was within the measurements for the pitch criteria as we'd checked before we purchased it. Which it was, after they measured it again with great ceremony. They had no choice but to take us to our pitch, having exhausted any valid reason for us not to be there. We had, after all, paid for it in full. One staff member asked us outright whether we were planning on living there permanently. 'Oh, of course not,' I lied, fluttering my eyelashes and smiling in what I hoped was a disarming manner, 'we just love the Lake District!' He grunted, clearly disbelieving our motives for being there, but became more cordial, grudgingly helping us to put our caravan in place on our pitch.

After a few short months of staying on the site, as they got to know us, the campsite staff's attitude towards us changed and we became an integral part of the campsite dynamic. I started hosting karaoke nights in the clubhouse with Tony the resident DJ and we often had get-togethers where the campsite manager would cook delicious curries for all of the regular campsite inhabitants (and for those of us who lived there permanently, of which there were quite a few). It was truly a fantastic community to be part of, with characters like Dunc the Monk, a gentle giant who practised Buddhism, Scottish Margaret, the clubhouse landlady, Pete the maintenance man and Hoody, an alcoholic who lived permanently in a tiny two-man tent – everyone looked out for Hoody; he helped out on the campsite and would always lend a hand putting up awnings or siting caravans. I'm sad to say that Hoody passed away a few years ago, another victim of alcohol abuse.

The campsite was a beautiful place to live; set in and among rolling green fields that were scattered with limestone boulders of interesting and mysterious shapes, copses of deer-filled brooding woodland, with views of the mountains beyond. During our time there, we were immersed in nature, hiking the snow-covered mountains in winter, swimming in the crystal-clear mountain pools in summer, watching twinkling showers of meteors and shooting stars in the autumn, and being enveloped by the heady fragrance of bluebells in the spring. It was a place of present moments, a landscape of grateful musings, a heart-filling space of life-affirming experiences.

January was fast approaching and, so far, Lee and I had been unable to find anywhere to live for the six weeks that the campsite would be closed. This was something that the campsite manager would not compromise on – no one was allowed to stay on site during the closure. As a last resort, we agreed that we would live in my campervan. We had been on holiday several times previously in my van with Peggy and, though it was a bit cramped and didn't have a heater, it would be manageable for six weeks. But it was going to be bloody cold.

Our campsite community knew of our predicament and had been asking around to try to find somewhere for us to stay. A week before the campsite closed, Pete, the maintenance man and gardener for the campsite, approached us with an unexpected and unconventional solution to our housing issue. How would we like to live in a nursing home for the winter or, more precisely, a supported housing project for the elderly consisting of individual flats with a communal dining room situated in the very heart of the Lake District? 'What about my dog?' I asked. Surely a fifty-kilogram American Akita wouldn't be allowed to live in a nursing home? Would she? Apparently she would. Pete's partner was the manager of the flats, which were privately owned, and she was more than happy to allow Peggy to come along. The deal was that, in exchange for tidying up the large, shared garden for the flats, we could live there and pay a reduced rent for the six weeks that the campsite was closed. It was brilliant.

The 'flat' was literally one room, with a tiny alcove for the kitchen and a small toilet and shower cubicle. Perpetually warm, frequently too warm, the central heating was on continuously, which made coming in from icy, snowy, slush-wet, numb-footed hikes absolute bliss. The residents were wonderful; a fabulous bunch of human beings in their later years. We'd been requested by the support staff to keep an eye on our neighbour, a glamourous lady in her eighties who was reluctant to relinquish her high-heeled shoes, shoes that had caused her to trip and fall on several occasions. She did indeed have a fall while I lived there, knocking her head quite severely on the corner of a table (ouch, yes, there was a lot of blood). It was pure luck that I wasn't at work or university that day, so I was around to hear her faint calls for help. The ambulance arrived quickly, and she was taken to hospital to be treated for mild concussion, before being sent home a day or so later. Two weeks after this happened, I looked out of my window to see her tottering precariously up the steep drive wearing her favourite black patent stilettoes. What can you do?

Nursing home life was a wonderful experience, but the weeks flew by and soon it was time to go back to the campsite.

The one thing that I missed while living in a caravan and at the nursing home was a bath – you can't beat a good soak in a bath. When the winter cold seems to have settled into your very bones, sometimes only a hot bath will take away the chill. Thankfully, we live in a world full of innovation and invention because, after some searching on eBay, it would seem that there is indeed such a thing as a portable bath. Made of the same material as your average Argos paddling pool and shaped like a hot tub, the inflatable bath was an absolute revelation. We kept it in the caravan awning as it was easier to empty from there, the outlet pipe steadily trickling spent bath water out on to the grass nearby. It took fourteen buckets of water to fill, each brimming bucket painstakingly carried from the campsite facilities block, something which became a Sunday night ritual. Due to the shape of the blow-up bath, it was only possible to sit in it, with knees tucked awkwardly under the chin, but the sensation of being in hot water while the cold air in the awning kissed bare, unsubmerged skin, was pure decadence.

The Lake District may have been an idyllic place to live, but things were far from perfect. While we'd been staying in the nursing home, Lee had revealed that he was unsure about our relationship and our future together. He explained that he didn't know whether he loved me or loved me *enough* to continue as we were. We discussed why he was having these doubts, and he made it clear that his feelings were related to alcohol and his resentment of me for being the reason that he was unable to drink. Our relationship had clearly moved out of the romantic stage and had entered into another, where his fear of not being able to drink now outweighed his fear of losing me. The anxiety and insecurity that I suffered from was particularly prominent at this time, likely influenced by the fact that I'd recently given up my home and was financially reliant on the success of a relationship that wasn't working. Although the costs involved to live in a caravan on a campsite were lower than if we had been living in rented accommodation, because I was studying with my only income being from a part-time job, I wouldn't be able to afford it on my own if the relationship ended.

Lee and I would argue frequently, friction that usually arose from my need for reassurance. Because I felt so unsettled, a few nights a week I slept alone in my campervan in the car park of the campsite. It was the only place where I felt truly safe. The relationship continued in emotional disarray; moments of deep love, connection and adventure, tempered by toxic insecurity and uncertainty.

Even though my mental and emotional health see-sawed precariously while I lived in the Lake District, from positively connecting with nature in a mindful way to despairing over my dysfunctional and insatiable insecurity, the experience of living in a caravan, of existing comfortably with so little, was a revelation so immense that I struggle to find the words to accurately describe it.

A tiny seed of possibility had awakened and was slowly beginning to unfurl within me. One stone, the first of many, had crumbled from the prison wall, and the view beyond, of open spaces and adventure, of debt-free peace of mind, was beckoning.

Chapter Six

Write the Way Out

When will the hobbits stop singing? All they do is sing, I thought, with the petulant resentment of the six-year-old child that I was. I desperately wanted the story to move forward, to find out what wonders, peril and excitement were laid out on the next page. Bring back the Ringwraiths; they were far less likely to break into song. I prayed for my mum to read faster. My brother and I were tucked up on either side of her on the living room couch, while she read *The Lord of the Rings* out loud to us. It was a bedtime ritual that lasted for the majority of my childhood and is one of the only happy consistent memories I have during that volatile time. My mum had chosen the middle school that my brother and I attended based on a single statement made by the school headmaster during an open day: he'd said, 'if a child can read, then they can do anything, and be anything, that they want'. The phrase, and concept, deeply resonated with my mum, who has been an avid bibliophile all her life.

Being introduced early on in my life to the infinite amount of worlds existing within books, it became clear that all I had to do in order to escape reality was to open the pages of one. Even after reading the first few lines, I would be transported, in a waft of musty dry air, to somewhere else entirely. Saturday trips to the local library were my favourite. I would sit, cross-legged, in the young adult section, even though I was only eight, and choose which worlds to visit next. I loved supernatural stories steeped in mysticism and mystery, folkloric tales of witches, fairies, selkies, mermaids and secret lands accessible only to those who knew the right stones to touch of a fairy circle on a waxing moon.

During the third year of middle school (I was eleven years old), my English teacher decided that I was too advanced in the subject to continue in the class that I was in. He explained to both the head of year and my mum that it would be detrimental for my development if I was forced to learn at a level lower than where I was. My obsession with stories, and my need for the escapism that reading brought, had increased my knowledge of vocabulary beyond that of my peers. I'd already progressed from reading the entire collection of *Point Horror* and *Goosebumps* books in the school library, which I thought were fabulous, to reading literature aimed at adults, rather than at a younger audience. The school drafted in a university lecturer to teach both me and another girl in a separate class. Even out of school, I already wrote my own poems and short stories; the new class, with the new teacher, gave me both the space and the encouragement that I needed to further develop my young literary voice.

At fourteen years old, I discovered drugs, boys and alcohol (not necessarily in that order) and my writing, though it continued, became a disorganised and tumultuous series of angst-ridden, self-pitying, hormone-fuelled, terrible poetry. Writing is writing, however, and even though the words of my teenage self were unfit to be read by anyone but myself, my artistry, if you could call it that, was still being developed by the simple fact that I was putting words on a page. Throughout my early to late teens, I was still an avid reader, even though I refused to read non-fiction. My genre of choice was always fantasy, with the odd historical romance thrown in as light relief from dragons, wizards and unicorns. In my head, life had been, and still was, complicated and traumatic enough without reading about someone else's.

When I was seventeen years old, I was introduced, through mutual friends, to two aspiring musicians. They were looking for a singer and, though I was terrified at the time, I put myself forward to audition. Throughout school, I'd been in the choir and was often picked for solo parts in productions, whether it was singing, acting or performing. I loved being on stage in general, and I loved singing. The audition went well and, from then on, I was officially in the band. My terrible, angsty poetry about poor mental health, cheating boyfriends and heartbreak was repurposed and put to use as song lyrics. Being in the band gave me a constructive creative outlet, beyond the drunk, morose, snot-stained, tear-streaked scribblings that were my previous operational standard. Channelling the hurt that I felt into music, rather than allowing it to consume me, changed the dynamic of the pain. A broken heart that would have previously had me locked in my room, drinking cheap sherry, listening to Jeff Buckley and pushing all the moisture in my body out of my eyes, instead became a humorous revenge song which had the unfortunate lyrics 'riding to the rhythm of your knock'.

One of the main positives from being in a band, certainly this band, was that I wasn't alone. We were a creative family, with the music studio that we worked in a place where I felt completely safe and supported. Everything that I went through, every emotion that moved me to write a song or to construct a melody, was shared and understood by my band mates, Adam and Sy. We created together and we supported each other. Not all bands are like this, which was something I discovered while I was in my mid-twenties . . .

I was working as a sound technician in a local music studio; setting up PA systems for bands who hired out the practice rooms, fiddling with knobs on complicated mixing desks pretending that I knew what I was doing, putting reverb on everything because I thought it sounded better, which is how I met Gary . . .

Gary was a very talented and experienced musician. Everyone in the scene knew him, so when he asked if I wanted to be in a band with him, it felt like a really big deal. I was blown away that he deemed my musical abilities good enough to collaborate with. Even though our musical influences were on opposite sides of the musical spectrum (Pentagram versus Peter Gabriel), I was willing to give it a try. Perhaps the vivid contrast in what informed our art would enable us to create music that would be something completely unique. We recruited a guitarist and a drummer, both of whom were phenomenally talented. Melodies, beats, riffs and lyrics poured out of us with ease and I was in my element. I would dress up in flamboyant ball gowns for live performances, use my voice in ways that I'd never done before and put on shows that were so much more than simply playing live music.

Inevitably, it completely and utterly fucked up.

Gary started to confide in me things that I felt were inappropriate – aspects of his life that I didn't want to hear about – that left me in a difficult and uncomfortable position. I didn't understand why he was sharing such intimate details. My responses were always non-committal and as vague as I could make them in an attempt to discourage these conversations.

The band continued to perform, to make music and to get our name out there. We were offered more gigs and, with them, came more opportunities. We were entered into a battle of the bands, the winner of which would play at a well-known local festival, where bands like James and the Kaiser Chiefs had played. I was beyond myself with excitement.

During a band practice prior to playing at the battle of the bands, I'd gone outside with Gary for a cigarette. He was again sharing details of his life that were inappropriate and made me feel desperately uncomfortable. 'Why?' I asked him. 'Why are you telling me all this?' He stared with an unnerving intensity and replied, 'because I'm in love with you.' What? Hold the fuck on a minute. Okay, we were playing in a band together, but he barely knew me. 'I'm really flattered, Gary, but I don't see you like that. We're friends. Band mates. That's as far as it goes. I hope this won't affect the band?' 'Of course not,' he replied. But, of course, it did.

Gary began to cancel band practices. He was rude and abrupt when I saw him. The final straw came when he refused to play the battle of the bands gig – the performance of our career. I couldn't tell the others in the band what Gary had said and why things had turned sour. I couldn't tell *anyone* what was happening. If I did, it would inevitably be brought back to me and twisted somehow so that I became the perpetrator. From what I'd witnessed in situations like this before (this happened prior to the 'Me Too' movement), women who spoke up about unwanted romantic attention were branded as troublemakers and home-wreckers. And all they'd done to warrant that toxic view was exist and be found desirable. I left the band without telling anyone why. It broke my heart more than any relationship breakdown ever had, namely because I now had nowhere to legitimately wear ridiculous ball gowns.

Writing lyrics and poetry, and creating music, taught me one of the most valuable lessons of my life: that I had the power to transform a difficult experience into something else entirely and, by doing so, I could change the very nature of that experience and how it affected me. Vulnerability is a superpower, anxiety is a superpower, and trauma can also be a superpower. The hardest experiences can sometimes be the most beautiful and the most rewarding, changing us in positive ways or directing our lives down paths which, though we may not have chosen them, lead us to wonderful things.

In my early thirties, I decided that it was time to get myself an education. I openly admit that it's entirely possible that my decision may have been motivated by the fact that I'd had enough of working forty hours a week. I applied to study a degree in fine art at Bradford College, even though the only qualifications I had were a couple of GCSEs above grade C and two NVQs – one in customer services and another in library and information services. As a mature student, it didn't seem to matter that I was, at least on paper, lacking an education. All I had to do was show the tutors at the college a few watercolour paintings, which I'd produced during a twelve-week evening class, and I was offered a place. Although I suspect I'd have still got a place if all I'd shown them was a coffee stain on a napkin; funding for all educational institutions isn't what it should be, and each course that the college offered required a certain percentage of students confirmed as attending before it could even go ahead.

Through the art that I created for my degree, as I had with my music, I transformed emotions and experiences into tangible compositions. Yet it was only during my last year of study at Bradford College that I began to allow my experience of domestic violence to actively inform the work that I was producing. It was a theme that I'd avoided up until that point, both as a musician and as an artist. The art that I produced from exploring that time in my life was both shocking and engaging. It's a heady feeling, and a great responsibility, to know that what you put out into the world, as an artist, as a musician or as a human, can have the power to change whoever views or experiences it. As I moved forward with my degree, it became apparent that words and language were an integral aspect of how I expressed myself, regardless of the medium or the platform. I was the first person in my family to have attended university, and I completed my degree with first-class honours. Poetry was part of the visual art that I was producing and, when I finished my degree, my wonderful tutor Carole, who is an amazing artist herself, encouraged me to pursue a master's degree in creative writing.

Lancaster University accepted my application to study a master's, even though I was unsure that they would. The only qualification I had in English was one GCSE, but my degree in fine art and a portfolio of terrible poetry secured me a place on the course. The year that I spent studying at Lancaster was the most informative of my life. My tutor pushed the boundaries of what we thought we were capable of as writers and encouraged us to work outside of our comfort zones. I had free rein to put whatever I wanted, however I wanted, on to the page. As is the case in the majority of creative classroom environments, the class, consisting of twelve or so students, was encouraged to critique and offer feedback on each other's work. The feedback that I received from my peers was phenomenal – it illuminated all the dark spaces in my mind where self-doubt was hiding and I began to think that maybe, just maybe, I might actually be good at writing. It was a liberating experience to be in a class full of creative people where I felt secure enough to share my work, and where I had the ultimate privilege of being party to theirs. The creativity of human beings never ceases to delight, inspire and astound me.

Life happened, as it does, and I didn't manage to finish the master's, having completed one year of the part-time two-year course. But I didn't stop writing. I began to put together a collection of prose, lyrical essays, poetry and letters, which I addressed to Ricky Gervais. Out of all the people in the world I could address my work to, he seemed the obvious choice. It was my friend Eleanor, who is the most creative person I know (and the one least likely to think that I was mental), who I eventually confided in regarding my writing project: 'Um, so I've been writing this thing, err, some poetry and letters and stuff, and it's kind of, maybe, addressed to, well, Ricky Gervais. What do you think?'

I first met Eleanor through my job as a stage-builder; the work that I did in stage-building would occasionally overlap with projects that had been set up via an international arts company that she had established. Initially, I was intimidated by the blinding vibrancy of her personality, her irrepressible drive, creativity and boundless energy, alongside her hula-hooping capabilities (which are at professional levels). But having worked with her on several occasions, it became clear that we shared a lot of common ground. Our life experiences of childhood trauma, our working-class background, our previous substance abuse issues, and the way that we both dealt with it all using humour, developed our working relationship into one of the most important friendships of my life.

Eleanor has worked within the art industry all her life – she passionately believes that art should be for everyone and anyone, regardless of their background. Her focus has always been to increase community engagement with art and use the power of art to break down barriers, inspire, create opportunities and expand inclusivity. She is a pioneer when it comes to conceptual and interactive art, and, before I knew her, once curated a live art installation that involved putting an epilepsy sufferer into a cage full of strobe lights . . . what is art if it's not pushing the boundaries? When her book comes out, which I hope it will, it will turn heads and blow minds.

Eleanor read my collection, and absolutely loved it. Since the start of our friendship, she has always been my biggest supporter and greatest inspiration.

The Covid-19 pandemic happened and I shelved my writing. I was too busy working for the NHS and getting over a broken heart to focus on anything else. It was a year or so later, when I first started living full-time in my van (I was thirty-six or thirty-seven years old), that I felt motivated to write again. I was living in Cornwall, where there had been a lot of negative press in the local newspapers regarding people living in vans. Most of the articles were outright discriminatory, unconstructive and lacking any compassion or humanity. No one was speaking up on behalf of the vanlife community. I toyed with the idea of writing an article as a response; perhaps if I told my story of how I came to live in a van, people would come to understand that I'm no different from them, just a fellow human being trying to get by in the world.

I penned an article in the style of an open letter, looked up some email addresses for a few local newspapers . . . and then got the fear. Who did I think I was – writing an article and daring to think that someone, somewhere, would actually publish it? The nasty little voice inside my head was on overdrive: 'No one wants to hear what you've got to say, you aren't important, you're just a working-class shit bag with nothing to offer anyone, you don't even have proper eyebrows [true], you can't boil an egg [also true] and you're crap in every way. Writing articles is for people better than you, who are more educated and have better eyebrows, so get some chocolate, keep watching reruns of *River Monsters* and sit the fuck down.'

I am so awful to myself, in my head. Thankfully, I had access to the divine power of Eleanor's belief in me . . . not just her belief in me as a person, as someone who can achieve anything that they put their mind to, but her belief in my writing skills. She has always taught me that possibilities in life are only limited by our imagination and our fear of failure. Fuck it, I thought, I'll submit the article. What did I have to lose?

Through Eleanor's art world connections, I managed to procure several email addresses for individuals who worked at the *Guardian* newspaper. Eventually, after sending a few emails, I was directed to the features editor of the newspaper, who I emailed my article to directly. To my utter surprise and immense delight, she loved it. The article required some subtle refining and editing, which she was kind enough to help with, but the story that I was communicating remained the same. Two weeks later, it went to print and I became an officially published writer. On the same day that the article was printed, my Instagram account went wild with new followers – I was inundated with messages from people all over the world and contacted by several literary agents. I remember being at work at the time and feeling hugely overwhelmed by the unexpected and unprecedented response.

In my experience, if we have the courage to put something of ourselves out into the world – our art, our truth – despite the uncertainty and fear of failure, then the universe will reward that bravery by opening doors and providing opportunities that we never thought possible, which is exactly what happened when I had my article published. Writing this book has enabled me to transform some of the more difficult experiences that I've had in my life into something beautiful, something creative, a piece of art that will hopefully inspire others. I am writing my way out of my past and, in doing so, I am fully inhabiting the present.

Chapter Seven
The Life I Took

It was street theatre, of a sort. A violent and horrific recital fuelled by excessive alcohol intake, PTSD and severe anxiety, intensified by hormonal changes that were, as yet, unknown. The stage was set: a narrow backstreet in between two towering, sand-coloured hotel blocks, their occupants an unwilling audience for the performance. They stood out on their balconies, open windows spilling subdued light into the hazy heat of the evening. It looked like they were waiting for a procession to fill the street below, a celebration of some kind. But at two o'clock in the morning, the only thing they would be celebrating would be my silence, when, and if, it came. Some jeered at me from their lofty lookouts, demanding quiet; others laughed at the drama unfolding before them, clearly entertained. My shouts and screams projected into the night, delivered at an almost superhuman volume, alcohol magnifying every trauma I'd ever experienced before spewing it out of my mouth in a tirade of toxic malice.

Kicking and punching, I attacked my seventeen-year-old boyfriend while he tried to physically restrain me. I was completely out of control.

We were on holiday in Malta, one of the most beautiful places I had ever been, not that I was coherent or calm enough at the time to fully appreciate it. My mum had finally divorced my dad the year before and recently decided that we all needed a 'real' holiday, rather than a few days at a cold, dilapidated Butlin's. My boyfriend, my brother, his friend, my mum and I had all come away together. My mum had paid for me and my brother, but everyone else had paid for themselves. A week away abroad was an extravagance that she could barely afford. I think it was her way of making up for all the years that my brother and I (and her) had spent in fear. But the damage done during that time wasn't something that could be fixed by a week in the warm, Mediterranean sun.

My boyfriend was two years older than me. We began our relationship when I was just fourteen years old. I lost my virginity, under the legal age, on a rickety bunk bed with Celine Dion's 'My Heart Will Go On' playing in the background via a cassette in my Argos karaoke machine. There are worse ways to lose sexual innocence. However, he was not the right person for me to become intimate with so early on in my life. Even at sixteen years old, he was a compulsive liar and a maestro of manipulation; he took pleasure in causing confusion and uncertainty. Even now, I have no idea what sort of childhood he may have had or what experiences had contributed to his character. He cheated on me frequently – rumours would circulate in our friendship group of his infidelities and, when confronted, he would tell me that it was all in my head; that I was in the wrong for questioning his faithfulness. This only compounded the negative effects on my mental health – from a fear-filled childhood lacking safety, straight into a toxic relationship with the same. My response to it all was to drink. I would drink to try to remove myself from how I was feeling and, in my inebriated state, I would turn violent. I blamed myself for my dad's brutal behaviour and I blamed myself for the infidelities of my partner. I wasn't good enough or well-behaved enough to be loved or kept safe, and I wasn't pretty enough to prevent my teenage lover from straying.

When my mum left my brother and I to live with her new partner in another town, once a week, she would do a food shop for us, dropping it off every Saturday to ensure that we were fed and that her feelings of guilt for leaving us were assuaged. It's not the most productive idea to leave two teenagers, both of whom had PTSD and who were just discovering drugs, in a house on their own. But I don't blame my mum for her desire to completely distance herself from her previous life, although I do sometimes blame myself for pushing her away. I was a difficult child, and an even worse teenager, for good reason of course, but still . . .

My boyfriend moved in with me at my mum's house after she left. She wasn't there to police the issue, or indeed any issue, so we did what we wanted. We had no external discipline whatsoever. We threw frequent parties that almost always ended up in a fracas of some description, and people of all ages would come and go from the house, at all times, day or night. The front door was never locked and anyone with drugs or booze was more than welcome. The neighbours detested us, and quite rightly so. When she found out that my young boyfriend was living at the house, my mum allowed it to continue (not that she could have stopped it without moving back in, which, for her, wasn't an option). Her view was that hormonal teenagers would find a way to explore their sexuality, regardless of any barriers that were put in place, and it was safer if that was done in a comfortable environment with access to condoms. I was duly marched down to the family planning clinic and given the contraceptive pill. But the issue with both condoms and contraceptive pills is that they have to be used, or taken, in order to be effective. I always forgot to take the pill and my partner disliked using condoms – he convinced me that using the 'pull out' method would prevent any pregnancy. As I was two years younger than him, with absolutely no self-confidence or experience, I didn't think to question his theory.

When we arrived back from the drunken, violent chaos that was our week in Malta, my boyfriend's mum collected us from the airport and drove us back to the house that my mum owned, but didn't live in. My irrational behaviour had ruined the holiday for everyone. The hatred that I had for myself was without limit. Mixed in with the feelings of shame, self-loathing and despair was a growing anxiety that my period, which should have arrived while we were away, was nowhere to be seen. I'd had a pregnancy scare previously, so I knew there was a spare test hidden in the back of the airing cupboard in the bathroom. While everyone was busy dragging their luggage into the house, catching up and making tea, I locked myself in the bathroom, urinated into the little pot provided and dipped the stick of doom (or joy, depending on your circumstances). Regardless of what the test revealed, I already knew what the result would be. I was right. And unfortunately, so was Clifford, my history teacher. The inappropriate, vicious, fortune-telling statement that he had delivered to me in class, two years before, had indeed come to pass (if only he had instead given me the winning lottery numbers). On the stick, two very clear and pronounced lines materialised. My heart rate increased. I ran out of the bathroom, stopping at the top of the stairs to shout for my mum, my voice hoarse and urgent. I think she already knew why I was shouting for her, so when she joined me in the bathroom and saw the pregnancy test result, there was very little surprise in her reaction, just exasperated disappointment.

There was absolutely no mention of the possibility of seeing the pregnancy through. The only option that my mum discussed with me was termination. For a brief moment, I thought about keeping the life inside me and vocalised this to my mum, but she swiftly stamped out any such thoughts, labelling them as being ridiculous and irrational, which perhaps they were. Frightened by what was happening, I allowed her to take control of the situation and, within the space of a week, I had an appointment booked at a private clinic in Manchester. Her efficiency was commendable.

The first appointment, which involved a scan of the foetus to determine how far along my pregnancy was, was a surreal experience. The nurse doing the scan asked if I wanted to see the foetus on the screen. I was shocked that she'd asked. After all, it would be sucked out of me in a matter of weeks. Perhaps it was to drive home the gravity of my situation, the life that would no longer have a chance to live because of my irresponsible behaviour. Still, when the nurse smoothed cool gel over my exposed stomach and rolled the ultrasound across my skin, I couldn't help but look at the screen by my side. I wanted to see what life looked like, at the very beginning of it all. Would it glow like a blown-out match-head, filling the screen with the light of aliveness? Or pulse like the floorboards at a party when the bass volume was too high? But it did neither. As I looked at the screen, my eyes were confronted by swirls and shapes in greys and blacks that I didn't understand.

My mum wouldn't allow me to have the termination on the NHS as she worked at the local hospital and knew most of the staff there. After my GCSEs were finished, it had been arranged for me to start an apprenticeship in library and information services at the medical library in the same hospital. She was ashamed that her fifteen-year-old daughter was pregnant, and concerned regarding how that would reflect on her parenting skills. As I was due to start work myself at the hospital, I think she felt that it would be inappropriate if the doctor who carried out my pregnancy termination was also someone whose books I would be stamping. Terminations arranged through the private healthcare sector aren't cheap, costing nearly £1,000, which my mum and my partner's mum paid. A thousand pounds to take a life, to change many futures and to buy the silence required to avoid the negative judgement of others.

In front of my friends, the only way that I could cope with being pregnant was to joke about it, to make light of the fact that inside me was a life which would soon be snuffed out (although for the life of me, or for the life of an unborn child, I can't think of any jokes right now). Using comedy and humour to deflect trauma was a technique that I'd learnt to employ which softened the edges of the horrific, smoothing them out so that instead they became simply unpleasant, which was far easier to process. There is humour to be found in any situation, however terrible.

I was a churning wreck of conflicting emotions. Alongside everything else, morning sickness started – a vehement reminder of the changes that were happening in my body. For me, it wasn't a case of feeling slightly nauseous during the early hours of each day. Instead, it took over my body with aggressive abandon. I projectile vomited anything that I ate with such force that it exploded out of not just my mouth, but also both of my nostrils. It was truly horrific. I'll never forget the Scotch broth incident, where pearl barley shot out of my nose like bullets from a machine gun. After a week or so of this, with my body getting progressively weaker due to the lack of nourishment, and my throat and nose sore from stomach acid, I was taken to A&E. They injected me with something that stopped the sickness immediately, and permanently, a pharmaceutical that they would only consent to give me because I was having a termination, which they'd had to confirm with the private clinic before administering it.

My parents never touched each other in front of me and my brother. Ever. There was only a single moment in my entire childhood when I saw them hold hands, which was during a day out to York. As children, we didn't lack completely for love – my mum read to us most nights – but the love was infrequent and always overshadowed by fear. Because my emotional needs weren't being met, I began to perceive 'things' as being the tangible evidence that I needed to prove that I was loved. I frequently demanded toys which my family couldn't afford to buy. When they refused, I'd have tantrums or sobbing fits, equating the lack of toy with being unloved, until I was placated with either verbal reassurance by my mum or subdued with terror by my dad.

The difficulties that I caused my mum as a child, and the anger that I provoked in my dad due to my tantrums, helped to cement what would become a core belief for me, something which I still struggle with today: that I was nothing but a burden, wrong in every way and a source of pain to those around me. Due to this early formed core belief, suicidal thoughts were nothing new to me. Even as young as six years old, I had moments when I thought my family would be happier without me, even if, back then, I was too young to truly comprehend the concept of suicide.

My bedroom at my mum's house was three flights up, a sloping roofed attic space with a skylight that opened wide enough to climb out of. During the time that I was pregnant and waiting for the abortion, around my sixteenth birthday, I didn't leave my room unless it was absolutely necessary. I was completely crippled with anxiety, my head full of intrusive thoughts, my system constantly flooded with limb-shaking adrenaline and tin-tasting cortisol. I honestly believed that I was completely broken, dysfunctional beyond any hope of repair. In my logic, the only viable option which would cause the least amount of suffering for everyone, including the child that I had inside me, was for me to die. However, taking my own life required a strength of will that I didn't have. Every time a thought came into my mind that caused me distress, and every time I seriously considered throwing myself off the roof, I would reach for a Terry Pratchett novel to distract me. The way that he softened serious issues with humour, expertly blending the inhumane with the mundane, the accessibility and humanity of his characters, and the fantasy world that he had created, somehow a mirror to our own, was the escape from reality, and from my own mind, that I desperately needed. Days would go by when I would stay in bed with my head under the blankets reading and rereading the same paragraph over and over again, while battling an almost physical urge to leap out of the window. I was so very alone at this time and incredibly unwell.

The abortion date was set. My GCSEs were now over, even though I'd barely attended any of the exams, except English, art, humanities and graphics. My last year at school was a blur of trauma, a fog of cannabis and a chaos of heavy drinking. On the way to the clinic in Manchester, I wasn't scared. I didn't really feel anything at all. My mind had shut down – perhaps going into some kind of survival mode, it refused to take part in the experience, which I was grateful for. My only concern was the needles that would be used in the procedure. I had a severe fear of needles and a consistent track record for fainting during the various injectable inoculations that we had received at school. My mum, with her knowledge of the clinical world due to her job as a medical secretary, requested a numbing cream for my hand prior to the nurse inserting the cannula, a device that goes into the vein and stays there, taped on to the hand, enabling direct access to the bloodstream. I didn't feel anything when the nurse fitted it, and I didn't look, choosing instead to completely ignore the piece of hard plastic and sharp metal that was slotted into my hand.

I was taken down to theatre in a wheelchair wearing nothing but a thin hospital gown. In a dream state born of shock, I was only vaguely aware of my surroundings and what was happening to me. The mind is an amazing instrument; it has the ability to work completely autonomously of conscious thought or direction. It will choose to disconnect and disengage from situations that it perceives are traumatic (I suspect that's why my memory is so poor, having spent a lot of my childhood and early adult life switched off). Once we arrived at the theatre, I was asked to lie on a hospital bed. They then injected the anaesthetic into my bloodstream via the cannula. And that was it. I woke up, feeling nauseous from the anaesthetic, but relieved that it was all over.

The clinic offered me counselling, but it was too far away from where I lived, and having counselling meant thinking about it, which I didn't want to do. After my discharge, which was the same day, I asked my mum for a McDonald's Happy Meal on account of being such a brave girl, and she acquiesced.

A human life in exchange for a McDonald's Happy Meal – there is much to unravel in that statement, which I'll leave to you, in case I, myself, unravel with the task of it.

Chapter Eight
She's Got a Ticket to Fly

The sea and sky fill my gaze as I drive along the coast road in west Cornwall. The road dips down steeply into Watergate Bay, as if you're driving straight into the ocean, before rising again, ascending into the cornflower-blue sky. I'm heading towards one of my favourite laybys, a large semicircle of rough asphalt on the side of the main road. It overlooks rolling green fields and has a view of the sparkling sea in the distance. This is a late spring and summer layby, as, once autumn arrives, the wind rises and the squalls come in, leaving any vehicles parked here exposed to the elements. As much as I enjoy being gently rocked to sleep by a moderate wind, some of the winter storms that arrive in Cornwall from September onwards have my three-ton van bouncing around like an enthusiastic child on a space hopper. For mid-autumn, winter and early spring, I seek out more sheltered parking.

As I pull in, the layby is empty of other vehicles, but I am confronted with a pile of unwanted furniture and refuse that's been unceremoniously dumped at the edge. Usually, in laybys where I have parked for the night, I will pick up stray crisp packets, empty lager tins and other such items to ensure that people like me, who live permanently in vans, don't get blamed. But the amount that's been dumped here wouldn't even fit in my van. The pile of detritus marring the beauty of the landscape reminds me of another time in my life, an incident, an event, of a similar nature . . .

When this incident happened, I'll openly admit that my knowledge of the UK justice system came almost entirely from nineties shows like *The Bill, Columbo* and *Heartbeat*. I was under the naive impression that, if the police had a warrant for someone's arrest, they would hunt down that person at all costs and, upon finding them, tackle them to the ground like a rabid dog. It turns out that they just use Royal Mail, which was frankly a massive disappointment.

The warrant for my arrest came in the form of a tersely worded letter, categorically informing me of the imminent familiarity that I would soon have with the inside of a jail cell. Upon opening the letter and skim-reading the contents, the whoosh of fear that shot up from my stomach to my throat nearly choked me. Fuck.

Shaking, I could barely read the details of the warrant; a veil of sheer terror had stolen all coherent thought and clouded my eyes with stinging, salt-filled fear. The letter recommended strongly that I hand myself in immediately at the police station (of course it would; why spend money on physically arresting people when it's far cheaper to get them to do it themselves for the price of a stamp?).

I called my mum. As always, she is the first person I turn to in moments when the cliff of life suddenly collapses and I am left standing on the edge overlooking the abyss. On the phone, after reading out the warrant in full, my mum was just as shocked as me. Unlike me, however, she was able to look at the situation objectively. She agreed that it was terrifying and unfair, but that it wasn't the end of the world, even if it felt like it. She advised me to take the next day off work so that I could go to the police station and hand myself in. She would come with me for support.

I spent the entire night in a panic, running through imaginary scenarios in my mind . . . being locked in a cell for days, weeks or years and attempting to tunnel my way out using the wrong end of a spoon. Or where the police had lost patience and had come for me while I was at work (I was a cleaner at a pub and restaurant at the time), slapping the urinal cakes out of my gloved hands in case I used them as projectile chemical weapons, marching me out of the building in handcuffs in front of all my colleagues. It was terrifying. I was, after all, being accused of 'a serious criminal offence which carries a fine of up to £50,000 for which an offender can be sent to prison'.

After a fitful and sleepless night, my mum announced her arrival in the morning with the high-pitched screech of the knackered wheel bearing on her blue Ford Fiesta. In anticipation of being thrown in a cold and uncomfortable jail cell, I wore my favourite loose-fit jeans and sea-green hoody – they reminded me of the good old days before I became an outlaw (like yesterday, before the warrant arrived). We were silent on the journey to the police station.

We pulled up outside the station, an imposing sand-coloured building in the centre of Bradford city, all edges and long lines peppered with tiny square windows that looked like weird, angular bullet holes. My mum switched off the car engine and the space that had been filled by engine noise and squealing bearings was now empty. I was loath to fill the silence. Speaking would lead to action and action meant my imminent arrest. How could this be real? How could this be my life?

It was time. We exited the car and stood at the bottom of the wide steps leading to the police station entrance. No amount of concealer could hide the eyes puffy from crying and the dark circles from no sleep. My mum flanked me like a bodyguard as we walked into the main reception area. Holding the paper warrant in my hand like a shaky flag of surrender, I approached the front desk and explained to the friendly desk sergeant that I was 'handing myself in'. He looked me up and down, took in my mum's smart green dress and registered a guarded look of bemusement as he took the proffered letter. Tapping away on his computer behind the reinforced plastic screen, he kept glancing up at me. Time seemed to stand still. All I could hear was the slow ticking of a clock somewhere and the tapping of keys on the computer keyboard.

The sergeant on the front desk seemed embarrassed and was almost apologetic after discovering the reason for the warrant. He explained that, out of protocol, they were required to formally arrest me, read me my rights and take me to a cell while my arrest was processed. I visibly blanched. I felt the colour draining from my face as panic began to rise. Another officer came out from behind the front desk and right there, in the reception area, he read me my rights. His tone was kind and he went through it quickly, sensing my distress. Somehow, the right sounds came out of my mouth at the correct time to respond 'yes, I understand', 'yes, that was clear'. He explained that he would have to take me to a holding cell while they processed my arrest. As he guided me away, I looked back at my mum, whose trembling smile was meant to be reassuring, but instead only served to communicate how upsetting this must be for her.

We went down a seemingly endless series of stairs, strip lights illuminating the bare white walls with their artificial light, presumably heading for the lower levels of the building, where the cells must be. Every hundred yards or so, we came to a locked door. Each one had to be opened; the jarring jangle of the sergeant's key card and myriad of key ring attachments bounced off the concrete walls like an alarm call. As each heavy door was locked behind us, my anxiety levels increased.

He stopped at an open cell and gestured for me to enter. Wild-eyed, I made my way inside. I was surrounded by thick, grey concrete walls. In a shadowed corner, I could make out an archaic metal toilet and matching sink. He asked me to take a seat on one of the barely padded concrete benches that were at either side of the tiny room, which I did, and he took the seat opposite. He opened the conversation by apologising for the need to be there and explained that he was purposefully leaving the cell door open. He told me that he would stay with me until my arrest had been processed, which he assured me wouldn't take long. He went out of his way to ask me questions about mundane subjects in a concerted effort to help me feel more at ease . . . 'Are you going on holiday this year?' and 'Gosh, hasn't the weather been shocking recently?' It was like being at the hairdresser, but instead of highlights, gossip and a trim, I was instead in the middle of being officially arrested.

After a reasonably short period of time had elapsed, another officer came to advise us that my arrest had been processed and that I was now free to go, pending a court hearing date, which I would receive through the post in the next few weeks. I was led out of the underground warren of concrete and locks, back to the reception area, to freedom, and to my mum, who was waiting to take me home.

The person responsible for my arrest was Brian.

There's always a Brian – in the office, in the warehouse, in any workplace. He's the guy who reads the health and safety policy on his lunch break; the kind of person who labels their lunchbox in case anyone might steal their damp corned beef sandwiches out of the shared staff fridge. You know the type – the guy sending emails to management that start like this: 'It has come to my attention that Tracey has been neglecting to adhere to policy 57a in the manual. As such, I feel that standards are slipping and the chrome effect on the coffee machine no longer holds a shine. Can you put this on the agenda for the meeting this morning?'

In the area that I was living at the time, there was a charity furniture project, which was a well-known community hub full of bric-a-brac, tat, furniture and hoarded 'treasure' donated from families of the recently deceased and house clearances. The furniture was then sold to people on benefits, claiming their pensions or who could prove that they were massively skint in a way that the government, and the project, deemed acceptable.

On this particular day, the day of the 'incident', I was in the process of emptying my home of everything in it ready to hand it over to my ex-partner. A friend had recently gifted me a beautiful cuddle chair, which was a huge armchair, bigger than your average armchair, but not quite big enough to be classed as a two-seater couch. It was brand spanking new. Expertly covered in a soft, plush light-grey fabric, without a single mark on it, I'd given it pride of place in my living room in the coveted spot by the big window. It was the kind of chair designed entirely for curling up in on dark, winter nights, armed with a good book and a massive hot chocolate. But, as with everything else in the house, it had to go.

Community projects, like the furniture one in my area, are lifelines for those of us with barely, if any, disposable income. People on benefits or in minimum wage roles simply can't afford to buy new (can anyone these days?). A good indicator of functioning poverty is whether or not you sleep on a second-hand mattress. The notion of bedding down on someone else's used springs is reasonably grim – a concept which wouldn't be entertained by some – but, for many of us (myself included), even the IKEA budget range is financially out of reach. Taking my beautiful chair to the tip, where it would have been consigned to landfill, never crossed my mind. It would have been a waste and socially irresponsible; the disposable, throwaway nature of society was something I didn't want to contribute to. Someone out there would love the chair as much as I had. So I took it to the charity furniture project. Obviously.

Meanwhile, it would turn out that Brian, the manager of the furniture project, had recently installed a shiny new CCTV system . . .

I'd driven my campervan into the mill yard, where the furniture project was based, having wrestled the cuddle chair that I was donating into the back of my van on my own. The loading bay doors were open and, from there, you could see right through into the warehouse beyond. There were other items of furniture already in the loading bay, waiting to be processed. I'd dropped off donated furniture here many times before. There was no one around. I opened the van doors and carefully wrangled the heavy chair out, which was a difficult and undignified affair, but successful. I left it almost inside the warehouse, on the edge of the loading bay doors. In my dubious wisdom, I'd decided that rather than ask the staff there for help to get the chair out of the van, I would make life easier for them and do it myself. Satisfied that I'd done a good deed, I closed the van doors, hopped in and drove back to my house to continue the task of emptying it.

During the court hearing, Brian told the judge that he'd watched me on his new CCTV the entire time that I was at the charity furniture project. He'd actually sat and watched me struggle on my own to remove the chair from the back of my van. Rather than speaking to me or helping me, like any other reasonable human being, he'd simply allowed me to drop off the chair and then watched me drive away, before contacting the police.

After I'd handed myself in at the police station, it took a while for the court hearing date to come through. In that time, my home was repossessed, I had an operation on a collapsed vein in my arm, my dog Peggy, who was fourteen years old by this time, died traumatically of a twisted stomach and I relocated to the Lake District to live illegally in a caravan. It's amazing how drastically life can change in such a short space of time. It certainly wasn't the easiest time in my life. It's just a real shame that those changes hadn't included a substantial lottery win.

The hearing date finally came. Arriving at the magistrates' court was very similar to arriving at an airport: scary, busy, loud, confusing and full of security guards. Uniformed men flanked two screening gates at the entrance. Our bags were checked as my support group, consisting of my mum, her partner, my partner and my best friend, were guided through the gates in quick succession. Once we had all successfully passed the security checks, we made our way to the correct court and sat in a row on dated, uncomfortable plastic seats that were reminiscent of a benefits office or a bus station café.

I wore my favourite smart outfit: an A-line eighties floral print dress in white and cornflower blue. I'd pinned one side of my hair back and applied minimal natural make-up in an effort to look presentable and, more importantly, innocent. In the suspended moment of time before being called in, terror and panic overtook me. The fear of standing up in front of complete strangers, people who had the power to take away my freedom entirely, was too much. I started to cry, silent, fat tears rolling down my cheeks in monsoon rivulets. As the usher called me in, necessity shut off my tears like turning off a tap and I found a resolve that I didn't know I had, scrubbing a tissue over my damp face before following him in.

As I entered the court, it was like being on a film set. The room was huge, with a cavernous ceiling and rows of church-like wooden benches at the back of the room, with desks at the front. Three female magistrates sat in a line on the raised platform that was the 'bench'. They shuffled papers and made an effort to look busy as I was shown where to stand, which was in a raised box structure to the left of the bench. The dark, austere wood that surrounded me up to my waist was like a tiny prison in itself. I later found out that it was called a 'dock'. I had to swear on the Bible, just like in the films, that everything I said would be the truth, the whole truth and nothing but the truth. The two magistrates on either side of the main magistrate seemed friendly – they smiled encouragingly at me, which helped ease my barely controlled anxiety. The central magistrate offered no such pleasantry and was steely-faced and officious, clearly enjoying the role of power that she was in.

They began by detailing the charges against me, the middle magistrate making it quite clear how serious the offence was.

They questioned me regarding my version of what had happened. I explained that I'd donated a lovely item of furniture to the project in order to benefit the community, something I'd done frequently in the past without issue (I had a well-known habit of changing the couches in the house and an obsession with retro furniture). The two judges at either side responded first – they were very vocal regarding their opinion that my actions were reasonable. The central judge was not in agreement. She fixated instead on the fact that I hadn't spoken to the staff at the project prior to donating the item of furniture.

They then asked Brian to detail his version of events. To my utter dismay, Brian told the judges that the chair I'd donated was in a sorry state, covered in marks and stains and that it wasn't fit to be resold. I responded without thinking, my outrage outweighing any rational thought, and told the magistrates that this simply wasn't true. The middle magistrate aggressively chastised me for speaking out of turn in court and warned me that, if I did so again, I would face serious consequences.

It was at this point that I lost my tentative composure and started to cry again – out of anger this time. I couldn't believe the injustice of it. When requested, I explained to the judges, through a stream of tears, that it would have taken me the same amount of effort and cost me the same amount in fuel to take the chair to a nearby recycling centre and consign it, instead, to landfill. Which I hadn't done because it was brand new and would have been a waste.

The central magistrate seemed determined to make an example of me. It was clear that she had taken a dislike to me from the start – I have no idea why. She announced my conviction to the courtroom with a booming, self-satisfied voice. I was so distressed by this point that I barely heard what she was saying. It was like being underwater; the sounds were muffled and disjointed. All I could think about was getting out of that room, away from the lies and the injustice before my faith in humanity was shattered beyond repair.

I was convicted of 'depositing controlled waste without a licence' and fined £180. I was also ordered to pay £570 in costs, with a £30 victim surcharge.

After justice had been apparently served, the usher collected me from the dock and I was led out of the courtroom in a daze. My family and friends, who had been sitting in the benches at the back of the room, filed out behind me. I was desperate to get outside into uncontaminated air. As soon as I'd given my bank details to an administration assistant for the courts, we were allowed to leave. I was so thankful for the support of my family and friends, who took me out for a meal later that day to celebrate my fly-tipping conviction.

I considered appealing against the conviction. Not only did I feel that it was unjustified and unfair, but I was concerned that it would have a negative impact on my future. But with the recent loss of my home and four-legged companion, alongside the upheaval of moving and commencing study for a master's degree, I didn't have the mental capacity to fight for my good name. Nor did I have the financial resources.

The fly-tipping conviction is something that will be on my criminal record for the rest of my life. It hasn't negatively affected me so far, but these days most employers will google potential new staff members as a matter of course. And when they google me, not only will they discover the array of poorly recorded YouTube videos from the various bands that I've sung in, but they'll find the article detailing my fly-tipping conviction.

I don't hold a grudge against Brian. In my experience, unhappy people sometimes do or say things that may not be perceived as positive or constructive. I should know. That's been me on many occasions and will probably be me again at various points in my future. It's part of being human.

Chapter Nine

Less Room, More Space

The mirror, propped up on the storage shelf above my bed in the van, reveals a ghostly visage . . . which is my face, plastered profusely in white clay. The mask, designed to smooth, detoxify and moisturise, is a mixture of shea butter and kaolin, a type of clay mined in Cornwall for the production of fine china and porcelain. I have decided to have a pamper day in my little home and, while the cool silk of the mask imbibes my skin with its softening properties, my feet are soaking in a washing-up bowl of hot water, lavender essential oil and Epsom salts. As the water that I use in the van requires me to fill bottles manually via an external source, I am conscious that my pamper day is something of an extravagance. In order to have a day, or a few hours, of this nature, it has required planning; ensuring that I have enough water in the van to cover both my foot soak and the water required to rinse off my face mask, as well as drinking water and water that I will use to cook with later this evening.

Living off-grid, in any format, automatically increases awareness regarding the resources that are required for both comfort and survival. My pamper day involves extra resources that I wouldn't normally use: gas to heat the extra water on my stove, diesel for the heater to warm the space in the van while I am there (rather than in a public library, a café or at work), the purchasing of Epsom salts, sourcing and buying good-quality, locally made products, and an extra five litres of water. I have made the judgement that my increased positive well-being from allowing myself these extra resources is a fair trade. Pamper days are a rarity, not least because I seldom have the time or the disposable income, but also because I'm not very good at sitting still.

It's winter. Rain intermittently envelops my van, driven in by offshore gusts in visible sheets that ripple and weave in horizontal lines across the surface of the sea, like a Cornish version of the Northern Lights. It's mesmerisingly beautiful. I watch it for some time. My clay-caked face in my window would be a frightening vision for anyone walking past, but the heavy downpours of rain have sealed everyone inside, houses and vans both. All I can hear is the rumble of the occasional car driving past, the background tick tick tick of the fuel pump for my diesel heater and the rain being pushed and pulled this way and that by the gusting winds.

Being careful not to cause a spill, I delicately take my feet out of the bowl and, as I disturb the water, I am swathed in the calming floral scent of lavender. I dry each foot one at a time with a vintage mustard-yellow cotton towel, before placing my newly softened feet on the multicoloured rag rug carpet that covers the blue vinyl floor of my van. I have purposefully parked the van on a road where there is an overflow drain on the same side that I am parked, a few metres away. Because the water in my foot soak contains only natural ingredients, I have no qualms tipping it down my tiny sink, where it will flow, diluted by the rain, into the metal grate of the drain. Carefully rinsing out the bowl in my sink, I place the kettle on my stove to boil it again, ready to refill the bowl so that I can wash off my silky white clay face mask. Once the bowl is refilled, I bend my face over the sink and start to rinse off the mask. An ache in my lower back prompts me to make a mental note that in my *next* van, I will make the worktop and sink area a little higher.

With the mask washed off, I pat dry my face and wipe up any residual clay from my sink area using biodegradable, lemon-infused wipes. The skin on my face feels soft and new, and my feet still pleasurably thrum from being immersed in hot water. I sit back on my bed, propped up by a pillow, and continue to watch the storm outside. Rivulets of rain running down the glass of my window chase each other in a race to reach the bottom. I feel safe. I feel happy. I feel secure.

To be secure, in the dictionary, means to be fixed in place. Fastened down. Immovable. Is that a good thing? Is that how we are meant to live? What's the difference between being secure and being trapped? The bank took away what I perceived as being my island, my place of safety. They took it away and I lost everything in the storms that followed. For a time, I was adrift. Treading water in a dark place, consumed by grief, overwhelmed by my failure and loss, wondering if the simplicity of sinking was the most painless option.

And then I found another way.

Who I am now understands that the stability and security society taught me to reach for are nothing but constructs and illusions. True stability, in my opinion, is not a house, but rather a state of being, an acceptance of what is, consciously letting go of expectations, judgements and toxic ideals. Success is a concept that I previously measured by my material and financial worth, which always left me feeling wholly inadequate and a complete failure, which simply isn't the case. I now measure success more constructively; by how happy I feel, how content I am and how supportive I can be to those around me (animal or human). The chance of being born at all is one in four trillion – surely that in itself is success enough.

Being free means something different to all of us. We yearn for it, we spend our entire lives working towards it. But what does freedom really mean? The media, and society, told me that, in order to be considered successful by my peers, I would need to put 'things' in my stone box, wear the right clothes and drive the right car. So I borrowed more money. I worked, sometimes in jobs that I despised or in roles that made me ill, to pay the debt and interest charged for my stone box and the things in it.

Out of the seven days in one week, I worked five, if not more, in order to generate enough income to keep the stone box running and heated, alongside the other essential costs of living. In the not-so-distant past, a household could be run on a single wage; those days are now more extinct than T-Rex. At least one day per week I spent catching up on housework and administration: laundry, cleaning, bill-paying, maintenance, and so on. If I was lucky, out of the seven days, this left me with one day to do with as I chose before the cycle began again, but, even then, this one free day was often taken up with social obligations – ailing grandparents who needed to be visited, friends who needed support, lunch with the in-laws (when I had in-laws). At what point, during my seven-day week cycle, was there time to just be; to create; to learn; to tune into what I needed as an individual in order to thrive; to properly connect with friends and family? On an evening, when I was tired and stressed from work?

As I continued through this cycle, attempting to grasp some sort of meaningful existence beyond my financial and employment commitments, my thoughts and emotions were constantly taken up with worry, stress and fear. Holidays were an unaffordable luxury and, if I wanted a week away, I had to borrow more money, sinking myself into more debt, which meant more stress.

Looking at my life as it was, I tried to predict my future – the years would go by and I would now have all the things that I could possibly want. The money that I had borrowed would eventually have been paid back, alongside the inordinate amount of interest. At this point, perhaps when I was in my late sixties, I would have some vague semblance of freedom. A reflection of freedom . . . if true freedom were to look in a dirty pond and all that could be seen was the distorted and misshapen image on the surface. What I wouldn't have, the one thing that money can never buy, is time.

I've heard stories about, or have been directly connected to, people who have reached this point in their lives, their mortgage finally paid off, pensions cashed in, the big holiday booked . . . and then they've died, having only experienced 'freedom' for a matter of weeks or months.

It made me wonder, is that really all there is? To live and die in debt, with only a few short years of freedom, before our bodies start to fail? To constantly experience the stress of existing with the knowledge that, at any moment, due to unexpected ill health, death, a lack of work, the home and shelter that I was in could be taken away from me by the bank (and was)?

I didn't want it. Any of it. I wanted a life now, not later. And I wanted a life that was free from stress, or as free as I could possibly make it. For someone who wasn't born into money and who has spent the vast majority of their working life in minimum wage employment, the only option that I had available, which didn't rely on anyone else, was to live in a campervan.

You may be reading this and thinking 'but I don't live in a van' or 'I have no plans to live in a van' but, crucially, everyone can live in a *virtual* van. Living with less, decluttering, consuming less, making more informed choices regarding how money is spent, measuring success in different ways and prioritising experience over ownership are all aspects of vanlife that can be applied to conventional living. Reducing the space that we take up in the world, with all the things that we think we need but don't, creates *more space*, space of a different nature: headspace.

Stripping back the non-essentials of life is something that you already do: when you're packing for a holiday and you have to downsize your things to what is truly needed, every time you go to work and pack a bag that contains only what you need to survive for that day, going on a road trip or a camping trip which requires a completely edited down version of your home. The reason why we feel more untroubled when we are away from home isn't simply because we are disconnected from our immediate worries by putting hundreds of miles between us and the bills coming through the letter box, it's also because, for that period of time, whether it's a day, a week or a month, we are living with less.

Living with less has a profound effect on how we think, feel and behave. When we are no longer surrounded by heavy clutter, things and stuff, our mental state, our very being, is lightened and, as a result, we have more energy, we are more likely to interact with strangers, to connect with others, to experience new things and to have the courage to be more adventurous than we may otherwise be.

As a child, I had no control over the domestic abuse that I experienced. With no knowledge of how the world worked, that was my 'normal'. My small body, constantly flooded with adrenaline and cortisol, grew to be a larger body with the same chemical imbalances, even though the immediate threat had gone.

As an adult, regardless of how hard I tried, I couldn't fit into the space that society had marked out for me. It seemed that I was a jigsaw puzzle piece with the wrong edges, taken from a different image. My parents had fit into the puzzle for most of their lives, both working full-time. My dad, his body negatively impacted by his job after nearly fifty years of strenuous labour, eventually arrived at the point where he was unable to physically work anymore, and my mum, the most successful puzzle piece of us all, managed to pay off her mortgage. The relentless seven-day cycle, focused entirely on financial need, is all-consuming, a trap like no other. And while I was in it, it was destroying me. I wasn't thriving. Exactly the opposite was happening. With no space or time to look within and process the trauma of my childhood and early adulthood, I turned to drugs and alcohol to self-medicate; to quieten the internal voice that constantly told me what a failure I was; to soften my edges so that I could somehow fit in.

I was, and I am, a human being healing from trauma, searching for meaning, happiness and freedom outside of what western society taught me I should be content with.

During the time of reflection that many of us experienced throughout the pandemic, it's clear, from the people I have connected with and chatted to, that priorities have changed. Months spent in lockdown allowed time and space, in a way that has never been experienced before, to connect with nature, to become more involved with neighbours and the community, to reflect on what was truly important in life, to look for meaning beyond the material. From my experience, it seems to be part of the human condition to have what feels like an empty space within, a black hole of discontent, an unfulfilled restlessness, which we try to fill with new things, with sex, with desire, fast cars, drugs, alcohol, food, the latest beauty fad, celebrity gossip . . . the list is endless. The only thing that will fill this void is love, in all its manifestations; love being the complete, non-judgemental and compassionate acceptance of the self and others. It takes immense courage to look within and say, 'Hey, you're fucking awesome, I love you', and it takes even greater courage to extend that love to the people who may have been the catalyst for suffering, like my dad, whose behaviour, words or actions were likely driven by their own lack of self-love.

Chapter Ten

Next of Kin

'Hello, is that Charlotte Bradman? This is Airedale Hospital . . . your dad has been admitted. He's in a stable condition, so please don't worry. We have you listed as his next of kin. Would you be able to come on to the hospital?'

Fuck. 'Yes of course I can,' I stammered, my voice hoarse with shock, 'is he okay? What's happened?'

'I'm not able to say over the phone, but he's okay. Please can you bring some spare clothes and pyjamas with you? He's on ward thirteen.' Oh God. A thousand scenarios began to play out in my mind: a car accident, an accident at work, a heart attack. She had said that he was in a stable condition – did that mean he was unconscious? In a coma? Hooked up to some kind of machine on an intensive care ward? I was at work, selling perfume in a department store, dressed in an outfit that made me look more like an air hostess than someone who sold fragrance. I was eighteen years old.

The hospital had called the department store directly in order to get hold of me, which was worrying. I could only presume my dad was well enough to be able to tell them where I worked. Quickly snatching up my handbag and jacket, I explained the situation to my manager, who released me from work immediately. I rushed out, the silly, red pencil skirt that was part of my uniform frustratingly restricting the length of my strides. I drove first to my dad's house in order to collect the items requested, adrenaline fuelling my body and sharpening my reactions. I'd never been in his house before when he wasn't there – one of the many rented properties that he'd lived in since he'd separated from my mum. Grabbing a carrier bag, I filled it with a spare set of clothes, underpants, socks and his pyjamas. I threw in a coat too – the wind was sharp and there was a nip of winter in the air. I packed his washbag, toothbrush, toothpaste, shaving stuff and shower gel. I was well-versed in the art of packing bags; it was something I'd done nearly every weekend for most of my childhood, when we'd had to flee his violence in the middle of the night.

Arriving at the hospital, I went straight to the ward detailed by the nurse on the phone. I knew my way around the maze of corridors as I'd previously completed an NVQ there. I explained at the ward reception desk who I was here to see. The nurse must have wanted to prepare me before I saw my dad as she took me to one side to kindly explain that he was absolutely fine and that it looked worse than it was. She informed me that he'd been beaten up by a gang of young lads the night before. Though she didn't say, I knew that he would have been drunk. There was no doubt in my mind that he would have provoked them in some way, or possibly attacked them first. The nurse said that he was found unconscious on the roadside near his house and a passer-by had rung an ambulance. She led me down the corridor to the room where he was. I was absolutely terrified of what I would see. My heart racing, I gripped the carrier bag with his things like it was an anchor to normality – mundane objects like underpants and toothbrushes offering relief from the situation that was currently unfolding.

The door to his room on the ward was open and, as we came to the rectangle of light, I saw what must have been my dad lying on the bed beyond. He was unrecognisable. His face was so swollen that it was a landscape of lumps, bumps and shiny, stretched skin.

His nose was clearly broken, both his top and lower lips were cut, crusted with dried blood, and the skin around his eyes was dark purple with deep bruising. I started crying. 'Hi love,' he said, his words slightly muffled by his swollen mouth, 'it's okay, I'm okay.'

It wasn't the first time I'd been called to the hospital as my dad's next of kin, and it wouldn't be the last. From the age of sixteen, I had somehow taken over the role that my mother had played, which was putting my dad's life back together each time he got drunk and shattered it. Instead of my mum, it was now me who received abusive text messages when he'd been drinking, followed by apologies the next day. I was the new scapegoat for his unhappiness. Rather than walk away, I felt responsible for him, not just because he was my dad, but because there was no one else. My brother had stopped speaking to him, unable to forgive him for the years of violence and fear that we had all endured. But like a kidnap victim experiencing Stockholm syndrome, I still felt the need to please my dad, alongside a sense of misplaced responsibility. He had no other family: his mum, dad and brother had all passed away, so the only person left to deal with it all was me.

When I was twenty years old, he remarried. When he told me that he was in a relationship, my first thoughts were that I was finally off the hook regarding looking after him, and that someone else would be able to take over from here. Thank fuck for that. Perhaps, as I left my teenage years behind, I could have some semblance of normality as I headed into my twenties. My second thought was how soon it would be before the violence started.

When I first met my dad's new partner, she was loud, scatty and hyperactive, but friendly. And, for a few months, it seemed things between her and my dad were going well. She had moved in with him, with her children, and I was given a much-needed break from being his main support. She worked as an account manager for a cosmetics company in a nearby town and, when a vacancy came up on the make-up counter next to hers, she was kind enough to recommend me for the role. Though I was young for the responsibility of the position, the department manager was impressed by my maturity and I was given the job as an account manager for the cosmetics company Clarins.

Clarins was an exceptional company to work for. During my employment with them, on several occasions, they paid for me to stay at five-star Radisson hotels in central London in order to attend week-long training seminars and new product workshops at the head office there. It was an opportunity and experience which wouldn't ordinarily have been possible for someone like me (an experience that I haven't had since, and one I am unlikely to have again in the future, unless that Lucky Dip I put on the lottery yesterday comes through). At the launch of every new product, they would ensure that each staff member received one for themselves, for free, and every two months, as a standard Clarins staff allocation, I was able to choose eight products to take home, again, for free. They are the most generous employers that I have ever worked for – I honestly felt like a modern-day Cinderella.

For a few months, things were reasonably settled. I was thoroughly enjoying my new job, despite still suffering with anxiety and having the occasional alcohol-induced breakdown (which I'm sure is standard for most twenty-year-olds). The other girls in the cosmetics department were friendly and fun, and, on quiet days, we'd give each other dramatic makeovers worthy of any red-carpet event . . . not that we had many of those, but we did have a 'club' where we showcased our on-trend make-up to middle-aged alcoholics and depressed call centre staff.

As everything in life seems to revolve around alcohol (I have no idea why), it wasn't long before the cracks started to show. My dad and his partner would drink together and, after a certain level of inebriation had been reached, they would argue. On some weekends, either my housemates or I would find him asleep on our couch, having let himself in at some point through the night.

Alongside these arguments, my dad's partner became frighteningly fixated on the notion that she thought my dad loved me more than her. When she was drunk, she would send me text messages with alcohol-addled language, but my understanding of the message was always clear: she hoped that I would die so that she could have my dad all to herself. It was so surreal, like being in an episode of *EastEnders* or *Brookside*. How was I supposed to deal with that?

It was too much for my young mind to handle. I was already suffering with severe anxiety, likely as a result of PTSD from the violence of my childhood; I was living alone, without support, as my mum had moved in with her new partner; I was frequently self-medicating with alcohol and drugs, unable to deal with my poor mental health any other way. And now, on top of everything, my new jealous stepmum, who I worked with, was probably going to kill me. Talk about being Cinderella . . .

I transferred my employment to another Clarins counter in a different town. I didn't have the capacity to deal with the surreal and toxic nature that was my dad's relationship. I tried to disconnect completely, ceasing all communication with my dad, and, for a few months at a time, I would experience calm (at least from the situation with them), but then they would argue, and my dad would start it all up again by arriving, drunk, at my door, with nowhere else to go.

Inevitably, after three years, they split up. While the divorce went through, Dad moved in with me – he had nowhere else to go and, as always, I felt responsible for him. He's lived with me, on and off, frequently over the years, like a child returning to their parents' house when, for whatever reason, they are unable to surmount the challenges of living independently.

In many ways, from being as young as sixteen, the role that I played in my dad's life was that of the parent, rather than the child. And even though the pressure of that responsibility had a negative impact on my mental health at the time (prior to having counselling), the skills that I learnt as a result of that situation have been invaluable as I progress through my life. According to Harvard University, mental and emotional resilience is built through supportive relationships, positive experiences and adaptive skill-building. However, that situational ideal isn't always possible – it certainly wasn't for me. I have found that resilience can also be built through facing and overcoming adversity, frequently rising to unexpected challenges and developing coping skills through necessity for survival . . . situations which my childhood and early adult life provided in abundance.

Chapter Eleven
Can't Drive, Won't Drive. Mum?

The vans that I've owned over the years have been a wide range of sizes (initially having a big dog meant that I needed a big van), and I loved the jaw drops and expressions of disbelief when people saw a tiny slip of a girl, with a face full of make-up, driving a huge Mercedes 308D like it was no bigger than a car. However, it took me years to pass my driving test, partly because I was either drunk or stoned on lesson day, and subsequently had to cancel, and partly because I was so scared of failure. I had lessons, on and off, from the age of seventeen to when I finally passed my test, in my early twenties. It's hard to remember a time when I was terrified of driving any vehicle bigger than a three-door Vauxhall Corsa, but I was . . .

Shortly after my brother and I were born, my parents set up two separate savings accounts for us. Every month, via standing order, they would transfer a small amount of money into each account. My mum has always been, and still is, somewhat obsessed with ensuring sibling equality, not just regarding finances, but also the love and attention that we receive. It's possible that this stems from my almost clinical insecurity as a child. As young as six years old, I would accuse my mum of loving my brother more than me. He seemed to take all of the violence and volatility in his stride, retreating to his room to quietly play computer games or Lego. Unlike me, he didn't cause my mum much trouble (before he hit his teens, of course) and I guess, in my child's mind, that made him more lovable than me.

Even now, with both me and my brother in our forties, if Mum pays for me and her to have a meal out or a cream tea (a favourite of ours, or mine mostly), she will either buy my brother something which costs the equivalent amount or transfer the money into his account. Her reasoning behind this is that mums and daughters tend to do more together than mums and sons, like going for days out, visiting museums, looking around art galleries and shopping. Mostly shopping.

These days, because I live three hundred and seventy miles away from her, I'll occasionally receive a text saying, 'I bought your brother a bookcase so I've put £50 in your account'. And I'll call her up laughing, admonishing her for maintaining this foolish, but truly lovely, obsession, explaining yet again that we are proper grown-ups now and that I'd rather she spent her money on herself.

When both my brother and I turned eighteen (he's a year and half older than me), we were given the money that our parents had so very kindly saved up for us. It amounted to approximately £2,000 each, which, back in the early noughties, was a substantial sum of money, especially for a teenager from a struggling working-class family. I think my brother bought a car and insured it with his money. I had the notion to do something similar with mine, except, instead of a car, I had my heart set on a campervan, even though I hadn't yet passed my driving test.

To this day, I still can't pinpoint a reason why I was adamant that I wanted a campervan. Trauma does interesting things with memory and the ability to recollect (mostly it buggers it up), and I have no memories of anyone I knew at the time owning a campervan. There must have been something which planted the seed of that idea – I only wish I could remember what it was. It might have been that I was instinctively drawn to the concept of having a place of safety that was entirely mine, something which I could move if I felt the need to. A den, something we used to build as kids out of bits of old wood, cardboard or corrugated iron, except this one would be made of steel and have wheels powered by a big engine. After years of feeling and being unsafe, this was the first opportunity that had presented itself for me to exert some control, to have something that wasn't owned by my parents and that they had no jurisdiction over.

The idea was completely stonewalled by both my parents, who had, at this point, divorced and were living separately. They didn't see how owning a campervan would benefit my life in any way; it would be too cumbersome to drive to work, difficult to park, uneconomical to run and inappropriate for an eighteen-year-old. So instead of investing the money in a campervan, I spent the entire £2,000 on alcohol, drugs, clubs, make-up and clothes from Topshop. I was eighteen with severe anxiety and low self-esteem – what else was I going to spend the money on? I'd never even *heard* of spa breaks at this point.

The campervan dream, however, was still very much on the list of 'things to buy when I'm a grown-up', so at the age of twenty-three, I must have considered myself grown up enough as that's when I finally bought my first campervan. In all honesty, to call this first van a 'campervan' is to do it something of a disservice. It was literally a house on wheels.

A cream coach-built Bedford CF, with eighties leaf-green racing stripe decals down each side, it had a double bed above the cab, a seating area at the back, a separate dining area, a full kitchen, with an oven and a fridge, a shower and a toilet. It was also intimidatingly large to someone who had only ever driven a three-door Corsa. However, I'd fallen deeply and irrevocably in love with this van, and nothing was going to stop me from getting it, including my own anxieties. I paid the deposit via eBay before I had a chance to overthink things and talk myself out of it. This time, I didn't need permission or consent from a parental figure; I did, however, need a lift to Coventry, which was where my new van resided.

Unable to contain my excitement and new-found passion for all things Bedford-related, before even collecting my van, I joined the Bedford CF online forum; a dedicated space for Bedford obsessives (of which, you may be surprised to hear, there were many). Introducing myself to the other Bedford owners and lovers, I told them of my new purchase and how excited I was to go and collect it. They were a great bunch of folk and, even though I couldn't understand most of the conversational threads on the forum as they were in engineering speak ('What do you do if the flange capacitor has split the crank on the dual fly lubricator?'), they made me feel incredibly welcome.

All I had to do now was get a lift to Coventry, pick up the van and drive it home. Which is where my old dear came in. My mum was the example for me over the years when it came to driving large vehicles, and the confidence that I have nowadays regarding driving pretty much anything is all down to her.

With my dad caught drink-driving, not just once, but three times, it was left to my mum to tow his massive fishing boat or the massive caravan with the massive Range Rover down single-track roads and up vertical hills to some random location at the arse-end of Scotland in order to try to catch massive fish.

She learnt how to tow vehicles and manoeuvre them safely, and how to map-read and navigate, taking into consideration the added width and length of either the boat or the caravan. Every time we embarked on a new fishing or caravan adventure, she grew more confident, although there were several nerve-wracking moments, not least because my dad was an intolerant, angry wanker. I knew that if my mum could successfully learn to be a competent and confident driver of large vehicles, then there was no reason why I couldn't do the same.

After I'd revealed to her that I'd put down a deposit on the Bedford van, she was surprisingly supportive, considering her previous views on me buying a campervan. She agreed to take me to Coventry in order to collect the van, and also promised to drive the thing home if fear got the better of me and I bottled it.

Finally, it was campervan collection day. I could barely contain my excitement! Logging on to my computer in the morning, I shared my update with everyone on the Bedford forum: we were setting off to Coventry to pick up the van. They cheered me on, nearly as excited as I was at the prospect of having another Bedford CF in the group. The drive down to Coventry was smooth and uneventful; the traffic was on our side and we arrived in good time. When I came face-to-face with my new van, my heart nearly burst with joy. It was even better in person than it had been in the photos from the initial advert, which were all I'd seen before agreeing to the sale. It was everything I'd imagined and hoped for. With this van, my world would open up, I could go anywhere, do anything or be anyone, and I would always have a safe space. The previous owners assured me that the engine was in good working order, that it was legally roadworthy and ready for new adventures. With my mum's encouragement, I decided to drive it home myself. She would drive in front of me so that all I had to do was follow her. Simple, right?

After handing over my cash and signing the relevant paperwork so that the DVLA knew who to send any speeding fines to (which was massively unlikely considering the van was about as aerodynamic as a brick), I climbed into the plush upholstered captain's chair, complete with armrests, ready to set sail on the tarmac seas. This was it – the campervan adventure had begun!

We set off in our mother–daughter convoy, following the main roads back to the motorway. The van was surprisingly easy to drive and, with my mum in front giving me a wave of encouragement as she checked on me in her rear-view mirror, I settled into the rhythm of the road, switching on the radio and winding down the window so that my joyful, smiling face could feel the breeze of this new-found freedom.

The joy didn't last.

Bugger.

I noticed the smoke starting to billow out from under the van bonnet at exactly the same time that I took in the alarming drop to my left, where the motorway I was driving on was suddenly exposed to the elements as it became a dizzyingly high bridge spanning another busy main road beneath.

The amount of smoke spewing out from under the bonnet increased by the second, unhelpfully impairing my view of the road ahead and my ability to prolong my life. Juddering like something in the last throes of death, the van wasn't responding to my efforts to slow it down via the brakes or steer it on to the extremely precarious hard shoulder. Battling wildly with the heavy, unresponsive steering wheel, my wide, terrified eyes took in that the only barrier between me and the massive drop to the road below was a small, metre-high, thin concrete wall. I remember thinking that a strong wind could probably blow that down – what chance did it have of stopping a three-and-a-half-ton van from careening over the edge? At some point during the madness, I managed to switch on the hazard lights to indicate to other road users that I would probably be leaving this world shortly. I'd say that my life flashed before my eyes, but for most of it so far I'd either been blind drunk, riddled with anxiety or terrified, so the only flashing going on was from the hazards. By some absolute miracle, the van, finally giving up the fight for life, slowly shook itself to a rolling stop and, somehow, during the roll, I managed to wrestle the steering wheel so that the van (and me) ended up on the hard shoulder and not, thankfully, through the wall, discovering whether Bedford vans could fly.

My mum, who had been leading our convoy of two, had witnessed the billowing smoke of doom from her rear-view mirror, but due to how fast and busy the motorway was at the time of the Bedford's demise, she was unable to stop. I switched off the ignition and swiftly exited the vehicle, just in case it blew up. Standing next to the concrete wall on a motorway bridge far from home, my small body buffeted and battered by the wind caused by the continuous high-speed passing of lorries, cars and vans that were just metres away, I watched my campervan dreams go up in smoke. Literally.

Within five minutes, my phone starting ringing; it was my superhero mother, who shouted over the wind and traffic noise that she was making her way back to me. While panicking, she advised me not to panic and to stay away from the moving traffic and the edge of the motorway bridge. Which, to be fair, didn't give me much to work with as there was only three metres between the two. Dutifully, I stood in the middle of the hard shoulder to await rescue, terrified by the ninety-mile-an-hour cars flying past, but equally terrified by the drop below. The smoke from under the bonnet was starting to dissipate. In all honesty, I think I was in shock. I'd been close to death via accident or circumstance on a few occasions previously, but this was the closest I'd ever been.

A car was coming up slowly on the inside lane next to the hard shoulder, its hazard lights flashing; it was my mum. She pulled in and climbed over to the passenger seat to exit her vehicle, ensuring that there was less chance of being mown down by a truck. Her hair whipped by the blasts from the traffic, trying desperately to hold her jacket closed, she was a mum on a mission. With her extensive experience of crisis situations, she immediately took charge, calling the person we'd bought the van off to explain where we were and what had happened, attempting to determine what had caused the van to destruct so spectacularly and endanger her daughter's life. The seller was incredibly unhelpful, to the point of being aggressive over the phone, stating that the break-down must have been our fault in some way, even though I'd only owned the van for all of two hours. She very rarely displays anger, my mum, being generally placid, understanding and with an ability to be objective that almost defies human nature. But not so much on this occasion. She told the seller that we were getting the van recovered back to his address and demanded a full refund or she would be calling the police. I could hear a tirade of angry protests, even above the heavy traffic noise, which were cut off abruptly when my mum uncharacteristically put down the phone.

Thankfully, we had breakdown cover and the recovery truck was quick to arrive – a huge flatbed vehicle, pulling up in front of my broken van to join our little party on the motorway bridge hard shoulder. After the mechanic opened the bonnet and took in the melted mess that used to be the engine, he determined that I'd set off without any water in the radiator, hence why the cooling system had failed to cool. Such a simple thing. Why hadn't the seller, or me, thought to check the water or the oil before I'd set off? Surely that was standard practice? In my excitement to be on the road, I'd completely forgotten, assuming that the seller would have checked those things prior to us collecting it. He was, after all, selling it as a working, roadworthy vehicle.

The broken dream of my Bedford van was expertly loaded on to the recovery truck and off we went, me and my mum in her car with the recovery truck following behind us, back to the seller's address. It was a tense and unhappy drive given that we were heading for what was clearly going to be a difficult confrontation with an angry man who definitely didn't want to swap back a broken van for £3,000 in cash.

He was waiting for us outside his house when we arrived, primed and ready like a loaded gun, flecks of spittle at the corners of his hard-edged mouth indicating his extreme anger. This was not going to be a productive exchange. He point-blank refused to give me my money back and, when my mum rang the police, they advised her that it was a consumer rights issue and not something that they could help with. We were at a stalemate, with the recovery driver unable to wait much longer before a decision was made, the broken Bedford still strapped on to the flatbed recovery truck. At twenty-three years old, with crippling anxiety, I didn't have the self-confidence or self-assuredness that often comes with life experience or age, and so I was unable to fight my corner. Instead, I simply cried. The seller offered to refund us £500 towards fixing the Bedford, even though that was a fraction of the cost of a new engine, which it would undoubtedly need. We had no other choice but to accept. With the £500, the broken van and a broken heart, we headed home.

The recovery mechanic, who was sympathetic regarding what had happened, kindly dropped the van outside my house, making sure that, when he carefully winched it down from the flatbed truck, it was parked in a suitable position. The chances were that it would be there for a good long while. My mum was a rock, as always, reassuring me that we would find a way to fix it. After she'd gone, I took a cup of tea out to the van to process the day's events. Sitting in my beautiful, broken new purchase, that had also left me financially broke, I despondently watched the shadows caused by the setting sun slowly creep across the unfamiliar shapes of the fixtures and fittings. As darkness filled the space, a welcome partner for my sadness, the streetlights suddenly came on and my self-pity was dispelled somewhat by their warm, orange glow; the light that streamed in through the Perspex van windows gave hope a new home.

The next day, I was galvanised. When it came to getting things done, projects which I considered important or essential, I had (and still have) a single-minded doggedness that often compensated for my distinct lack of planning. I always have the will, but not necessarily the way. However, in my experience, if your will is strong enough or persistent enough, the world will, in one way or another, acquiesce. Logging on to the Bedford CF forum, I divulged the details of my van misfortune, understandably worried that this community of seasoned mechanics, engineers and van and truck enthusiasts would judge me to be the silly little girl that I'd judged myself to be for not checking the oil or water before driving the sodding thing. They were incredibly sympathetic and supportive, and the name 'Phil' was mentioned by several people: 'Oh, you need to speak to Phil', 'Phil will be able to sort it out', 'Wait for Phil to get in touch, he logs on most days'. Who was this Phil, uncrowned King of the Bedford CF forum? And could he really fix a completely melted engine? I had my doubts. I'd seen the smoke-blackened chaos that was under the bonnet.

As foretold, Phil contacted me that evening, sending a private message via the forum. He asked me for as many details as possible regarding the breakdown of the van and arranged to come over the following week and assess the damage in person. He made no promises, of course, regarding whether he could fix it, but the fact that he was even willing to have a look was a reason to hope.

Phil arrived as a wiry, petite man in his early sixties. He had long, white hair, which he tied back in a ponytail, looking more like an ancient warrior or wizard than a mechanic. Perhaps it would take a wizard with the right kind of magic to fix the knackered van. Welcoming him to my home and thanking him profusely for taking the time to come over, I put the kettle on for a brew. Everybody knows that pivotal moments, life-changing events or new connections always begin with a hot drink of some description. He told me of his life as an ice cream van mechanic some years ago, a time when nearly all the ice cream vans on the road were Bedford-made, which he had a passion for. He had since retired and now spent most of his days fixing the vehicles of poor sods like me. Brews drunk and introductions made, it was time to assess the damage on my van.

Phil pulled on a pair of well-used blue overalls and some latex gloves, and popped the bonnet with a practised hand. He poked around for some time, pushing at parts, pulling at others, wiping the black dust off components before lying on the floor beneath the engine to see what damage he could find there. I stood and watched him with worried anticipation, waiting for a diagnosis, occasionally topping up his tea levels and bringing him biscuits. He closed the bonnet, indicating that his expert assessment was now complete, and removed his overalls. We sat in the back of the Bedford to discuss what, beyond scrapping it, could potentially happen now regarding the future of the van. Phil explained that the engine would need to be stripped down and rebuilt entirely, advising me that most of the components of the engine were still okay and it was worth saving. Yay! The wheels in my head were instantly turning: who could I get to rebuild the engine? Who did I know who was a mechanic? How much would it cost? Phil's voice cut through my racing thoughts with the phrase, 'I can do it.' What? Did I hear that right? 'I can rebuild the engine,' he said again, 'but it will take time as I can only come over on weekends and evenings.' I was overjoyed! 'That would be so brilliant!' I said. 'As long as you don't mind and you're sure you have the time? How much will it cost?' He told me that I could pay him whatever I had to spare over the weeks and months that it would take to rebuild the engine. He didn't ask for a set amount of money that I would struggle to find. His only stipulations were that I assist him, where I could, and that, at the very least, his fuel costs were covered.

He became known to my friends as 'Phil the Wizard'. It took four months to rebuild the engine, with Phil working solidly in all weathers throughout the winter months; snow, ice, wind and driving rain. The entire rebuild took place on the pavement outside my house. It's difficult to comprehend a task as mechanically complex and physically taxing being accomplished by one man and his inexperienced assistant (all I ever really did was clean parts and get covered in oil and grease) without a workshop or indeed any shelter of any kind. He was, and still is, a hero – and one of the most compassionate, intelligent, open and aware human beings that I have ever had the privilege to meet.

The Bedford, my first ever campervan, was reborn, like a phoenix from the ashes.

Communities of individuals who share similar passions, either based online or as a physical group, can be the gateways to receiving the help and support that we need. For me, this was very much the case. Had I not joined the Bedford CF online forum and found the courage to explain my waterless radiator engine melting situation, something which I saw as *my* failure and which made me feel vulnerable, who knows what would have happened to my broken Bedford van? It may have received a new engine, eventually, but it would not have been rebuilt with the care and expertise of someone whose life has centred around those vehicles. I viewed this exchange as a valuable life lesson, something which I desperately needed to learn: that showing my vulnerability did not make me a weak person or a failure; instead, it was evidence of my strength. Learning to ask for help and support, to admit when I'd made a mistake or when things hadn't gone to plan, was a key part of becoming who I am now. There was an openness forming within me which enabled me to reach out and connect, moving past the barriers that my mind had constructed in the form of fear of judgement, fear of rejection and fear of failure.

In the end, I am ashamed to admit that I never even slept in the Bedford. In fact, I only drove it once after Phil the Wizard had worked his magic. After the scare on the motorway bridge, my confidence – a fragile thing that was barely there to begin with

– regarding driving large vehicles had shattered. I sold the Bedford soon after the engine had been rebuilt. Applying logical thinking to the situation (which was very rare for me in my early twenties), I decided that it would be best if I started small and worked my way up. Using the money from the sale of the Bedford, I bought a Volkswagen Transporter, one of the most compact vans on the market. It would be my training van, the gateway vehicle which would hopefully build my confidence.

I didn't know it then, but the experience with the Bedford was to set me up for what was ahead of me, in more ways than one.

Chapter Twelve

Up the Creek with a Paddle . . . Board

After nearly two years, our time living on the campsite in the Lake District was coming to an end. Lee had decided that he wanted to do an optional placement year as part of his degree. The flexibility of how we were living meant that we could go anywhere in the country, or at least anywhere that we could feasibly pitch a caravan on a long-term basis. We both agreed to move south for the year. I was desperate to live by the sea and he had found a job in the Dorset area learning skills that would benefit his degree. I put my creative writing master's on hold with a view to finishing it the following year and Lee began contacting campsites in order to find somewhere for us to site our caravan. On a recommendation from the man he would be working with for his placement, Lee contacted an organic farm and campsite not far from Lyme Regis. The owner of the farm was happy for us to live there and, in exchange for use of the showers, toilets and electric, we would work one full day each per week and help out in the polytunnels where the vegetables were grown.

The farm was fairly remote and only accessible via single-track roads which were hemmed in by tall hedges on each side. The nearest supermarket was a thirty-minute drive away. For a girl who was used to having a B&M around the corner and access to a twenty-four-hour Asda, even while living in the Lake District, it was a little out of my comfort zone. Which was a good thing. In a world of increasing demand for instant gratification, living in a place where the only shop in the local village closed at six o'clock in the evening taught me valuable lessons regarding the difference between want and need. The facilities on the campsite consisted of three gas-powered showers situated in a wooden hut and three individual composting loos. Neither the shower block nor the toilets had lights, and so torches were a necessity for farm life. There were other people already living and working on the farm when we arrived, inhabiting a fabulous array of trucks, vans, caravans and shepherd's huts. It was my first real experience of being around people who lived permanently in moveable homes.

The vegetables on the farm were no longer grown for commercial use and, instead, were solely for the people who lived on the farm; from curly kale, carrots, potatoes and green beans, to four different varieties of tomatoes, fresh salads and sweet cantaloupe melons. If I hadn't cancelled out the vitamins by smoking, I would say that I'd never been as healthy as I was when I lived on that farm. I would walk through the small apple orchard, the sea sparkling in the distance, the late afternoon sun warming my skin, carrying a basket down to the polytunnels, where I would dig up or pick the food that we would be preparing for dinner. It was wonderful and the closest I'd ever been to living, what may be considered by some, an idyllic life. But despite having somewhere to live for free and having access to free, organic food, I still needed a job. I had my campervan to run, debts to pay off and other financial obligations, like my mobile phone bill and the ever-present standing order set up to my mother's account to pay off money I'd borrowed from her over the years.

I decided that I wanted to become a paddleboard instructor. This was for no other reason than my great love of the sea and the fact that I'd been on a paddleboard . . . once. How hard could it be? It was a job that would enable me to be outside all day, either in or on the sea, which was exactly where I wanted to be. Using my passion as momentum, before I talked myself out of it, I contacted a water sports company in Lyme Regis and managed to convince them that I was an experienced paddleboarder looking for a job as an instructor. Either they were desperate for staff or they genuinely liked me, because they gave me a job. Not only did they employ me without first testing my ability to paddleboard, but they also paid for me to officially qualify as a paddleboard instructor and put me through my first aid at sea training. I still have no idea how I managed to wing it so spectacularly – I expect that it was only sheer determination that kept me upright on the paddleboard the first few times I went out.

On one particularly sunny Dorset morning, I arrived at work ready for the day's lessons. The business had a great location on Lyme Regis seafront, mere yards away from the beach. One of the other instructors pulled me to one side to excitedly inform me that there had been a dolphin sighting in the bay the day before. I had lessons booked in that morning and again in the afternoon, which meant that I would be out on the water for most of the day. If the dolphin was still in the area, I had a good chance of seeing it. Wow, a dolphin! I'd never seen one before! I felt like every event in my life had surely been leading up to this moment, this day when I would commune with the second most intelligent animal on the planet (arguably the first, let's be honest). I was ready to meet the real-life Flipper, we'd be best friends by the end of the day and maybe we'd play 'catch the seaweed' just like the dolphins in *Blue Planet*. Me and Flipper forever! (Obviously, none of that was said out loud – I wouldn't want people to actually *know* how ridiculous I am, although you are reading this book, so you'll probably have some idea by now.)

My first lesson of the day was with a teenager and his dad. I was beside myself with excitement that the dolphin might still be out in the bay so I explained to my students that, though this would indeed be a paddleboarding lesson, it was mostly going to centre around finding the dolphin. They were just as keen to see it as I was. The first part of the lesson took place on the beach – simple things like how to fall in the water correctly while paddleboarding (yes, that's a thing – if the water isn't deep enough and you fall in incorrectly, you could potentially knock yourself out and drown). Health and safety done, we then headed out on to the water, ready to begin our search for the dolphin (oh, and the paddleboarding lesson, of course).

In Lyme Regis bay, a long line of orange buoys marks the entrance to the harbour. The buoys also indicate that any engine-powered boat must stay behind them, leaving the ocean between the buoys and the shoreline safe for swimmers, kayakers and paddleboarders. I'd been told that the dolphin had been last spotted near the entrance to the harbour, so we headed out in that direction. Both the teenage boy and his dad were proficient paddleboarders within minutes of being on the sea – it's not a difficult sport, but it does require balance.

Twenty minutes into the lesson, the dad starting waving his paddle and shouting, 'He's over there!' Sure enough, perhaps fifty metres away from where we were, we could make out the dorsal fin of the dolphin right next to one of the orange buoys. I was filled with a rush of excitement. 'Let's go!' I said and started to paddle my way towards Flipper.

All three of us arrived next to the buoy as the dolphin frolicked in the water, just centimetres away from our paddleboards. It was huge – so much bigger than I ever imagined or could comprehend. If I'm honest, fear was definitely mixing in with my excitement. I watched as the dolphin swam around the buoy, dipping and twisting through the ocean, nimbly avoiding our three huge paddleboards. He turned sharply and, when he did, I saw the underside of his belly and . . . hang on. What was that? A weird, curly stringy thing was hanging off the dolphin's tummy, like an undergrown turnip. I turned to the dad urgently, thinking it might be fishing line or some other flotsam that we might have to try to remove from the dolphin, but before I had a chance to speak, he calmly stated, 'Horny bastard isn't he?' What? 'What?' I said again, out loud this time. 'Oh yeah, he's got the horn big time. I've seen it before with dolphins in Florida.' 'How can you tell? What do you mean? Are you saying that curly weird thing is the dolphins NOB?' 'Yeah, yeah, it's his man part, see what he's doing with it . . .'

I looked on, feeling less enraptured and more distressed as I watched the huge, grey mammal purposefully rub his curly weird nob thing on the rope connected to the buoy. This was supposed to be a mystical, magical experience, engaging with nature, creating a rapport between two species, transcending the language barrier and exchanging gestures of friendship, one intelligent being to another . . . what I actually had was a dolphin wanking itself off on a bit of old rope.

The dad, totally unperturbed by this particular development, announced, 'I'm going to get in the water with him for a swim.' He jumped off his board and his son did the same. They were literally right next to the dolphin, who was bigger than either of them. The dolphin, whose focus seemed to be entirely on the bit of rope and his curly nob, didn't even notice the swimmers.

When I was younger, I remember trying to drag my neighbours' huge dog off my friend as he enthusiastically attempted to hump her. He wasn't keen on the interruption and bit me for my troubles, which left puncture holes in my arm, followed by a trip to A&E and a stinging tetanus jab. What would happen, then, if a half-ton dolphin's happy time was interrupted? I didn't really want to find out. But the dolphin simply carried on as if we weren't there, with the dad and his son treading water next to him while he continued, with vigour, to rub his curly turnip widget on the frayed rope. It was all very surreal and rather disconcerting.

Still, I had been up close with one of the most majestic creatures on the planet, even if he was on the horn and tossing his little flippers off. After the lesson, I didn't see the dolphin again that day, or any other day for that matter. He'd obviously got what he came for from the poor, unsuspecting rope and then buggered off to pester another rope in a different bay. It was definitely a lesson in letting go of expectations and, instead, allowing the present moment, an experience, to be exactly as it is.

It was a brilliant summer, despite the occasional difficulty that arose with my relationship with Lee, and, as a result, my sometimes poor mental health. Being on the water teaching paddleboarding, growing vegetables, spending time with great people, swimming in the sea most days and living a simpler life showed me how things could be, which was far removed from the conventional status quo. I felt empowered by my success at becoming a paddleboard instructor; from what was initially nothing more than a thought, a desire, a dream, to then what became a reality, manifested by my own energy, determination and drive, showed me the possibilities of what I could achieve if I put my mind to it.

The vanlife community on the farm was a vivid example regarding the level of freedom that could be achieved by choosing to live permanently in a home that could be easily moved. Some of the other van residents would spend their summers working in the UK, saving money, before packing up their vehicles to spend the winter months travelling around Europe. Their lifestyle, alongside how open and welcoming they were, and my time living on the farm, inspired me to reflect on what was truly important to me, what I actually needed to survive and how little that amounted to in the way of material things.

When Lee's placement year was complete, I made the decision to move back to Yorkshire for a time. My decision was entirely motivated by finances, or my lack of them, more to the point. Teaching paddleboarding was exceptionally good fun, but it wasn't a particularly lucrative career. I knew I could get employment within the NHS through contacts that my mum had, and I desperately wanted to get some money in the bank. Lee and I decided to continue our relationship by meeting up on weekends. He would move back in with his parents and we would figure out our future together at a later date.

Chapter Thirteen
The Beauty of Violence

Nearly every inch of my skin bloomed with sickly purple, sulphur-yellow and charcoal-black bruises. Dirty red dots, where blood had broken the surface of the skin, added a brutal, defined contrast to the almost watercolour softness of the contusions. My face was left untouched, marked only by tear-streaked mascara and the swollen shiny skin consistent with prolonged crying. The explosive violence, which had seemed to last for hours, or days, had finally subsided, the energy changing from uninhibited savagery to one of shocked disbelief at what he'd done. I sat, hunched over on the couch in the aftermath of the violence; broken ornaments, holes in the walls, smashed pictures, shards of glass scattered over every surface, and decimated furniture, its original purpose unrecognisable. I was barely able to move. It was as if my body had ceased to function, defensively withdrawing from all sensation, initiating a protective numbness, likely a result of shock. 'What have I done, what have I done, oh my God', the words tripped out of his mouth as the rage in his eyes was replaced by horror. Tears streamed down his face as he sobbed apologies, 'I'm sorry, I'm so sorry, please, I'm so sorry.' And I knew, with ripped-edge clarity, that he wasn't sorry for me, for what he'd done, but that he was sorry for himself, filled with fear that he would be made accountable for his actions.

James and I had met through a mutual friend. He was a year older than me. I was infatuated from the moment I saw him, teenage desire coursing through my veins, sweet and hot like melted chocolate. He had full, beautifully defined lips, almond-shaped eyes, which turned down slightly at the outer corners, high cheekbones, which framed a strong jawline, and hair worn in a carefully dishevelled mop of jet black. The first night we kissed, he stayed over, an excess of cheap cider, desire and raging hormones leading to physical intimacy quicker than a diving peregrine. After that first night, he more or less moved in with me. With my mum living with her new partner in another town, I had no parental supervision, no one to answer to; I was completely free to lose myself in this passionate new connection.

In the beginning, our relationship was everything that a blossoming young adult, with idealistic views of love, could ever hope for, despite, and in spite of, the poor example that my own parents had set. He was like a character from a romantic film – learning my favourite songs on the keyboard and performing them for me, his heart in his voice, his love evident with every note played. He would write me endless love poems, telling me constantly, in written and spoken word, how beautiful he found me to be and how much he loved me. It was both overwhelming and empowering to be loved so much, to fill someone else's thoughts so completely. It seemed too good to be true, and it was.

After the emotional intensity of the first few months began to diminish, things started to change. He initially became jealous and possessive, discouraging my friendships with other men, becoming angry when I wouldn't acquiesce. At one point, he threw a crate of glass bottles full of cheap lager at me, narrowly missing my head. I was shocked, but not overly so. I had witnessed similar acts, and worse, in my childhood, so I didn't see it as a warning sign. For me, it was relatively normal behaviour, almost expected. I viewed the extreme highs and lows of a volatile relationship as being proof of love, evidence of passion; true love is pain, I thought, such was my experience of it so far.

After it became apparent that James was unable to exert control over me through anger and tantrums, he then began to withdraw from the relationship, subtly disconnecting, paying me less and less attention as the weeks went by. When we were out together, he would flirt with other girls in front of me, and then deny it when I later confronted him, telling me that it was all in my head, that I was the one with the problem. It felt like a repeat of my first relationship – the same patterns and behaviours happening all over again. My young mind assumed that all relationships must be this way, that this was how it was if you didn't want to be alone.

He started going out drinking straight after work, purposefully switching off his phone and not returning home until late the next day. On those nights, I am embarrassed to admit that I would go out looking for him, scouring the pubs and clubs of the town. This new method of control and manipulation that he was employing played directly to my insecurities and extreme anxiety, to my fear of being unloved, of not being good enough. I was completely at his mercy, and he knew it. Irate, irrational and often drunk, I would plead with him to stop treating me this way, begging him to tell me that he loved me, to reassure me, to come home, sobbing and crying in the middle of whichever bar he was in. Then, when he refused, I would become angry. His callous derision for my suffering, his calculated responses and behaviour designed to belittle me, to induce hurt, would turn my distress into incandescent rage. I am deeply ashamed to admit that I would physically attack him, flailing at him in an alcohol-fuelled frenzy. With my dad's behaviour as an example, it was unsurprising that I would also turn to violence when I felt out of control. Unsurprising, but completely unacceptable.

Over the time that our horrifically toxic relationship continued, I developed a reputation in our locality for being completely, and dangerously, out of control. And I was. But they only saw my violent outbursts, witnessed my drunk, uninhibited reactions, whereas James's behaviour went under the radar. While we were together, I was living in my first house, bought with the hefty deposit my mum had lent me. James never moved in with me, although he often stayed over, as the relationship was too volatile and I knew that the chaos could not continue. At some point it would come to an end, one way or another.

I lost count of the amount of nights when I couldn't reach him on the phone and the number of different women friends had told me that they'd seen him out with. Every time I confronted him about his infidelities, he denied it. He vehemently maintained that I was mentally ill, that my lack of trust was pushing him away, that I was in danger of losing him, and that no one else, except him, would put up with my issues. He was adept at covering his tracks; there was never any clear evidence that he had been unfaithful. Unable to validate my suspicions, I began to believe that he was right – that it must all be in my head.

Gaslighting, as a form of psychological abuse, wasn't a concept, or a phrase, that was particularly prominent in those days, but I suspect that's what I experienced.

To deflect from the shaking, anxious misery and self-hatred, I would drink to the point where I was completely out of control. Then the violence would start, with me as the perpetrator. Pushing, shoving, slapping, my tiny balled fists would flail ineffectively while he easily restrained me. Poor mental health and substance abuse issues had negatively affected my weight and, at five foot three inches tall, I then only weighed seven stone (I'd been a curvy ten stone when I'd first met him). In my alcohol-addled, confused and traumatised state, I wanted to hurt him, to communicate with anger and physicality what I didn't have the words to articulate.

There were moments when the violence escalated beyond a push-and-pull scuffle: I once bounced a full pan of cold stew around his head, splattering the walls with inexpertly cut chunks of turnip (my stews are pretty awful, making him eat it would have been worse); I smashed his keyboard; I once bit his nose until I felt it crunch (he was pinning me to the ground at the time). He once held me upside down by my ankles, swinging my head repeatedly against a wall while I tried, unsuccessfully, to twist off his balls.

Violence begets violence. It is a self-perpetuating cycle, powerful enough to sweep those who have not been subjected to it, or who are not violent in nature, into its devastating grasp. Any violence that had occurred before, from either side, was like an overly enthusiastic game of Twister compared to what was coming . . .

I'd been selling T-shirts at a gig for my mum's partner's band; I'd also been drinking. It was a gig after all, and it wasn't as if I needed an excuse. It took some time, after the band had finished playing, to pack down their equipment, so it was one o'clock in the morning when Mum dropped me off outside my house. Fumbling with my key in the lock, my vision and coordination affected by both brandy and the dark, I eventually managed to open the door. Once my mum had seen that I was safely inside, she left to go back to her partner's house, waving at me from inside the car as she drove away. Waving back, I closed the door quietly behind me. As my eyes adjusted to the darkness of the living room, I could make out the shape of a person lying prone on the couch. With silent steps, I moved closer, the shadowed, angular features of James's face becoming distinct in the dull, orange glow of the street lamp outside the window. He must have let himself in with the key I had lent him.

Rhythmic sounds of steady, deep breathing indicated that he was asleep. I could smell the alcohol on him, his expelled breath permeating the air with stale ale. Lowering myself to the floor, I sat cross-legged, swaying slightly with receding alcohol levels, and watched him. Maybe I should wake him, I thought. He'll only get a crick in his neck or a bad back if he sleeps all night on the couch. He was fully clothed, and had even neglected to take off his boots, an indication of how inebriated he was.

Out of the corner of my eye, I noticed a small black, oblong shape on the coffee table next to the couch. It was his phone. My heart skipped a beat and my breathing quickened. He was usually incredibly careful with his phone, ensuring that it was either on his person at all times or inaccessible (except to him) in some way. Without thinking, I reached out and picked it up, my touch causing the screen to illuminate alarmingly, casting an instant glaring light over my partner's sleeping face. Panicked that he would be roused, I snatched the phone into the darkness of my lap and held it there, watching his face for signs of awakening. He slept on. Shaking slightly, I lifted the phone and held it close to my face, clicking the side button to switch it on. To my complete surprise, there was no lock or security password. I had full access to whatever secrets were hidden within. My sinking heart knew what I would find, but my head, which had been filled with lies, hoped against hope that the lies would be true.

Clicking into the phone's text message function, I saw that the last message he'd sent had been to a number which wasn't saved in his phone. And with that tiny detail, I knew. I didn't need to read the messages, but I couldn't stop myself. Scrolling down, the words blurring as my eyes filled with pricking, hot tears, I had finally found the evidence which proved my sanity, but it wasn't a comfort, it was the painful breaking of an already fractured heart. 'Come over', 'I love you. Shall I come over? I can't wait to touch you again', 'I miss you so much', 'You were amazing last night – how long will I have to wait till I see you again?'

I carried on scrolling. The message exchange between them went back for months and, though they'd been very careful not to mention names in the messages, I knew who she was from the content of the messages. We'd had arguments previously, with her as the focus. Several times, when we'd been out and she had been there, I had caught them exchanging meaningful looks – eye contact, facial expressions and body language that had shouted louder than any voice. Another person may have missed these subtle exchanges, but an upbringing of domestic violence had honed my skills at reading communication beyond what could be heard. Being in a constant state of anxious hyperawareness meant that I actively searched, often unconsciously, for indicators of how I might be hurt so that I could mitigate the pain.

Previously, when I had confronted him about these silent exchanges, he had denied any involvement with her. He maintained that it was my anxiety that was the problem, that I was seeing things that weren't there, and that I needed professional help for what was clearly severe mental illness. As part of his manipulation, he would then threaten to leave me, declaring that he couldn't be with someone who didn't trust him.

Rage filled me, coursing through every cell and vein in my body, from the soles of my feet, to the top of my tingling scalp, burning the alcohol from my bloodstream and replacing it with something far more destructive. There was no room for thought. Rising from my cross-legged position, his phone gripped tightly in my fist, I began to hit his prone, sleeping figure, smashing both his phone and my fist into his back. I was screaming, shouting barely coherent obscenities with each connection of my fist to his body.

He was awake in an instant, from drunken slumber, to vicious, teeth-baring fury. He flung me to the other side of the room, where I bounced off the edge of the kitchen worktop to land awkwardly in a heap on the floor. Though I was winded, I felt no pain; the blind rage in me offering a dangerous immunity. Picking myself up, I continued my onslaught, windmilling my fists, landing blows on his chest and shoulders. Even in the chaos of the moment, I noted a terrifying change in his face and eyes. He became unrecognisable, my violence having triggered something primal in him, beyond his control . . .

He attacked me with a cold focus that was almost without emotion, terrifyingly methodical, raining blows on every part of my body, except my face. There was no restraint. He shoved me next to the closed front door, and I was cornered, unable to get away. Snatching his phone out of my hand, he pounded the hard plastic of its case into my breasts and chest. He kicked my legs, the hard rubber soles of his desert boots causing welts on my shins and thighs. I tried to fight back, to pull his hair, to disable him, but all I achieved was to escalate the violence. The force of his fists caused instant colour to appear on my pale skin. The fight seemed to go on for hours, with me throwing whatever I could reach, and him continuing to pound my body with heavy hands, hands that usually built scaffolding towers and lifted heavy steel. He swung me across the room, and I put out my arm instinctively to prevent myself from hitting the fireplace. My hand connected with a lamp, smashing the glass from the bulb, which cut deep into my palm. At the same time, my shredded skin connected with the live filament and I was electrocuted.

I collapsed in a heap on the floor as blood coursed down my arm, which was tingling with numbness. I was still conscious, but the electric shock had broken my momentum and I couldn't take anymore. The sight of so much blood seemed to force him to return from the state of primal rage that he had been inhabiting and into the stark reality of what had just enfolded. Without speaking, he wrapped my hand in a tea towel and lifted me, almost tenderly, from the floor into a seated position on the couch.

It was done. It was over. There was nothing left in either of us to give or to take.

And it was my fault. I deserved the blood and the bruises, the beautiful black-and-yellow blooms on my skin, the deep purple shades of shame, the ache of damaged muscles and the heavy burden of blame.

He cried when he saw the marks on my body, silent sobs of remorse: 'I'm sorry, I'm so sorry', he repeated over and over again. Night had somehow turned into day, and the light streaming through the windows was merciless in its illumination of the devastation that had been wrought. He left, walking out of the front door and into a world that had inexplicably changed, reflecting back what had altered within him – a capacity for violence that he never knew was there.

For a while, I sat unmoving, the adrenaline and cortisol rapidly leaving my body, and, as they dissipated, so did the numbness. My ability to feel was returning. Every part of me throbbed. I felt heavy and contorted, like my whole body had been twisted hard and wrung out. My hand was still bleeding and I was worried that shards of glass would be embedded in the cut. It needed cleaning, and so did I. My mind wasn't functioning as it should, unable to follow through thoughts or focus, and I knew that I didn't have the capacity, or physical ability, to sort myself out. My handbag was where I'd dropped it when I first came in. I reached out from my seated position on the couch and dragged it slowly towards me. My phone was in there, flashing with unanswered messages and missed calls. I ignored them all and called my friend Donna, who was the one person capable of dealing with what had happened with the least amount of fuss. I had no idea what time it was, what day it was, I just rang and prayed that she would answer. 'Hi, it's me, I'm sorry to call, I'm not sure what else to do. I've had a fight with James, and it's pretty bad.'

Within ten minutes of me making the call, Donna arrived, bringing her mum with her. I registered the shock on their faces as they came into the house, confronted with a scene of destruction usually synonymous with the aftermath of an earthquake. Everything was smashed or broken, the curtains had been torn down, there were holes in the walls and broken glass glinted sharply across the carpet. 'Fuck me,' was all Donna said, before she took charge of the situation, exactly as I knew she would. Firstly, I was bundled into the car and taken to hospital, where my hand was X-rayed, cleaned and bandaged. The young doctor who triaged me at A&E, after he had seen the bruises and lesions covering my body, was insistent that I call the police. I mumbled that I would when I got home, but I had no intention of involving the law. In my head, I deserved every mark; after all, it was me who had started it. He checked me over for any indications of possible bone fractures (he didn't find any) and advised me that I would be very sore for a minimum of seven days, and that the bruises could be there for up to three weeks.

After the hospital, Donna and her mum took me home. While Donna's mum made something for me to eat, Donna ran me a bath. She helped me get upstairs and undress, before she practically lifted me into the bath. The mottled bruises covering my naked body were almost beautiful, like the coat of an Appaloosa horse. We both cried, and I was so sorry that she'd had to see me this way, sorry for the distress that it had caused her. She washed me, gently wiping the dried blood from my arm and taking great care with my highly sensitive bruised skin. I was then dressed in clean pyjamas, put to bed and encased in soft sheets. I slept for hours, or maybe days. With trauma of any sort, time loses relevance, replaced instead by emotion and sensation, by feeling.

When I awoke, my body was so sore that I could barely move. But my head was much clearer. Gingerly, I swung my legs out of bed and carefully staggered my way downstairs. As I entered the living room, my breath was snatched in a gasp of shock and tears filled my eyes.

It was beautiful. New curtains hung from a new pole at the window, a new rug blanketed the floor, the holes in the walls had been filled in and repainted, the broken furniture had been removed, there was a new lamp and the whole space had been cleaned, dusted and vacuumed. Donna and her mum, Elaine, had thought of everything; their kindness was overwhelming. I can never thank them enough for their care and generosity at that time in my life.

It wasn't long, perhaps a few days, before word of what had happened reached other members of my friendship group. I hadn't yet told my mum, and there was absolutely no way that I would ever tell my dad. If my dad had seen my body, the black bruises, the swelling, there would have been every chance that he would have hurt James to the point of no return. I didn't want that for either of them. I didn't want my dysfunction and poor mental health to have any more impact, than what it had already had, on anyone else's life. James may not have beaten me at all if I hadn't attacked him first.

My two bandmates, Sy and Adam, came to see me. They were already aware of how volatile my relationship with James had been. They asked me to show them the bruises, and I did. It had been nearly a week since the violence, but, if anything, the bruises, rather than fading, were now even more pronounced. Their anger at what I had experienced, rather than being loud and demonstrative, as I thought it might be, was instead tightly controlled and worryingly serious. They asked me to come to the police station with them to report what had happened. I protested, explaining that I'd started the violence, that James was a victim as much as I was, but they would not be dissuaded. Their view was that he could have walked away at any point, that he could have restrained me rather than attacked me and that he should be made accountable for what he had done.

It took me half a bottle of wine and constant persuading to pluck up the courage to go to the police station. I was a young woman and absolutely terrified. Sy and Adam drove me there and walked me in. They stood with me at the counter and, when I couldn't find my voice, Adam spoke on my behalf: 'I'd like to report a case of domestic violence.' Both of them were a few years older than me, and I trusted the increased life experience that they had alongside the unshakeable view that this was the right thing to do. And perhaps it would have been, in other circumstances . . .

The officer assigned to my case was called PC Plod (of course, this isn't his real name). I was taken by PC Plod into a small room in order to issue a statement on record. Sy and Adam were unable to accompany me and waited in the car outside the station. Another officer was also present, a female officer, who advised me that the conversation would be recorded on tape. They requested to see my bruises, which I showed them, explaining that the incident had happened six days ago. PC Plod was brusque, and almost accusatory, when he asked me why I had not come to the police station earlier. I said that I hadn't come before because I was scared and I didn't want to cause any trouble. Something didn't feel right with his tone and attitude, and I started to cry, feeling decidedly unsafe in a place that was supposed to be exactly the opposite. He asked me what had happened, and I told him that I had come home drunk to find evidence of my partner's infidelity and that I had initiated the violence which had resulted in the beating which I had received. PC Plod, his voice raised, almost spitting with anger, then proceeded to give me his version of events; that I had apparently caused the bruises on my body myself, that I was going to ruin the life of an innocent young man and that I was nothing but an out-of-control drunk.

Dissolving into sobs, I don't remember much after that, except wishing that I'd never come to the police station in the first place. I left in a fog of hysterical despair.

Even though a police photographer took pictures of all my bruises and I was advised that they had arrested James and taken him in so that he could make a statement, four days after my traumatic experience with PC Plod, I rescinded my statement and dropped all the charges. I didn't want to ruin anyone's life. A police record for assault or violence would have had a negative impact on the career that James was aspiring to, and I didn't want any future repercussions from reporting the violence. PC Plod was right; I *was* an out-of-control drunk. But did I deserve the beating that I'd received? Probably not, but then equality between the sexes, in my mind, must be inclusive of every aspect and difference between them. Even though James weighed nearly twice as much as me, why should he be expected not to hit me back if I hit him first, just because of my sex? True equality would mean that he had every right to hit me back (but maybe not quite as much as he did, which really fucking hurt).

It's people like PC Plod, however, and his inappropriate behaviour, who dissuade victims of domestic abuse from reporting it. Hopefully, by speaking about my experience, it may bring about positive changes in the system regarding how victims are treated, and people will be less afraid to come forward and talk about their own experience.

Perhaps because violence was all I'd known, it was all I had to give and all I could hope to receive; it had been normalised as part of my everyday life since childhood. Or perhaps I was simply a young, mixed-up person, self-medicating with alcohol for anxiety and PTSD, who had been gaslighted by a complete fucking arsehole and let down by West Yorkshire Police. The answer is entirely subjective.

Chapter Fourteen
Escape from Glastonbury

There were thousands. The sounds of their revelry could be heard across the valley: loud rave music; heavy basslines, like drums of war, shaking the very hills; shouting; laughing; and, worryingly, a few screams. Such a large amount of people together somehow became a single entity, one animal with one purpose: to party. They were camped out at the top of the hill waiting for the festival gates to open, having a pre-festival festival. The excitement and tension spilling down past the currently closed gates was like an elastic band pulled taught, ready for release. I was parked in a staff campground surrounded by towering circus-size tents, currently beyond the reach of the loud revellers, already within the coveted space of the festival.

It was night-time, but there was no true dark here. The shadows had been chased away by the glaring, multicoloured illuminations of the festival and the multitude of bright flood lights, offering regular, flickering swathes of artificial daylight. I'd covered over the thin curtains in my campervan with blankets, towels, shawls and scarfs, but still the light came in. I couldn't sleep. My body was shaking with anxiety, my heart was beating too fast and my breathing was short, sharp and shallow. It was four o'clock in the morning. In four hours' time, the gates to the festival would open, and the immense mass of revellers would stream in: wild-eyed and sleep-deprived, brimming with alcohol, propelled by excitement or drugs (probably both), glittery paint smeared across their faces, trampling all their inhibitions into the dirt with sequined Ugg boots and sparkly wellies.

Over the winter months, while I was still living in the home that had yet to be repossessed, a few years before I'd met Lee and moved to the Lake District, I'd been doing occasional work for a pyrotechnics company. I use the term 'company' loosely . . . it was one man – Tim.

Tim was eccentric, brilliant and the most self-centred person I've ever met, but perhaps you need some level of self-absorption in order to be a successful innovator. And he was. He invented, designed and built several incredibly creative installations, the most impressive of which was a huge, gas-fuelled flaming sculpture that mimicked the solar flares on the surface of the sun in real time.

Working in pyrotechnics sounds like it should be, or could be, rather exciting and glamorous. It wasn't. It involved lifting heavy steel frames and staking them into place, hammering their supports into the hard, frozen ground of mid-winter. Stripping wires with cold, numb, claw-like fingers, fiddling with fuses and long cables in the freezing, pissing down rain until the hands had completely lost all feeling and any reasonable dexterity. Of course, once the set-up was complete, the firework shows, or flame displays, were phenomenal. I've yet to see a firework show to rival one of Tim's. I'd fallen into this type of work through stage-building, which is basically glorified scaffolding. My work in stage-building had transpired through the connections of a previous romantic partner, who worked in that industry, which had, in turn, led to my role as a pyrotechnician (or 'heavy lifting cable fiddler', which is a more accurate job title).

Tim had been putting on shows at Glastonbury Festival for years, both firework arrangements and flame installations. He attended every festival without fail, taking a select group of lucky people to work for him, some of whom had been going with him for over twenty years. I was absolutely desperate to go. At twenty-eight years old, I'd never been to Glastonbury (crippling anxiety doesn't really go hand in hand with crowds of people from whom there is no escape, but I was determined not to be dictated to by my irrational fears). Life was passing me by, and it was time for me to make a stand, feel the fear and do it anyway. I begged and pleaded with Tim to take me to Glastonbury, and he eventually acquiesced, exasperated by my relentless onslaught. I was beyond myself with excitement, and anxious terror. Mostly terror. We'd be on site for two full weeks, setting up before the punters arrived, and packing down after they had left. Two weeks was a long time to be persistently in the company of others, and for five days straight I would be surrounded by continuous stimulation provided by one of the world's largest festivals in full swing; music that never stopped, flashing lights, laser shows and the constant noisy rumble of thousands of people.

In the run-up to the festival, I took my attention away from the nerves and anxiety that I felt by meticulously planning. I'm good at planning. I love it. Often, I enjoy packing, planning and writing lists for a holiday or an adventure just as much as the holiday itself, if not more. I openly admit to being one of those people who always has paracetamol and clean tissues in their bag. And I wouldn't even *dream* of going *anywhere* without a full first aid kit and emergency foil blanket – you never know when you'll need it, or when someone else (human or animal) may need it more. Being an anxiety-riddled control freak is a superpower in my eyes, and hopefully in the eyes of all the people I have come across in my life who needed a clean tissue, pain relief, a blister plaster or a wound bandaging (perhaps Marvel would consider developing a new superhero called 'Captain Full Bag' . . . or maybe not).

Tim had allowed me to take my campervan to the festival, which I was incredibly grateful for. It would mean that I had a safe space to retreat to if I felt overwhelmed. He didn't know that I suffered with anxiety, and I wasn't going to tell him. His immense ego meant that he had the same capacity for empathy and compassion as a recently deceased crab. There would be no support from him. I would deal with my anxiety on my own; I'd had plenty of practice through the years (not always successful, I might add). I began to pack all of the things that I could possibly need, not just for the festival, but for general existence: first aid kits, emergency blankets, sun cream, aftersun, tinned food, water, ridiculously sparkly clothes (it was a festival, after all), colouring books, crayons, wool, knitting needles (you never know when you might have to speed-knit an emergency scarf to calm a busy mind), torch, back-up torch, spare batteries, jump leads. Most of these items were already in my campervan (a white Vauxhall Movano, which had originally started life as a patient transport vehicle), but as I wasn't living in it full-time at this point in my life, I needed to ensure that I had enough clothes to see me through two weeks, preferably without needing to wash my knickers in the van sink.

The day arrived. Those of us who were working for Tim at Glastonbury had been directed to meet up at his unit – a dark, dirty and damp space permeated by the smell of sulphur. It was his cave of inventions, his workshop, and the place where he stored all of his explosive paraphernalia and flame-throwing contraptions. We would be travelling down in a convoy consisting of four vehicles: my campervan, a dilapidated Jeep, a trailer full of explosives and Tim's old army truck. The truck was huge, with tractor-size wheels and a decommissioned machine gun turret on the top. The entire vehicle had been painted with wild abandon in seventies hippy designs featuring swirls, curls, peace signs, robots and magic mushroom-inspired compositions. Tim told me that the artwork had been done by a renowned graffiti artist; I can't remember who, but not Banksy, I don't think he goes in for rainbow-coloured mushroom people, but you never know.

The drive down to the festival was reasonably uneventful, other than the extreme heat and my anxious chain-smoking. It was one of the hottest summers on record. When I hit traffic, which I did frequently, and the van was stationary, the lack of breeze coming in through the open windows made it almost unbearable. We arrived at the festival gates, along with a train of other vehicles, all full of festival staff in some capacity or other. We were directed to park up in orderly lines by high-visibility-clad security staff. Reams of busy people were attending to each vehicle, checking festival tickets for their authenticity, but also doing a quick search for drugs, which was slightly worrying, namely because I had some weed (it wasn't mine) stashed in a secret location under the dashboard.

It was soon my turn to get checked. A young lad, wearing the fluorescent yellow fashion statement that indicated his elevated status, inspected my ticket and proceeded to do a half-hearted search of my van for any untoward substances. I struck up a conversation with him (namely to distract him from finding the stash of weed, which remained unlocated, thankfully) and was distressed to learn that he would be out in the relentless heat, checking staff into the festival, until twelve o'clock that night. It was far too hot to be working outside all day, hot enough to be dangerous. The sun was beating down relentlessly with hammer blows of heavy heat and the silly bugger didn't even have a hat. Thankfully, I had everything he could possibly need in the van, plus spares of everything anyone could possibly need. I gave him a peaked hat, a tube of factor thirty sun cream, a bottle of water and a cautionary tale of how I'd once passed out in a Spanish restaurant, ended up hospitalised with sunstroke and had flown home early as a result, crisper than a bus station café bacon butty and peeling like a snake. He was very grateful, for the hat, sun cream and water at least.

After the check-in was complete, we were directed to the area where we would be living for the next two weeks. It turned out to be a small patch of grass directly behind an enormous, circus-size big-top tent, close to one of the main entrances into the festival. I was happy to note that it was situated next to a direct vehicle route out of the festival. My main anxiety regarding working at the festival focused on being trapped and having the choice of whether I could leave, with my van, taken away from me. The thought of being hemmed in freaks me out, even now, and car parks with any sort of barrier are no-go areas. It's not like I hadn't been to festivals before – I had, well, I'd been to one small festival multiple times, but I'd always attended as a performer (I sang in a rock covers band for many years). As a performer, I had an access-all-areas pass, which meant that I could leave whenever I wanted and use staff entrances and exits. It helped that I also knew the organisers of the festival, which is the Beat-Herder Festival in Lancashire – a grassroots event with all the creative magic of a larger festival, but concentrated into a smaller, more accessible space. They didn't mind if I parked my van at the very edge of the camping field, next to the exit.

The staff camping area at Glastonbury was already full with other live-in vehicles and various interpretations of tents when we arrived. It seemed that no one wanted to park next to the dirt track road, but I definitely did; last in, first out is a motto that I live by. We arranged our vehicles and tents in a horizontal line directly behind the big-top tent. The non-vehicle residences (tents, tarps, wigwams, bivvy (bivouac) bags) were pitched in between each van, with a large gazebo erected in the middle. The gazebo would be the community hub and kitchen for our little pyrotechnics group. There was no barrier between my van and the adjacent dirt track festival version of a road, which I was parked next to. This made me incredibly happy. Being next to the road meant that I could leave whenever I wanted to, which, conversely, allowed for a higher probability of me staying. My anxiety was alleviated greatly by the fact that I didn't feel trapped.

The next day, we started work. The sun was relentless, with the air as hot and dry as a sauna. Work involved rigging small flame throwers in sequence on to scaffolding towers and festival walkway bridges, some of which were hundreds of feet high. It was fucking terrifying, I won't lie. Being up so high in relentless extreme heat wasn't an ideal situation to be in. But I'd done similar work before as a stage-builder, so I wasn't particularly fazed. Tim buggered off to do whatever it was eccentric and prolific inventors do at festivals not yet open to the public and left us to it – 'us' being me, his son and his main assistant. In between rigging the flame installations, we wandered around the festival grounds, watched the stalls, stages and installations take shape, sunbathed and chain-smoked. This was the general pattern of events for the next few days.

The evening before the festival opened, after the sun had set, we explored the festival grounds. Huge, robot-like structures loomed out of the shadows looking like something you'd see in a sci-fi film. Lights of every colour twinkled across the valley, and those putting on shows with lasers tested their equipment, illuminating the night sky. I marvelled at the creativity that was on display; the sculptures, the artwork, the robotics, the immersive, sometimes intimate, at other times, wildly expansive, installations designed to transport festivalgoers to other worlds. As midnight approached, the site was both ethereal and visceral. My awareness was heightened, not just by my anxiety regarding being there, but by sleep deprivation, overstimulation, dehydration, nicotine overdose and overexposure to the sun. So when I returned to my campervan to find both it, and our staff campground, completely surrounded by tall, metal fence panels, all meticulously locked together with bolted clips, fear rose faster than a feather in a tornado. I was trapped.

Everyone was still awake, hanging out in the gazebo, drinking beer, smoking joints. Someone had produced a portable speaker, which was bravely attempting to drown out the sound of the awaiting punters on the hill above us. It was one o'clock in the morning. In seven hours' time, the gates to the festival would open and the mass of humanity would pour in, like a burst dam. And when that happened, I wouldn't be able to leave the festival site with my van until it was officially over. All vehicle movement was restricted after the festival opened to the public, for obvious safety reasons. With that in mind, and the cage of metal fences now blocking my exit, I felt the familiar rush of overwhelming panic. What was I going to do? My outward-facing persona was reasonably stable – holding conversations, laughing in the right places, cracking jokes – but underneath, like the frantic legs of a paddling duck, I was fighting to stay calm. I began to formulate the idea that if I spoke about how panicked I was, and my feelings of anxiety, perhaps it would lessen, especially if I felt supported. Maybe my assessment of Tim was wrong and he was harbouring underground streams of hidden compassion beneath the mountain of his ego.

It took all of my courage to ask if I could have a quiet word with him in private. We walked a few metres away from the group at the gazebo, to stand in the shadow of his huge, painted ex-army truck. 'I'm feeling a bit anxious Tim – a bit panicky. I think it's nerves about being here for the first time and being locked in. I'm really sorry.' His facial expression initially registered shock, moving to incredulousness, then to anger. When he spoke, it was to shout, 'Oh for fuck's sake! You're not going to have a fucking panic attack, are you?!' Everyone in the gazebo heard him and turned to look at us, before ducking their heads and pretending that they hadn't. What could I do? I felt my face flush with embarrassment and shame. 'Ha ha,' I laughed, brittle like a bone bleached in the sun, 'no, of course not! I'm fine. I just wanted to let you know. Don't worry, everything is cool. I'm fine.' I smiled widely to reassure him, cracked a joke about something else in order to change the subject, and he was pacified. I was too good at being inauthentically authentic, which was thanks to a life being spent, one way or another, pacifying and navigating the dangerous waters of violent men. Even now, I have no idea where I, Charlotte Bradman, begins and what I've had to learn to survive ends. What is human authenticity truly, if not the sum of what we have learnt?

We returned to the gazebo with the rest of the group and carried on as if nothing had happened. People were beginning to slink away slowly, searching for their beds. But something had happened – in my head. I had slipped, with quiet, pale-faced accuracy, directly into flight mode. The hidden streams of compassion that I thought might exist within Tim were more accurately like rivers of liquid wankerishness, which had tipped the balance, or blown any semblance of balance into tiny pieces. I said my goodnights to whoever was left and made my way back to my van. There was a tepee tent set up next to it. I noticed that, while I'd been exploring the festival site earlier, the owner of the tepee tent had tied reams of triangle bunting, flags and other festival paraphernalia to the back of my van. The tepee and my van were now inexplicably attached. In my panicked brain, this was yet another bar on the cage that was swiftly closing in.

For a few hours, I sat in the back of the van, quietly hyperventilating, trying to calm myself by colouring in the outlines of waves and shells in my *Mindful Colouring Book for Adults*. It wasn't helping. I took out my battered, well-used copy of *The Little Book of Calm*, flicking through with agitated urgency, hoping against hope that my anxiety could be cured by a single sentence. It couldn't, and it wasn't. Sleep was all but impossible. I was running on adrenaline, an excess of nicotine and shaking with anxiety and sunstroke. Wild-eyed, and barely rational, I made a decision: I was getting out of there.

By this time, everyone had gone to their various beds. Gently, and quietly, I opened my van door. It was four o'clock in the morning.

The hazy light of dawn was just peeking over the horizon, but above, the sky was still dark. The stars flickered in the heat of the night, keeping time with an ageing, dying bulb in one of the floodlights. The metal fencing which separated my van from the road, and from getting out, presented a slight problem, as did the bolts on the clips connecting the panels together. Thankfully, I always had my toolkit in the van (and still do), which is where I kept all of my stage-building and scaffolding tools. I knew from looking at the bolts that they were either a size nineteen or seventeen, and I had both sizes in my socket set. Quietly, and quickly, using a scaffolding spanner and an adjustable wrench, I undid the bolts on the two panels that I would need to move in order to get my van out. The panels were heavy, but I'd lifted and shifted similar types of fencing before. Carefully, and as silently as possible, I hefted each of the large, metal fencing panels out of their ground supports and moved them away from the rest of the line, leaning both gently against a block of Portaloos nearby.

It was time.

I climbed back into my van, quietly closing the door and stashing my tools in a place where they wouldn't roll around while I was driving. Starting my engine would wake everyone in the staff camping area, notifying them immediately of my desertion. Tim would not be happy. But then he was rarely happy, so there was no change there. Before I set off, I planned the angle I would need to drive the van in in order to get clear of the camping area safely, and on to the road beyond. The two fence panels that I'd moved had given me an opening, but it was awkward. It was now or never. Time was ticking and, soon, no vehicles would be allowed to move anywhere within the festival. I started the engine. It was as loud as a chainsaw in a sleeping forest. Fuck it. Off I went, flicking on my headlights and navigating the small opening leading to the dirt track road. Through the steering wheel and the pedals of the van, I could feel a slight resistance, the van not pulling forward as spritely as it should, and then, beyond the noise of the engine, I heard the twangs of snapping string. I had completely forgotten about the bunting and crap that had been tied to the back of my van. I didn't stop or look in the mirror to see the chaos that was evidently happening behind me; for all I knew, I'd completely pulled the tepee out of the ground and was dragging it, with its occupant, along for the ride. At this point, my anxiety was so completely off the scale that I didn't care. Once I was on the dirt track, I just drove. The festival was as big as any city, and I had no idea where I was. Getting away from Tim was the first part of the mission, before he could demonstrate his rage at me leaving, challenge my decision or hold me accountable for the potentially destroyed tepee (if people were going to tie shit to my van without asking, then it's their own fault if they get an impromptu night-time tour of the festival, alongside some light exfoliation from being dragged along a dirt road).

A quick check in all my mirrors indicated, to my relief, the absence of any attached tepees. I continued to drive, slower now that I was well away from immediate retribution. There was movement ahead of me, a figure illuminated by my headlights. He wore a high-visibility vest, the light glinting off his glasses as he waved at me to stop. He was middle-aged, with a beer belly hanging over his workwear trousers and the long, straggly black hair of an unwashed metalhead. Stopping, but leaving the engine on, I reached over to wind down the passenger window. Before he could speak, I told him that there had been a family emergency and I needed to leave the site, but I didn't know where the exit was . . . could he please help me? 'Shhure thing luuuv, I'll jumpsh in the van with yous and di, waaait, dire, direct youuu.' He was absolutely arseholed. But he was the only other person I'd seen since I'd made my escape and possibly the only chance I had to get out of there. 'Yeah, that would be great, thank you,' I replied, with a mixture of relief and trepidation. He jumped in the van, a sharp tang of stale sweat and stale ale following him in. Though he was drunk (or high, or both; it was hard to tell), he managed to direct me to the exit, which took twenty minutes, an indication of how big the festival is.

At the exit point, which led to freedom and the open road, he tried to kiss me. I *did not* see it coming. Faster than a bullet, the greasy sod managed to get his slippery, moist lips suckered on to mine, until I pushed him away in shock. Perhaps he expected a reward for his help, but I didn't really see how a blowjob (or whatever he might have been expecting), for a few slurred directions and the lingering smell of his body odour, was an equal exchange. The expression on my face clearly communicated my feelings without the use of words and he swiftly got out of the van, mumbling, with a less slurred voice, 'It was worth a try.' The van door shut, and off he went. For a moment, I felt sorry for any females at the festival, who, having taken excessive drink or drugs, might wake up to find my sweaty tour guide next to them in an unknown tent. They had my sympathy. Why is it always about sex, booze, drugs and rock 'n' roll? Myself, I prefer hiking (these days, anyway).

With only ten hours of sleep over three days, blood pumping and head buzzing with excessive cortisol, nicotine and adrenaline, body a husk of sun-exposed dehydration, I began the long drive home. It was five o'clock in the morning, and already the claustrophobic heat of the sun was closing in. Without a doubt, I was definitely unsafe to drive.

In a state of fraught panic, I managed to drive for two hours. For a good hour of that, I was driving without direction. There was no phone signal in the depths of the Somerset valleys, so I was unable to access my satnav, which I rely on heavily as my map-reading skills are patently non-existent. On a quiet country lane, surrounded by rolling green fields and a copse of young oak trees, I came across a big layby set back from the road. It was somewhere I could pull in and gather myself before attempting to drive the rest of the way home (according to my satnav, I had another three hours' worth of driving ahead of me). Parking up the van, I switched off the engine, lay down on the bed with an eye mask on and some ear plugs in, and tried to sleep. But I couldn't; I was far too wired, my head filled with self-loathing – I shouldn't have gone to the festival in the first place; I'm broken, useless and a burden to everyone around me. I got up and did what I always do when I'm heavily anxious, which is to try to lift the weight of my anxiety by reducing the weight of my existence – getting rid of things, tidying and organising. Because I felt out of control, in order to comfort myself and feel more grounded, I exerted control over the environment around me. Sorting, cleaning and tidying kept my mind and body busy, using up anxious energy until it reduced or subsided.

The amount of crap I kept in the van was unbelievable, given that I only used it for holidays at this point, but regarding content, the van was a much smaller mimic of my conventional home. Being brought up by a violent alcoholic conspiracy theorist prepper had prepared me for life in more ways than one – not only was I always ready to flee danger, but should my house burn down while I was away in the van, I would still have everything that I could possibly need.

There was a public bin in the layby and, by the time I'd finished getting rid of the things that I regarded as being either clutter or simply unnecessary, it was nearly full. Some of it should have gone to a charity shop, but I needed it out of the van, and out of my head, immediately. I cleaned the entire inside, from top to bottom – under the bed, in every cupboard, every pane of glass and the floor. I changed my sweat-soaked sheets for clean ones, the scent of freshly washed linen helping to soothe my frayed nerves. Finally, I lay down on the bed, feeling like a weight had been lifted. My eyelids began to close as my body gave in to exhaustion, my mind gradually unwinding from its tense, coiled state. I felt lighter now that I'd reduced the possessions that I stored in the van and I was safe.

Looking back, with better awareness and understanding, I now know that I was always safe while I was at Glastonbury (more or less – it is a massive festival full of drug-addled and pissed-up people after all). My mind had told me the story that I was unsafe and, if the mind feels unsafe, it then alerts the body, and the whole system is primed to fight or flee from whatever threat it may perceive. I've learnt that freedom from anxiety and from repeating the same negative unhelpful patterns, either in life or in relationships, lies in the knowledge that the past does not exist, except in memory. Whether I allow my past to affect my future is a choice, rather than an inevitability.

For me, preventing the negative experiences of my past affecting my future is still very much an ongoing process of growth and development, of challenging my anxiety and the patterns of fear that are part of my learnt behaviours, in order to move forward. Even now, at nearly forty years old, and as a qualified mindfulness therapist who has attended several counselling sessions over the years, I still struggle if I'm without my campervan. It's my getaway vehicle, my home and my safe space all in one. The only way for me to overcome this anxiety is to step into it, to purposefully put myself in situations that challenge me. I was unable to overcome my anxiety while I was at Glastonbury; of course it didn't help that my boss was a massive dipshit. But the fact that I went at all, knowing that I would feel anxious and unsafe, required courage, something that I wasn't able to see at the time, but which I now understand and acknowledge.

Chapter Fifteen
A Spotless Suicide

Did I want to die? I wasn't sure. I knew that I couldn't continue as I was, and that the quickest way to change my state of being, to end my suffering, would be to end my life. Also, I was absolutely arseholed, so not only would suicide end my suffering, but it would also enable me to avoid the hangover of all hangovers that was heading my way.

Three bottles of red wine coursed through my veins, filling my heart and mind with desolate, irrational despair. It was Friday night, or rather, early Saturday morning. As usual, I couldn't reach James on the phone. He would eventually call me, convincing me that I was psychologically unwell for questioning his faithfulness – that he'd stayed over at a friend's house. And, as usual, I would believe him … it was either accept his diagnosis of my insanity and keep him or confront the truth and lose him. Either way, I was sick of being sick, tired of the frantic volatility of my relationship, totally overwhelmed by my emotions and trapped by my mental illness.

I can't say that I was particularly coherent as I contemplated taking my own life, head filled with abstract thoughts pinballing around, disjointed and sharp. Paracetamol. The thought peaked in a split second of clarity, like a break in the clouds. No, I thought, with hazy difficulty, the red wine fog rolling back in. That would really hurt, wouldn't it? It melts your stomach from the inside, doesn't it? *Does it?* I want it all to end, but I don't want it to actually *hurt*, that would be *really* shit. What else? The window. I could throw myself out of the window. No. I'm too drunk. I can barely walk, let alone get to the upstairs window. For fuck's sake, I can't even kill myself with any reasonable level of efficiency. I drank more wine, Jeff Buckley whingeing away with dark melancholy in the background, and cried more tears of self-pity and despair.

Through the salt-water blur, my eyes caught sight of a small white box on the coffee table. It contained the promise of clear skin in the form of big, bright-red, round tablets; long-term antibiotics for cystic acne, a condition that I'd been struggling with since I was sixteen years old. Acne was yet another factor that had a negative impact on my mental health and on my sense of self-worth (or lack of it). I'd been taking the tablets for the last six months, three a day, and they were about as much use as a concrete sofa. My skin was still covered in huge, angry bumps, weeping pustules and volcanic spots. The tablets were the latest treatment that I'd tried in a long line of failed medications and painful procedures, from topical retinoids to paying for private laser therapy, where I could both feel and smell my skin burning. It was all for nothing as none of it had worked.

In those days, I only ever took off my make-up in private, and reapplied it straight away afterwards. I was so insecure about my skin that I would put make-up on to go to bed. In a way, my terrible skin confirmed the toxic belief that I held regarding how I saw myself – that my spots were somehow a physical manifestation of my brokenness, my terribleness as a human being, the badness inside bubbling up through my skin.

Maybe I could end my life by taking the acne tablets and, as a bonus, my skin might be beautifully clear, ready to be made up by some expert make-up artist in time for the open casket at the crematorium (drunk logic equates to the same line of thinking as putting no overnight parking restrictions in place to somehow make vanlifers magically disappear). Right, I thought, fuck it. I'll do that. I took another glug of red wine straight from the bottle while reaching for the box of antibiotics. It would be a spotless suicide. I laughed manically at my own joke, but the noise I was emitting soon turned into ragged, hiccupping sobs. Sat cross-legged on the floor, I began to pop the tablets out of their tin foil and plastic sheets, slowly building up a small mountain of them on the carpet in front of me. They were big tablets, like oversized Smarties. It would take fucking ages to swallow all these. I'd probably die via a blocked windpipe before anything else. Ah well, I thought, weaving back and forth drunkenly from my seat on the floor, I'll give it a go anyway. I put one into my mouth and swallowed it with the red wine. Then another, and another. I took about twenty of them, one after the other, before I began to think, hang on a minute, this might actually kill me. For real. Oh.

Fear, alongside a previously unknown instinct for survival, rose up, overriding the red wine fog, bringing a terrible and terrifying sober clarity: I wasn't sure if I wanted to die after all. But I'd taken the tablets. Shit. Grabbing the living room waste bin, I tried to make myself sick, sticking my fingers down my throat until the burning acid of red wine mixed with stomach bile reached my mouth. Mucky red vomit came up, and I heaved with the effort of trying to rid my body of the tablets, but none came out. How long does it take to digest tablets? Surely it wouldn't be that quick? Would it? Grabbing my phone, I rang 999 and told the operator that I'd taken an overdose. They took my details and dispatched an ambulance. I hated myself so much in that moment. My selfish actions had wasted vital resources, and perhaps meant that someone with greater need than me would miss out on life-saving care.

The balance between drunk and sober had now tipped into more sober than drunk. Standing up, I managed to stumble my way upstairs to the bathroom in order to have another go at making myself sick, and to clean my face, which was black with tear-streaked mascara. There was a hard knock at the door and I nearly fell down the stairs in my rush to answer it. Opening the door, I was confronted by two paramedics dressed in green, one of whom was carrying what appeared to be a large first aid kit and a defibrillator. Behind them, on the roadside in front of my house, was an ambulance. The side door was open, spilling light out into the darkness and offering what felt like a taboo look into the interior, which was full of scary-looking equipment.

'Are you Charlotte Bradman?' one paramedic asked. 'We've received a call to say that you've taken an overdose. Is that right?' I nodded. 'Can I ask you to come into the ambulance with us while we do a few checks? Everything is going to be okay.' They led me into the bright light of the ambulance interior, seated me on a chair and shut out the universe beyond by closing the sliding door. 'I need to ask you what you've taken. Do you have the box of the medication?' I didn't have the box, but I reeled off the name of the acne antibiotic. While he was asking me questions regarding my date of birth, when I'd last urinated, how much alcohol I had drunk and how many tablets I thought I'd taken, the other paramedic was checking my heart rate and oxygen levels with a little machine that clipped on to the end of my finger.

'Are you related to Paul Bradman then? He used to manage that pub at the top of the village? You know the one, it has that funny name.' The question the paramedic threw at me took me by surprise. 'Err, yeah. He was my uncle, but he passed away a few years ago.' Oh God, I thought, he probably knows my dad.

'I went to school with your dad you know, but he was a few years older than me. Great bloke he is, always up for a laugh. Does a brilliant take on Elvis on the karaoke. How's he doing? What's he up to these days?' For fuck's sake, I thought, you can't even plan your own death around here with any peace and quiet

– it's such a small town that everyone knows everyone. He took the machine off the end of my finger and started to roll up my sleeve in order to check my blood pressure. 'Yeah, my dad is fine, thanks for asking. He's still doing shutter joinery . . . he works away a lot. He does like a go on the karaoke after a jar or two.' It felt both strangely normal and freakishly surreal to be having such a mundane conversation while the paramedics checked, essentially, whether the tablets that I'd taken would kill me.

'Oh that's good, I'm glad he's well. Tell him Bob Milner was asking after him next time you see him.' Of course, I absolutely wouldn't, as then I'd have to explain how and why I'd met Bob Milner in the first place. I'm not sure either of my parents would take too kindly to their daughter's half-arsed suicide attempt with ineffective spot medication.

Having checked all my vitals and tapped away on some kind of iPad, he told me that the tablets I'd taken wouldn't have any adverse effects, to drink plenty of water and to get a good night's sleep – one that I would definitely wake up from. And with that, I was free to leave the ambulance. There was no mention of counselling or mental health crisis support in any capacity. Shamefaced, I thanked them both for their help and crossed the pavement to my front door with my head down, hoping my neighbours hadn't seen.

Now, as I sit in front of the roaring log fire in my friend Lorraine's hand-built cabin, spring sunshine streaming in through the windows, it's difficult to imagine that there was ever a time in my life when I felt like I couldn't go on. In fact, it's so hard to equate my previous life with the one that I'm currently living, at forty years old, that it's almost like I've lived two separate lives.

I have the privilege of looking after Lorraine's cat Pickle, and keeping an eye on the cabin and land while she is away for a few days. Lorraine and I met while I was walking the South West

Coast Path, and I still marvel at the ease with which new connections and friendships have come about in my life since I've lived full-time in a van. The land where Lorraine's cabin is built sits just below a small forest, at the top of a set of rolling green hills, which look out across the beautiful Cornish countryside. The land is only accessible on foot via a well-worn footpath, bordered at each side by briar, brambles, snowdrops and blackberry bushes. My van is parked at the bottom of the lane and, as much as I love the earthy and homely space that Lorraine has created, I'll head back down the path just after sunset and sleep in my van tonight. There's nothing better than your own bed, after all.

It's so peaceful here. There is no artificial noise at all – the only sounds that I can hear are the gentle crackling of the fire, the wind whistling through the eaves of the cabin and the occasional burst of tinkling birdsong. I watch the tiny white flowers of a hawthorn tree outside the window dance in the brisk, April wind, the flowers and clouds merging together with a backdrop of porcelain-blue sky. Barefoot, I head out into the garden, past the raised vegetable beds, the vivid tulips in pink, red and yellow, and the vintage caravan, and head up to a small, grassy clearing that has a low, sun-bleached driftwood bench. Pickle the cat meows a protest at being left out and scampers after me, all sleek and surefooted grace. Sitting down, face lifted to the sun, stroking the soft, downy fur of my feline friend, I curl my bare toes into the earth-scented soft grass. I feel so incredibly happy. Not just to be here, in this perfect place, on this sunlit hillside, and to be part of a beautiful friendship that I cherish, but to have made it this far. To have survived. To have triumphed over adversity. To have learnt to love myself enough to allow others to love me and, in doing so, opened myself up for all the magic of the universe to pour in.

Chapter Sixteen

Own the Moment

Tammy Girl, my favourite brand, was selling real suede Afghan coats. At twelve years old, that was all the confirmation I needed that they were the coolest thing ever and I had to have one or life wouldn't be worth living. The coat that I had fallen in love with was an ankle-length, beige-coloured, huge fur-collared monstrosity (seventies fashion must have been having something of a revival at that point in time). The fur on the collar went all the way down the lapels to the bottom of the jacket. It was a vision of skinned, dead animal presented in a horrifically flamboyant manner in the most unflattering colour on the spectrum. To my young, unethical and tasteless mind, it was the most beautiful thing I'd ever seen, and I simply couldn't exist in the world without it.

My mum, attempting to teach me the value of money, alongside budgeting skills (unsuccessfully, I might add), made me save up my pocket money in order to buy it. I was beside myself with fear that the object of my desire, the thing that would ultimately complete me as a person, would no longer be in the shop by the time I had enough money to buy it. After a few weeks of vaguely attempting saving, combined with relentless, full-on and intense pleading, my mum finally relented and bought me the coat (I had begging and pleading down to a fine art . . . 'but please Mum', 'I swear I won't ask for anything ever again', 'pleeeeeeease Muuuuuuum'). The parental figure had been worn down enough to give in and I had won! My prize: a coat made out of the skin, blood, tears and trauma of unjustly murdered animals in a colour that doesn't suit anyone, ever.

I remember the moment distinctly; the extreme high of elation fizzing through my veins, the anticipation, the drive down to the small shopping centre in Keighley, joyously taking the coat from its display stand over to the counter, and my mum handing her credit card to the assistant. It was finally mine and Mum *definitely* loved me (I was so insecure and felt so unloved that I needed physical evidence of her love).

I was exultant, filled with excited adrenaline. The feeling lasted all the way home and for at least an hour after getting in. It was then extended by prancing around the house and looking at myself in the mirror wearing my new coat of dreams. This coat would undoubtedly change my life, increase my happiness levels overall and probably turn me into some sort of fashion-based superhero. I would be someone else in this coat.

Unfortunately, it did none of those things. After a few hours, the adrenaline left my body and the coat didn't seem quite so amazing now that I actually had it. I'd spent weeks coveting the coat; my entire focus had been making it mine by any means necessary. Obtaining that awful coat had been my life's purpose for a short while. And now that the drive to own it had gone, the empty feeling inside was even worse. I'd harassed my poor mum for weeks, adding weight to her already heavy burden of keeping the family financially afloat, working full time, managing a household, looking after two difficult children and surviving the weekly bouts of domestic violence. In my naivety, I'd genuinely thought that owning the coat would change my life in some fantastical way, that I would feel better when I had it. But all it had done was make both myself and my mum feel worse.

Within a week of owning the coat of broken dreams, a friend and I decided it would be a brilliant idea to drink four litres of cider and then break into a nearby mill (what else is there for nearly teenagers to do?). I was, of course, wearing my new coat. Squeezing through a dirty broken window, we explored the mill, riding around inside the cavernous building on 'borrowed' bicycles that we'd found there. I got dirt from the broken window all over the coat and, by the time I'd finished riding around on the bike, the back of it was covered in sticky black oil. Our break-in had set off the mill alarm, which had automatically alerted the police. Hearing the sirens in the distance, which were swiftly getting closer, we frantically squeezed back out of the broken window, keeping hold of the big bottle of cider, which took precedence over cut fingers and imminent arrest. In order to get away, we waded through a three-foot-deep river, climbed a muddy embankment on the other side and then hid in the long grass of a nearby field, frantically trying to stay quiet as hysterical laughter started to bubble up. Half an hour passed, and it became clear that we had given our uniformed pursuers the slip. We thought it safe enough at this point to drink more cider and laugh until we were crying, no doubt brought on by the relief that we hadn't been caught. It turns out that oil and dirty river water don't mix well with beige suede. My mum did what she could to remove the oil stains, but the £70 jacket was consigned to a car boot sale shortly afterwards. I felt absolutely terrible – it was such a waste of money.

The coat hadn't enhanced or changed my life for the better in any way. But the desire that I had to own it had filled my mind and given me something to focus on that wasn't threatening or frightening. At twelve years old, there was nothing I could do to control or stop the violence that I was both subjected to and a witness of, but I discovered that I could change my mental state by choosing to focus instead on things, and their acquisition. It became a toxic cycle of distraction and a battle for self-worth that would continue well into my adult life.

As someone who lives in a very compact home, due to the lack of space, I have had to forgo becoming a collector and an owner of things, and instead, learn to be fully content as an experiencer and observer. From my progression of first living in a house, to then living in a large caravan, before moving permanently into a small campervan, I've found that by living with less, my capacity for happiness has substantially increased. Reducing the things that I own and changing my attitude towards material possessions has given me financial freedom and, most importantly, increased my capacity to connect with myself, my environment and the people around me. Fewer things, means more headspace. Less debt, means less worry and more free time. This is a principle that can be applied to any way of life and any choice of residence. Filling up my life with 'things', as I had before, or holding on to objects because of nostalgia and memory, left no space for the present or for the future. Not just physical space, but psychological and spiritual.

Tax and national insurance are measurable ways to calculate an individual's monetary contributions to society, but there are other ways of contributing that are of equal value, even if they can't be measured, like being happy, healthy and thriving. Happy, healthy and thriving people are the greatest asset of any society, and not simply because they cost the NHS less. If someone is happy and thriving, they are more likely to help and support others in need, to engage with the community, to create and to be innovative.

In order to thrive and be happy, I came to the conclusion that the simpler, and lighter, my existence was, the more space I would have in my life, and in my head, for the things that truly mattered to me: family, friends, being creative, learning new skills, adventures and spending time in nature. I didn't have to own 'things' to be happy or successful. Instead, I found that the way forward was to own the moment – to try to be fully present, as much as possible, for every experience.

Nature doesn't care how rich I am, it doesn't judge me based on the clothes I wear or the car I drive, so why should I judge myself or allow the judgement of others to affect me? I am part of nature and, as such, I am moving towards living a life of less that is more – full of moments, rather than things. However, nature can be highly unpredictable at times and there are some things – beyond the obvious, like air, food, water and shelter – that I consider to be essential (and I don't mean my small vintage clothing collection).

The items and objects that I see as need, rather than want, usually centre around well-being and being able to access nature comfortably and safely (although I did once see a young girl hiking up Pen-y-ghent in the Yorkshire Dales wearing two-inch-high wedge sandals, a miniskirt and a matching clutch bag . . . and she was rocking it, until she encountered actual rocks). A good waterproof coat and overtrousers, a pair of waterproof hiking boots or shoes, a well-stocked first aid kit, sun cream and hats (you can never have too many hats; they keep the head warm in winter and prevent sunstroke in summer, which is why I'm rarely seen without one – my ears are sensitive to the cold and I've had sunstroke before from spending an hour without a hat in the low thirty-watt sunshine of April in the Lake District) . . . these are some of the things I see as being essential.

Having the right kit enables year-round access to nature and the outdoors, which, for me, is vital for positive mental health. Although high-performance outdoor wear is often expensive, I see it as an investment. The person I was before – someone who would spend vast amounts of money on an Afghan coat, which had the waterproofing and thermal capabilities similar to that of a digestive biscuit, in order to *appear* wealthy and successful – is long gone. And thank goodness for that. My current ethos regarding how my finances are utilised goes something like this: by spending a larger amount of money than I would usually on a coat that is authentically waterproof from a brand that is sustainable, transparent and has a low carbon footprint, I am future-proofing my moments in nature, saving money in the long term, reducing the amount of clothes that go to landfill and loving myself enough to invest in my well-being. Being piss wet through and freezing my tits off at the top of a mountain (which has happened frequently in the past) puts my focus instead on how damp, miserable and cold I am, rather than connecting with the sense of achievement from reaching the summit, taking in the spectacular views and allowing the grounding vastness of five-hundred-million-year-old mountains to put my anxieties and worries into perspective.

'Oh wow, that's such a cute and pretty little box! What have you got in there then? Stationery? Art supplies? Jewellery?' my friend exclaims as she spots the sparkly mauve mini toolbox, complete with a little handle, on my shelf above the cab in the van.

She's laid out on my single bed, with a cup of masala chai tea with a splash of oat milk on the 'writing desk', a shelf that I fashioned out of cheap ply, painted sea green (like everything else) and screwed to both the van wall and my tiny bookcase next to the sliding door. I'm sitting cross-legged on my passenger chair, which has been spun around to face the van interior. Viewing my little home from the turned around passenger seat, my van seems far bigger than it actually is.

'Um, no, it's not jewellery. It's, well, it's the ashes of my dead dog.' I can't help but laugh as I watch her face drop in shock at my macabre revelation. Out of everything that could be kept in a sparkly little plastic box, I think the cremated remains of an animal was the last thing she was expecting. But she took it in her stride, and was soon laughing along at the ridiculousness of it.

Peggy, my dog, died four years previously from a twisted stomach. She was fourteen years old, which is a good age to reach for a large breed like her. A twisted stomach can happen to any dog at any age and vets still don't know why, but they do know that bigger dogs with larger chests are more susceptible. I was living in a caravan in the Lake District when she died. The home where she'd lived for most of her life had been repossessed and, as I couldn't bury her in the garden there, I didn't feel like I could bury her anywhere. So she was cremated. What was left of her, alongside the scattered hairs that were once keeping her living body warm embedded in the caravan carpet, threaded through my clothes and entwined with all the things and the places that we had shared together, was a ziplock bag of heavy grey ash delivered in a small, autumn-leaf-printed cardboard box.

My van didn't start life as a campervan and, as such, it doesn't have any of the designated ventilation that factory-fitted campervans and motorhomes do (unless you count the seal that has disintegrated on one of the side windows and the sliding door that doesn't shut properly). In winter, condensation can be a real problem; everything, and I really do mean *everything*, can end up going mouldy. Which is what happened to Peggy's final resting place. After a particularly wet Cornish winter, the cardboard box her ashes were in started to disintegrate, the autumn leaf print almost indistinguishable, covered by the downy white fur of mould spores. It wasn't rescuable (or healthy to be breathing it all in), so I took a trip to a Hobbycraft shop in order to search for an alternative box of a similar size. The new box couldn't be wooden, as that might go mouldy; it couldn't be cardboard either for the same reason. The new box had to be plastic or metal. And, unfortunately for Peggy, a dog least likely to be associated with sparkles (forgive me Pegg-shoe), the only box the right size for her dusty countenance had more sparkles than the dress of a Disney princess.

Peggy's box of ashes has always been in my campervan, ever since she passed away. It's all that I have left of her after her hairs were eventually washed out of my clothes or sucked into uncaring vacuum bags. And yet it, or she, is still a 'thing'. It's not necessary for me to keep her ashes. Indeed, my friend Warren, channelling what he refers to as 'mechanical sympathy', would tell me that the box is unnecessary extra weight, which increases wear and tear on the vital running gear of the van. The extra weight also increases fuel consumption, which, in turn, has a negative impact on the environment and climate change. And, though I hate to admit it, he's right.

All the moments that I have shared with Peggy are in my head, not in that sparkly box. She was the purest love I have ever known. She loved me, when I didn't love myself, and I loved her, above all else. I think, perhaps, it's time to let her go. To recognise that what's contained in that box is no longer her, it's just a 'thing' taking up space in my head and in my van that a bright, sparkly new moment could occupy.

Chapter Seventeen
Who Are You?

He told me in the white sheet, lurid purple, paint by numbers space that was a hotel room. A Holiday Inn Express at the end of a bleak, concrete cul-de-sac on an unfinished industrial estate on the outskirts of Shrewsbury. It was Valentine's Day. Cold, damp and grey. It was Valentine's Day and my lover of three years told me that he thinks he might be gay.

We had been living apart for the last few months, meeting up every other weekend in various cheap hotels in the Midlands, yet our relationship had been blowing hot and cold for some time. I was ready to commit; officially, conventionally, with rings and a white dress, but Lee had maintained that he wasn't ready, that he wanted to wait until the right time.

I arrived at the hotel first and checked in, communicating via text which room number we were in. As it was Valentine's Day, I'd made him a card and bought chocolates and other gifts, which I placed in a neat display on the desk where the tea and coffee tray lay idle. There was a knock at the door. My heart rate increased; I was excited, but also nervous – I hadn't seen him for two weeks and, as we had been living together previously, two weeks felt like a lifetime. Quickly smoothing my hair in the mirror, I reached out and opened the door. There he was, looking more handsome than I'd ever seen him, but the smile he'd pasted on his face didn't fit the picture of a romantic Valentine's Day reunion. It was strained and fragile, the corners of his mouth trembling with the effort of keeping it in place. He didn't hug me as he moved into the room. Instead, he put down his bag on the floor, sat on the end of the bed and lifted his gaze to mine: 'I have something to tell you.'

It was as if I'd been physically hit. The colour drained from my face, nausea rose as my stomach dropped, adrenaline flooding my body with its familiar sensory warning indicating that pain of some description was close by. My first thought was that he had been unfaithful, but that didn't feel right, he wasn't the type of person to cheat, but then, I rationalised, he did sometimes drink until he didn't even know his own name, so perhaps something had happened on one of those occasions. 'Are you seeing someone else?' I asked, the words thick in my mouth. 'No, it's not like that,' he replied.

'What is it then?' I heard myself ask. 'I'm having doubts about my sexuality.' Oh.

So many questions were trying to spill out, and why had he chosen today, of all days, to tell me this? I was distraught.

Lee was kind and thoughtful, and the most tactile partner I'd ever had, holding my hand everywhere we went, putting his arm around my shoulders at every opportunity. After being single for three years, and untouched for the same amount of time, it wasn't long before I was falling in love. He was supportive of my anxieties and insecurities in a way that I'd never experienced in any other relationship before.

Now that I was in a long-term relationship, contraception was something that I needed to consider. I didn't want to take the pill – I'd had negative experiences in the past with mood swings and weight gain; pumping excess hormones into my body wasn't a feasible option. That left the copper coil, a horrible little device that is inserted into the uterus, where it stays, causing all kinds of mayhem, for up to ten years. I'd used the copper coil as contraception some years prior and, during the procedure to fit it, I'd gone into cervical shock, which is as bad as it sounds – excruciating pain, fainting and nausea. While the device was in my body, my periods were so heavy that I would often leak blood on to my clothing, regardless of how frequently I changed my sanitary towel. And the menstrual pain was so agonising that I would vomit, unable to keep tablets in my body long enough to numb the pain. But I desperately didn't want to get pregnant and there were no other options available. Despite my knowledge of how difficult and life-changing having another coil fitted would be, I booked an appointment to get it done. If Lee and I wanted to have sex without pregnancy, this was the only option.

The experience was as horrific as the last time I'd had one fitted, as I knew it would be – laid out in a dimly lit, beige and brown clinical room in a beige and brown family planning clinic, while someone forcibly shoved a piece of metal and plastic into my body. The pain from the procedure lasted for days. I am only human, and I silently resented Lee for the need to have this foreign, sharp and painful thing inside me. I had to pretend to myself that it wasn't there or I would start to panic. Some nights, I couldn't sleep, my thoughts taken up with anxiety that this *thing* was in my body. At times, I wanted it out so desperately that I would seriously consider finding the strings that hung from the vile contraption, pulling them and ragging the thing out myself, regardless of the damage that might cause. But I left it in and said nothing of my concerns.

As the months went by, and we'd now progressed our relationship to the point where we were living together in the caravan, I realised how little I truly knew Lee. My instincts were crying out that something wasn't right, but I'd spent so long alone before I met him that I ignored them. And in that hotel room, on the day appointed for lovers to celebrate their romance, he finally revealed why our relationship could no longer continue . . .

We spent two nights at the hotel, eyes swollen with constant crying, while we tried to figure out how to move forward from this point. Somehow we arrived at the dubious decision that he would move in with me at my mum's house while we worked through this, which is where I was currently living. Despite the revelation regarding Lee's unresolved sexuality, we were still in love and wanted to be together, regardless of the challenges that we faced. After two weeks of living at my mum's, it became clear that trying to stay together while he found out who he was wasn't working and it was causing us both distress. He moved back to his parents' house, which was a six-hour drive away. We agreed to cease all communication for a time and officially split up.

I am not ashamed to admit that the breakdown of my relationship, and the nature of how it ended, left me suicidal – the ending of any relationship is a bereavement of sorts, after all. The difficulty I had in processing my relationship breakdown was that, throughout the entire, messy business, Lee maintained that he loved me deeply. Romantically. However, love, on its own, wasn't enough.

My poor mother was at a loss as to how to support me. My grief see-sawed between explosive and angry denial, to bleak and desolate acceptance. She was compassionate and empathetic regarding Lee's situation, allowing him to stay in her home after his revelation, but she couldn't forgive him for choosing Valentine's Day to share his news.

The weeks after Lee left went by in a haze of tears and grief, until I received an email advising me that I'd been successful in a job application that, if I'm honest, I'd completely forgotten about. My role as logistical support for two teams of community nurses began just before the pandemic started. While I was at work, there was no time to wallow in grief and heartbreak – I had a job to do and the nurses needed all the support they could get. GPs had stopped seeing patients in person due to the risk of infection, and it was the community nursing teams who stepped in to fill that gap, despite being short-staffed, underpaid and stretched so thin that the service was almost at breaking point. I've never known a set of people more dedicated, hard-working and altruistic than the community nurses I had the ultimate privilege of working for.

Three months went by, with only an occasional email exchange between me and Lee. I found it exceptionally difficult not to blame him for the overwhelming grief that I was experiencing due to our break-up. My best friend Eleanor was a huge support during this time and her level-headedness helped me to navigate my feelings, which were, at points, leading me to have suicidal thoughts. She listened to me, with compassionate and infinite patience, for hours, as I tried to make sense of it all.

After six, long months of what felt like moving through a thick, grey fog, Lee rang me out of the blue. The phone call can be summed up into, 'Hi, I'm no longer unsure regarding my sexuality, I love you, maybe we can think about getting back together?'

After all the grief, trauma, depression, suicidal thoughts, hopelessness and complete despondency, the phone call seemed surreal.

The heavy blanket of grief lifted in an instant. My mind and body were so familiar with extreme levels of emotion from my childhood, that I took it all in my stride. I was happy for us.

We met up the following weekend and spent the day together. We reconnected and rekindled our romance. After a few months of meeting up on weekends, through my friend Eleanor, we found a flat near to where I was working and moved in together. Lee was finishing his degree remotely, due to the pandemic, and I was still busy working for the NHS.

Initially, our relationship flourished; we were both so happy to be back together. But, as time went on, things became strained between us. I don't think it's possible to go straight from heartbroken, trauma-stricken grief, to happy romance at the push of a button. The lack of communication and reticence to talk about our feelings only served to widen the rift between us.

At this time, my friend Eleanor had received the devastating and life-changing news that her partner Michael was terminally ill with lung cancer. Everything else then took a backseat, including the issues Lee and I were having with our relationship. Lee focused on finishing his assignments for the last year of his degree, and my headspace was taken up with work and supporting Eleanor.

While we had been separated, Lee had secured a job for when he finished his degree. This new job meant relocating to the south, which I was unsure about initially, but it was too good an opportunity for him to pass up. I agreed to move with him. I wanted to support him with his career and, more importantly, continue with our relationship. He found us a house to rent, which wasn't far from where he would be working and, over the course of a weekend, using my campervan, I moved all of our things to the new property. The plan was for Lee to live in the house down south and start his new job, while I stayed up north and worked my four-week notice period for the NHS, before I joined him.

I had one week left of my notice period before I was due to permanently relocate to the south, move in with Lee and start our new life together. We'd been speaking on the phone every day since he'd started his new job, and things seemed fine, despite the continued feeling of slight disconnection, which I felt was something that would be resolved in time. He called me, as usual, after work, but rather than telling me about what he'd done that day for his new job, as he had done every day since he started, this time, the conversation began the same way as the conversation in the hotel room, 'I have something to tell you . . . '.

He went on to say that he didn't love me enough anymore and that he was ending the relationship. I asked him how long he'd been feeling this way for, and he replied that he'd wanted to split up for months. It's fair to say that there's never a convenient or appropriate time to end a relationship, but a week before I was due to move?

In that moment, I completely shut down. I didn't bother to ask why he hadn't mentioned the fact that he was having doubts about our relationship *before* I'd handed in my notice at work and transferred all of our belongings to the new house six hours' drive away. What was the point? It wouldn't have changed anything. I wished him well in his new job and the phone call ended. There wasn't much else to be said. I was relieved, more than upset, that it was over. I would miss him, of course. Despite feeling like I never really knew him, not truly, he was still one of the most understanding, patient and compassionate people that I have ever met. Yet he wasn't right for me, that much was clear. My mum, via email, arranged for me to be compensated for the belongings that were mine at the new house (Lee transferred £400 to her bank account); sofa, TV, bed, mattress . . . things that I wouldn't need now that I wouldn't be living there, and things that, if I'm honest, I didn't particularly care about.

Three days after Lee abruptly, and unexpectedly, ended our relationship, Eleanor's partner Michael died.

Eleanor had booked two nights away at an Airbnb in Saltburn, a seaside town in North Yorkshire. She desperately needed a moment of respite from the intense emotional and physical demands that came with caring for her terminally ill partner. Michael was medically stable at home, receiving care and pain relief from Macmillan nurses. During his illness, he had moved in with his mum so that he could spend his last few months surrounded by the people he loved. Eleanor had invited me to stay with her in Saltburn, in a tiny cottage overlooking the sea, to be there for her and offer support while she navigated her turbulent emotions. In a way, though Michael was alive, she wanted to say goodbye to him on her own terms.

The relationship breakdown with Lee, and the abrupt change to my immediate future plans, was pushed to one side. The only thing that mattered was being there for my friend in any way that she needed me to be.

It was emotionally intense as Eleanor worked through her pain and grief. On the first day of the trip, she wrote a goodbye letter to Michael and, together, we swam in the cold, grey sea, releasing both the words she had written, folded into a tiny paper boat, and her tears of loss into the wide expanse of ocean.

On the second day that we were in Saltburn, Eleanor received a phone call in the evening from Michael's mum. His health had declined unexpectedly and dramatically, and he had been transferred to a hospice, where he was now in a coma. She explained to Eleanor that the doctors had advised that he would likely pass away within the hour. It was a three-hour drive from Saltburn to the hospice. With great compassion, Michael's mum advised Eleanor to say her final goodbyes to Michael from Saltburn, as it was unlikely that she would make it to his bedside in time. Eleanor was beside herself with grief, inconsolable. Michael had been sending her text messages for most of the day and she'd spoken with him on the phone just that morning. It was almost unbelievable that he had deteriorated so rapidly. Overwhelmed, distraught and in shock, Eleanor took herself to bed, taking two sleeping tablets in order to sink into emotion-free oblivion.

At four o'clock in the morning, despite taking the sleeping tablets, Eleanor woke. Even now, she has no idea what prompted her from her chemically-induced sleep, whether it was a sound, a feeling or something more inexplicable. At the side of her bed, her phone flashed to indicate an unread message. It was from Michael's mum. Michael was still alive and had woken up from his coma to demand nothing other than a cheese sandwich. Eleanor dressed and rushed into my room – she woke me up both crying and laughing at the comedic absurdity of Michael's mid-coma request. He was still with us, still on this earth, and we could make it to the hospice.

In moments, I was dressed. I threw everything we owned into black bin liners, which were then launched without ceremony into the back of my van. Every second counted. We were on the road within fifteen minutes. On the empty, early-morning highways, we were able to make good time, breaking speed limits when it was safe to do so (and when I wouldn't get caught), flying through the hazy light of the new day in a race against death itself.

We arrived at the hospice, where I dropped Eleanor at the front doors, and she ran inside. I didn't stay; it wasn't my place to be there. Instead, I took her belongings to her house, unpacked them and ensured that the space was tidy for when she came home. I was heavily sleep-deprived and emotionally overwrought, holding it together by strength of will alone. While I sat in her living room, gathering myself, Eleanor rang me to say that Michael had died. He had passed away within an hour of her arrival at the hospice. He had fallen back into a coma during our fraught drive to the hospice, but she was able to talk to him and play him his favourite songs, to touch his warm skin while his spirit still inhabited his failing body and hold his hand while he passed. The raw grief and heartbreak was unbearable. After the phone call had ended, I lost my tentative grip on my emotions and was wracked with sobs, overwhelmed with fathomless and all-encompassing loss.

It was too much. My relationship breaking down with Lee, not once, but twice; Michael's death; my own poor mental health; supporting Eleanor while she navigated the turbulent waters of terminal illness (which was, though difficult, one of the greatest privileges of my life so far); working full-time in a stressful job; paying bills; hemmed in by the looming, decaying grey buildings of a poverty-stricken city; debt; anxiety . . . I couldn't do it anymore. Any of it. In that moment, I made the decision to set myself free.

Chapter Eighteen
Making a Home

The screen of my laptop is flooded with a kaleidoscope of shifting hues, a rippling dance of colour and movement as sunlight reflects off the waves of the sea outside my window. The words in front of me blur as my attention is captured, redirected momentarily by the beauty beyond the rectangular pane of glass – the rugged coastline of Cornwall, towering wind-sharpened lines and torn slate edges, surrounded by clear, turquoise ocean. This overwhelmingly beautiful place is where I currently live. You would be forgiven for assuming that I must be wealthy to have a residence with sea views in this county, a county which is considered to be one of the most desirable locations to live in England. I am certainly not wealthy, if wealth is measured solely by financial worth and material possessions. Yet my home has coveted sea views, the outdoor space that I have access to includes a beach on my doorstep and I live in a highly sought-after area.

The loss of my bricks-and-mortar home opened more doors than I could have ever imagined and it changed my perspective entirely regarding living my life in a more meaningful way. It also resulted in opportunities that simply wouldn't have occurred had I still been stagnating in an unmotivated, motionless and despondent state overwhelmed by financial pressures and surrounded by crumbling, ageing plaster, dangerous electrics and broken boilers.

The repossession of my conventional home was the beginning of a journey that set me free, the gateway to financial and psychological liberation. It is the reason that I now have a sea view from my window, a beach as my garden and a swimming pool the size of the Celtic Sea. My new home is transportable, moveable and manoeuvrable . . .

I've had several campervans throughout my life, some – like the Bedford CF – that were the size of small bedsits and others that were no bigger than estate cars. My current home is a size that I would class as being perfectly in between. It's spacious enough for one person to live in comfortably, yet small enough to navigate the often hazardously narrow roads of the rolling Cornish countryside. As with several of the campervans I've owned over the years, this one wasn't originally manufactured to be a campervan – it began life as a patient transport vehicle, full of rows of seats with a wheelchair ramp at the rear. Throughout my van ownership history, I've cultivated and developed contacts with various professionals relating to converting standard vans into campervans: auto-electricians, cabinetmakers, metal fabricators, caravan-breakers, carpet-fitters and mechanics. I've also developed my own practical skills, not just through my campervan obsession, but via the various jobs I've had throughout my life. I've frequently been employed in roles that involve practical, hands-on skills, like putting up scaffolding, chopping wood, welding, angle grinding, building partition walls and setting up pyrotechnics displays. I'll generally have a go at anything, especially if it either saves or earns me money, except electrical or gas installation – those are two areas that I leave to the experts.

Professional campervan conversion is big business these days with the advent of wanderlust, vanlife and travel vloggers on social media, all selling us the dream of permanent or prolonged periods of adventure – a dream that is attainable for everyone and anyone. The life I live is certainly proof of that. Van conversion tends to be a male-dominated profession, which means that some van interior designs, from my observations, don't seem to take into account the issue of personal safety . . .

Most current campervan conversions partition off the front of the van from the back, dividing the driver's seat and passenger seat from the living space. This layout is designed for more efficient temperature regulation in the living space; heat is lost via areas that are not insulated, the largest area being the vehicle windscreen, so separating that area from the living space does, in part, make sense. However, this layout wouldn't work for me. If I was in the main living space and I felt threatened or frightened by something outside the van, I would be unable to drive away without first exiting the vehicle, potentially putting myself in danger. As a woman living in a van alone, for me, safety is paramount. It is an issue that I feel must be factored in with any campervan conversion.

There are fundamental differences between campervans that are designed for infrequent use and campervans that are designed to be inhabited permanently. I've found that this often relates to the internal layout of a vehicle. Campervans designed for permanent living will usually have a fixed bed of some description, rather than one which folds out. I can tell you from experience that there's nothing more frustrating in the vanlife fraternity than fighting with a heavy, rock and roll bed (a style of foldout bed) twice a day. I had a bed in a previous van that was so difficult to fold away, my shins were constantly purple with bruises as the positioning of the bed meant that I had to push it back with the front of my legs every time I put the sodding thing away.

Space, or the illusion of space, is so important with any vehicle designed for permanent living. The majority of factory-built campervans seem to focus heavily on storage. I think the psychology behind this is to entice individuals who are new to campervan holidaying and who may be attached to their possessions. Perhaps being able to bring as much as possible from their bricks-and-mortar home helps them feel more comfortable in their temporary van holiday home. However, excess storage simply equates to less space. For me, the key to a functional and comfortable campervan layout is space. Whether it's a van conversion for a holiday or to live in permanently, being surrounded by less stuff creates more headspace, which has a multitude of benefits. In my experience, living lightly, with fewer material things to take up my attention, allows me to have an increased capacity to engage with my environment, the people around me, my creativity and activities that enhance my feelings of well-being.

If you are considering owning a campervan, either to live in permanently or to use for wonderful adventures, I would strongly recommend undertaking the conversion yourself (if you're not buying one that has been already converted, that is). It is often cheaper than hiring the skills of a professional conversion company and you are then guaranteed that the layout and functionality of the van will be bespoke to your exact needs. There are thousands of incredibly brilliant instructional videos on YouTube that detail how to convert a van in accessible, step-by-step formats. Regardless of whether you think you are a practical person or not, if my mum can change the brake discs and pads on her car using instructional YouTube videos, then frankly we are all latent rocket scientists. All it takes is the courage to give it a go.

With the help of a few talented friends, I converted my lovely little light-grey Citroën Relay myself – the luminous birch ply storage cupboards/kitchen unit (the wood left natural and unvarnished) were designed by me and made by a friend (who completely ignored my shit designs and then made even better versions), the slate-blue speckled worktop is from IKEA, the van floor was levelled, ply-boarded and expertly covered with midnight-blue durable vinyl by BCF Carpets (based in my hometown of Keighley), the white fibreglass roof was made by a company called

Shapes in Truro, I sourced my steel sink and drainer from a great bloke known as Caravan Bob in Halifax (he breaks caravans for a living and sells all the parts), my mum made the deep teal curtains and my dad made the bed from wood that we'd 'borrowed' from a skip. The overarching colour scheme of the van interior is synonymous of the various shades, tones and moods of the Cornish ocean, from turquoise, mint green and cobalt blue, to aqua, teal and cyan (which is pretty much the same as my entire wardrobe . . . I do like to colour-coordinate).

Though I am incredibly embarrassed to admit it, I never actually insulated my van. The interior of the van was already carpeted throughout when I bought it, which looked smart enough to leave in. I was too impatient regarding making it liveable to put in the required effort to insulate it, which would have meant stripping the back out completely, all the way to the bare metal walls, which was time and effort that my uncontainable excitement didn't have to spare. If there's one piece of advice that I would give to anyone embarking on a campervan conversion project, it's this: insulation is life. It keeps the van warm in winter and cool in summer, it helps prevent condensation (which I have rivers of) and contributes towards a more consistent temperature in your living space. As my van was originally a patient transport vehicle, it has windows all the way around. Some people may think that this style of vehicle, along with minibuses, make ideal campervans, but the truth is, they absolutely don't. Too many windows in a van present a multitude of problems, including reduced temperature regulation and more condensation, which can lead to damp and mould. The only good thing about having more windows is that there's more natural light in the living space and an increased capacity to take in the beautiful views (depending on where the van is parked, of course).

Last winter in Cornwall, there was one frost. One. And the winter sun melted it away within half an hour. Which means that living here full-time in a campervan, even one that is more glass than metal and which isn't insulated, is still comfortable. The temperature doesn't drop particularly dramatically and, when it does, I have a diesel heater (it is my hope that electric vans progress in their development to the point where a campervan can have all of its living components, including a heater, powered by a rechargeable source rather than fossil fuels). Living in my van as it is now, say, in Yorkshire where I'm from, would be a very different experience. In fact, it would be exceptionally uncomfortable. There have been times in recent Bradford winters when the temperature has remained below zero for weeks on end. To live in a vehicle comfortably in those conditions would certainly require a van with fewer windows, *all* of the insulation, and maybe an inbuilt sauna.

My campervan has absolutely none of what I would consider to be 'mod cons', unless you count a sink as a luxury amenity. I have a gas canister stove with a single hob and, well, that's about it, oh, and a pretty, blue cool box. I don't have an oven, a fridge, a grill, a shower, running water or a boiler. I'm always astounded by how little I truly need to live incredibly comfortably. My water is stored in five-litre bottles (I use three), which are kept in the cupboard under the sink. I fill them up for free at various harbour taps, graveyard garden taps and drinking water taps, depending on where I am. If I need hot water, I boil it in the kettle on the stove.

My clothes and bedding are washed every two weeks in whichever laundrette happens to be local to wherever I am (I have an abundant collection of knickers, in case you were wondering). My favourite laundrette is in Falmouth and is called The Laundry Room. It has an entire cork wall dedicated to the advertisement of community events, local businesses, therapy services, items for sale and items wanted, and an art installation compromised of pinned-up lost and lonely single socks. I can happily spend hours taking in the artwork and creative writing of the hand-drawn flyers. It's a warm and inclusive space, filled with the comforting scent of clean linen, of things made new, where life pauses for the duration of a spin or two.

Showers are a fun affair which usually involve either sneaking on to a university campus nearby (they always provide accessible free showers for cyclists), gyms, leisure centres and swimming pools. In the summer, it's easy to simply walk on to a campsite and have a free shower using their facilities – not just in Cornwall, but in any busy tourist location in the UK. There are so many people on the campsite that you and your washbag get lost in the chaos (my sincere apologies to the various campsite owners who may now feel the need to invest in retina-scanning technology for access to the shower blocks). Of course, if I'm having a dip in the sea, I will also have a wash. Salt water is very good for the skin – it is a natural exfoliant and full of microminerals, like magnesium, a mineral essential for muscle and nerve function, and one which can also alleviate anxiety. Three seasons out of four, I will swim nearly every day in the sea and only have a conventional shower once or twice a week. In winter, I try to swim at least once a week in the sea, not just to stay clean, but for the health benefits of cold-water immersion. As my sea-swimming activities decrease in winter, my conventional showering increases. I wouldn't want anyone to think that I'm a grubby sod – I can assure you that I'm as clean as a whistle.

Loneliness can occasionally be a grey and sad companion, especially during the long winter nights, and it will almost always knock on my door in the days prior to boarding the fun train that is menstruation, when I'm usually feeling particularly emotional. But, as with all feelings, it does pass. Rather than distracting myself from uncomfortable feelings with Netflix or chocolate (which I sometimes do – I am only human), I try to sit with them and allow myself to feel whatever it is that I'm feeling. Of course, I have a phone and I have friends, so if, at any point, the loneliness becomes unbearable (which it hasn't so far), I would simply phone a friend. Something that I've found to be particularly empowering, which I believe is a direct result of living full-time on my own in a van, is my increased capacity to be happy in my own company. From being an anxious person who felt like I needed someone there all the time, I now participate in and enjoy activities like hiking and swimming outdoors, visiting museums and art galleries, and enjoying decadent cream teas in boutique cafés, entirely on my own.

I suppose we'd better talk about bodily functions which focus on waste disposal – it's often the one aspect of living permanently in a van that incites the most curiosity. Tinkles are done in a little Portaloo, which is stored under the bed. Instead of using chemicals to control odour, I add a handful of baking soda into the main tinkle collection compartment. As there are no hazardous chemicals involved, I'll either empty it into a public toilet or, if I'm out in the wilds, I'll empty it into dense vegetation. It's exactly the same principle as using a soakaway or a composting loo – both function by allowing wastewater to be absorbed by soil, rocks and vegetation. The Portaloo is then cleaned with biodegradable antibacterial wipes and rinsed out with a warm solution of baking soda and lemon juice. Never put boiling water or bleach into a Portaloo – both will degrade the rubber seals inside and you'll end up in a world of piss. Literally. If you felt that harsher chemical cleaning products were necessary to sanitise your tinkle pot, then it would need to be emptied either into a public toilet or into an appropriate designated unit, found on campsites, that cater for campervans and touring caravans.

Disposal of solid bodily waste usually involves accessing the multitude of facilities that are available in most areas: supermarkets, public toilets, coffee shops, and so on. If I am in an area where these facilities are not accessible, then it's a case of using a biodegradable dog faeces bag placed into a lovely little turquoise sandcastle bucket, with biodegradable wet wipes and alcohol gel at the ready. It is then disposed of in a designated dog faeces bin or, if there isn't one available, in a standard council bin. It's all very clean and highly sanitised, I can assure you. There are all sorts of contraptions out there designed to function in exactly the same way as my sandcastle bucket (which might be a little on the small side for some people and certainly requires reasonable yoga skills). My friend, who also lives permanently in a van, invested in a collapsible toilet; it's the same size as a standard bucket (fourteen litres), uses larger biodegradable bags and can be folded away after use. It is arguably much more comfortable than my method.

The electrical system in my campervan isn't particularly complex; the fewer components involved in any system or process, electrical or otherwise, the less there is to go wrong. I have one leisure battery, which is a battery designed entirely to power the living functions of a campervan, separate to the main van battery. My leisure battery is charged via a relay system when I drive the vehicle. That charge is then supplemented by two small solar panels fixed to my van roof. The solar panels trickle power into my leisure battery constantly (when the sun is out) which means that I am not reliant upon driving the van to ensure that I have power. This reduces my carbon emissions as I use less diesel, which also saves me money. The leisure battery is the source of energy for my internal lights, my twelve-volt plug sockets (which I use to charge my phone and laptop) and my diesel heater. Because I don't have a fridge, running water, an oven, a shower or a boiler, I don't need much power at all. A campervan conversion which has these extra components may implement the use of two leisure batteries, instead of one, and use larger solar panels.

Having a built-in shower in a campervan is great – it's certainly more convenient than sneaking around university campuses trying not to look shifty with your washbag, but regardless of how tiny they can be made (which is ridiculously tiny in some cases), they still take up a relatively large amount of living space. The water they use is also substantial, meaning that water tanks need to be filled up more regularly, which may mean paying to use a campsite, rather than just 'borrowing' water from free sources. One of the main attractions to living permanently in a van is the substantial reduction in financial outgoings. With my particular set-up, I have no need to use paid campsites. However, for a couple or a family living in a van, the use of a campsite once or twice a week in order to access the facilities and refill water supplies is still financially viable and considerably cheaper than paying a mortgage or rent with everything else that comes with it.

The food I eat isn't imaginative, not least because I only have one stove to cook on. I've never been adventurous when it comes to food – proper cookery is like maths or science to me (neither of which were my strongest subjects). I don't have the attention span required for complicated recipes and, if I'm honest, I'd rather be doing other things with my time, like freezing my tits off swimming in cold water. Food is simply fuel for the machine that takes me to the places which bring me joy and, as such, I try to eat in a way that hopefully prolongs the existence of my machine, but also prolongs the existence of those places. For breakfast, if I'm feeling like I need to be healthy, I'll opt for low-sugar granola with chopped nuts, dried goji berries and coconut milk. When the whole food health kick clean-eating thing is sucking my will to live, I'll toast up some crumpets and slather them with dripping, tangy and creamy salt-infused butter. For lunch, it's either soup with a flatbread or raw carrots with low-fat hummus and a few cherry tomatoes. Dinner is usually something like rice, broccoli and mushrooms fried in a pan, or tinned new potatoes, green beans and vegetarian sausages. Sometimes, if I'm feeling energetic, I'll make a chickpea curry or a vegetable stew.

Even in summer, I don't eat much salad as, without a fridge, it simply turns to mush within hours. I try to make up for the lack of leafy greens in my diet by eating lots of green vegetables, namely broccoli. If I'm having a 'fuck it' day, which is more often than I'd like, I'll really push the boat out and treat myself to a toastie in a café or, if it's an exceptionally difficult day, I'll sod off to Wetherspoons for either a halloumi burger with chips or a pizza, slathering it all in mayonnaise with reckless, hormonal abandon. Regardless of political, housing or financial position, the sanctuary afforded by the Wetherspoons chain to skint vanlifers and, indeed, all financially challenged people alike, is something I am always grateful for, especially in winter. When the nights draw in and the weather turns cold, in a Wetherspoons pub I can purchase an endlessly refillable hot drink for less than £2, hang out and reset in the warmth and space of a beautifully restored building (my favourite is the old Palladium theatre in Llandudno), charge my phone and laptop, if required, and settle in for an evening in front of an open fire.

Parking my van is easy; I park it where it's free and flat. No one likes to sleep on a tilt, except perhaps my mum's partner, who read somewhere that it's good for the vascular system if his head is raised six inches above the legs when catching forty winks. Maybe it is, but I have no desire to find out. The only rule that I follow when it comes to where I park/sleep in the van is self-imposed: I try not to park directly outside someone's house. The last thing I would ever want to do is cause anyone distress or anxiety. Having an unfamiliar vehicle parked overnight on your street, especially a van, which is a vehicle more often associated with male drivers, does cause worry for some people. Men, or individuals who have what society would perceive as a traditional masculine appearance, are unfortunately more likely to be viewed as being a potential threat than a woman would be.

As a single woman, I feel more vulnerable the further away I park from built-up areas, so I tend to stay within the boundaries of small towns. There have been occasions when I've parked in an empty layby, away from any residential area or housing, and a car has pulled in. The car has then been exited by an individual male, who has proceeded to stand in front of my van and stare at me for an inappropriate length of time through my van windscreen before I've managed to close the curtains that separate the driver and passenger seat from the living space in the van. This has happened more than once. Countryside laybys are not always the quiet, out-of-the-way little park-ups you would think. Especially after the sun has set. As I spent my entire childhood and young adulthood in fear, these days, I refuse to be intimidated and will constructively address situations that arise which cause me to feel unsafe. On the occasions when I've been stared at, or scoped out, by these layby wanderers, I've opened either my van window or door (if I felt safe to do so) and directly challenged them. I'm always polite, but very direct. Depending on what mood I'm in and how scared I am, my approach ranges from, 'Hi there, are you okay? Do you need any help?' to 'Why are you staring at me?' They always drop their heads and mumble something incoherent before getting in their car and driving away. Obviously, after these encounters, I don't stay in the layby and, instead, drive somewhere I consider to be safer, which is somewhere my screams could be heard by creatures potentially more helpful than squirrels.

Chapter Nineteen

Reservoir of Fuck-ups

'You complete fucking tit, Charlotte,' I splutter out loud, my breath coming in little gasps, part physical exertion, part anxious hyperventilation. For once, it didn't really matter that I was talking to myself out loud, something which I frequently do.

Having been caught mumbling to myself, 'Hmm, what shall I have for tea? Crumpets? I'd better not, I'll end up turning into one, and not the non-politically-correct sexy lady crumpet kind, but the stodgy, doughy, holey, messy crumpet kind . . . ooo, that looks nice . . .' (I really do have full conversations with myself, I'm ashamed to admit), I have been known to cover my tracks by looking around the aisle in an exaggerated manner and proclaiming loudly, 'Where's he gone? He was here a minute ago – he's always wandering off!' referring, of course, to the imaginary person I was apparently holding a conversation with.

Rather than being in a supermarket, this time I was instead on a remote clifftop, balanced precariously on a very slim dirt path at the arse-end of nowhere, with the crashing waves of the sea a sheer two-hundred-metre drop to my left, the cruel wind trying its damned best to drag me to my death and the sun sticking two fingers up at me by deciding to set faster than normal.

As darkness began to roll across the exposed cliff edge, an absence of light more solid than a brick in the face, it became clear that things were not going well.

It began with an end, as most things do. You have to have an end before there can be enough space for a beginning. The end, or endings, manifested themselves over the course of a few short years: the loss of my home, the death of my beloved dog, the breakdown of my relationship (twice), my criminal conviction for fly-tipping, the suffocating weight of constant financial hardship and the traumatic passing of my best friend's partner. At thirty-seven years old, I was done. The bleak, built-up, industrial grey of Bradford had been a murky-edged backdrop for the gritty turbulence of emotion that I'd experienced and I knew that, in order to heal, I would need to drastically change both my environment and the way that I was living.

Throughout the pandemic, I'd worked full-time for the NHS. Most of my friends had been furloughed (lucky bastards), but for me, not much had changed, except the commute to work. During the pandemic, it was like driving on the set of a zombie apocalypse film, the roads almost completely devoid of other vehicles, and also devoid of the casual, friendly morning road rage that I'd come to rely on as a replacement for caffeine to start my day. The closure of all shops, apart from supermarkets, had not only forced me to re-evaluate my relationship with consumerism, but had also meant that I'd managed to save up some money, something which I'd never been very good at in the past. It wasn't much money – £2,000 – but, if I was careful, it would be enough to fund the change that I desperately needed.

Some years before, I'd considered hiking the Camino de Santiago, which begins in France and ends in Spain, as a 'do or die' way of getting over my anxiety, but I'd bottled it, and had instead gone on to complete a degree in fine art. Two thousand pounds wasn't enough to fund a prolonged trip abroad, taking into account the cost of flights, hotels, hostels and food, but it was definitely enough for me to pack a rucksack and embark on a long-distance hike in the UK. The walk would push me out of my comfort zone, change my environment and give me the head-space that I desperately needed. Cornwall has always been a special place for me; in all honesty, it's a special place for anyone who visits. The raw power of the rugged coastlines, the beauty of the transparent turquoise sea and the ethereal quality of the light there is a soothing balm for any wound, whether it's emotional, physical or spiritual.

Over the years, I'd holidayed there many times and spent several summer seasons working in various bars or hotels in Newquay. I already had friends there and, with it being one of the warmest counties in England, it made sense to complete a long-distance hike in that area. Not only would I be less likely to freeze to death in my tent on a night, but if anything went wrong, support wouldn't be too far away. The South West Coast Path was perfectly placed to offer what I wanted. With other inland walks, I may have needed maps, apps, charts, a compass, and the mental capacity to use all of these things effectively, which I didn't have. The South West Coast Path follows the coastline from Minehead in Somerset to Poole Harbour in Dorset. As long as I kept the sea on my right-hand side, I couldn't go far wrong. The prospect of six hundred and thirty miles of sun, sea, physical movement and mental stillness filled me with purpose and, as I began to plan my escape from conventional life, I also began to heal.

I've always been an active, outdoor type of person (even when I took copious amounts of drugs and drank my body weight in cheap sherry, occasionally combining the two for interesting results), hiking up mountains, swimming outdoors, completing lengthy day hikes, exploring old ruins and castles. But I'd never done any prolonged hiking or backpacking, where I would be carrying everything that I could possibly require in a rucksack and sleeping in a tent every night. Sure, I'd camped out before, loads of times. I'd had several tent-based holidays in Cornwall, and even two weeks in a tent on a road trip around France. By any-one's standards, I was clearly a seasoned tent lifer. And as for carrying a full rucksack? No problem. My time as a stage-builder and the year that I spent weightlifting at my friends' home 'gym' (a freezing cold warehouse full of car parts and rats) had more than prepared me for carrying a bit of weight in a little backpack. Or so I told myself.

There's only one way to learn, and it's always the hard way. Which can be a right bastard sometimes.

The first mistake I made was while preparing for the walk. Even though I'd done a reasonable amount of research regarding which camp stove to buy, what sort of sleeping bag and tent was best, and so on, I completely ignored all of that and, instead, bought most of my gear based on whether it colour-coordinated with the vintage board shorts that I'd planned on walking in. With that kind of nonsensical fuckwittery, I deserved whatever fate was coming my way. Let's not forget that I was restricted by my small budget, which meant that the higher end brands, and more technical backpacking equipment, weren't an option. The one thing that I didn't hesitate to spend my money on, though, was footwear, which is probably the most important part of any kit when undertaking a long-distance hike.

In my late teens, I'd somehow fallen into a job working in a shop which sold equipment for specialist hiking, climbing and camping expeditions. At the time, my anxiety was almost unmanageable, so I don't remember much from the few, short months that I worked there, but the one thing that I did remember was how good Teva sandals were. If there was any shoe in the world that could get me from Minehead to Poole, while navigating a multitude of terrains, it was the four-wheel drive sandal that is the Teva Terra Fi 5 (like the sandals that your old geography teacher used to wear, if they'd been injected with super soldier serum and made by Jeep). This was Britain though, where rain is inevitable in all seasons, so I also spent another hundred pounds on some mid-range waterproof hiking boots.

After I'd made the first mistake of buying gear based on colour, rather than weight or performance, the flood barrier to the deep reservoir of total fuck-ups was structurally compromised, leading to a torrent of fuck-ups that just kept on coming. Packing my pretty (and very heavy) teal and turquoise rucksack was an organisational experience that fed my list-making obsession to the point that I was almost high with elation. What would I actually need for seven whole weeks on the trail? A book of poetry by an obscure author that I'd never heard of? Yes, definitely. A first aid kit similar to the size that paramedics use? Obviously, goes without saying. Three different hiking outfits that colour-coordinated with each other, three bikinis, a sparkly dress (just in case – you never know who you might bump into), fourteen pairs of knickers, eleven pairs of socks and three jackets (waterproof, insulated, fleece)? Yes, yes, yes, all absolutely essential. I packed a notepad and pen, so that I could journal in the evenings (or use it to write my last will and testament if things didn't go well), three torches with multiple spare batteries, a South West Coast Path guidebook, a water filter, three litres of water, water purification tablets, two emergency blankets, two microfibre towels, a bar of soap, toothbrush and toothpaste, body wash, shampoo, conditioner, phone, spare phone, battery bank, a knock-off GoPro camera (I couldn't afford a real one, and still can't now), eight packets of tissues, a lightweight down sleeping bag, a small pillow, an inflatable camping mat, a one-man double-skin tent, a compact stove with gas, a titanium cooking pot, tea bags, hot chocolate sachets, trail mix, noodles, flapjacks, apples, dried fruit and breakfast biscuits. All in all, with the rucksack packed, it came to a lightweight and manageable nineteen kilograms (please note the sarcasm here).

My lovely friends, who lived in Newquay, had agreed to drive up and meet me in Minehead, the start point for the walk. The plan was to have a night together on a campsite, me in my campervan and the two of them in theirs, before they drove my van back to Newquay, where they would look after it for me while I completed the walk.

Everything that I owned, my entire life, was now in my van. After the final and permanent break-up with Lee, I temporarily lived at my mum's house while I worked my notice with the NHS, a notice period that they'd kindly allowed me to extend after Lee had ended the relationship unexpectedly. The added time enabled me to continue to support Eleanor after her partner Michael's death and the extra money was helpful as I prepared for the walk. It was at this point that I made the decision to transition from using my campervan solely for holidays, to using it as my permanent, full-time home. I'd gone from having a planned future with Lee, to now having the freedom and exhilaration of wide-open space in front of me, full of possibilities.

With my rucksack packed, a brightly coloured sweatband encircling my head and wearing my vintage board shorts, I looked like a cross between an eighties aerobics instructor and a colour-blind Scout leader. I said goodbye to my friends at the sculpture which marks the start point of the walk, and off I went.

The sun was shining, the sky was blue, the sea was, well, brownish grey (it is Minehead, not the Maldives, after all), and I was infused with a sense of excited anticipation, buoyed by the ultimate freedom of moving through the world with nothing to worry about beyond putting one foot in front of the other. Everything that I needed (and loads of crap that I didn't) I was carrying on my back. I've found that, in most travel scenarios, whether it's long-distance or short-distance travel, for the period of time spent in motion, moving between point A and point B, everything gets put on hold, including everyday stresses, worries and anxieties. The same often happens during vacations. It's as if the mind knows to automatically switch off the worries that can't be addressed from, say, Majorca, or from a long hike on the southwest coast. Here I was with no responsibility for anyone except myself, minimum financial commitments (mobile phone bill, vehicle tax and insurance), some money in the bank, no house, no rent, no mortgage, a clear mind and an empty heart that was ready to filled by the beauty and wonder of nature.

With the guidebook in my hand and a smile on my face, I set off on my grand adventure. The path initially went through a forested area, taking me on a steep climb through dense, dark woodland, which really hit home just how heavy my rucksack was. I wasn't deterred or worried; yes, it was ridiculously heavy, but it was manageable. I'd done no training at all to prepare for the walk – I didn't feel it was necessary. My fitness level was already reasonable and, as the days went by, it would gradually improve. If I felt tired, I'd simply stop and rest. The only training anyone needs to do to walk is to, well, walk.

The guidebook advised me that the first stage of the hike was nine miles long, beginning at Minehead and finishing at Porlock Weir. At the top of the forested hill, the path opened out on to beautiful, rolling moorland, blanketed in purple flowering heather. The china-blue sky, the vivid cobalt of the sea in the distance (transformed from the murky brown of the sea near the shore by increased nautical miles and fathoms), teamed with the gold, lilac and sage green of the heather hills, brought a lightness to my being and a sense of elated happiness that no over-stuffed rucksack could ever hope to squash.

As the morning sun warmed my skin and I settled into a steady walking rhythm, I felt myself letting go of the tension that I'd been carrying, both consciously and unconsciously; finding stillness and peace in the movement of my body and the natural environment surrounding me. My mind, body and soul all exhaled an immense sigh of relief.

The section of walk between Minehead and Porlock Weir was relatively straightforward – the only occurrence of any note (besides my complete rebirth) was the rescue of a tiny, baby rabbit that had somehow managed to get itself on the dinner menu of a hungry crow. I noticed the crow first, swooping and pecking at something which was obscured by the dust on the path, but, as I drew closer, the crow retreating to observe from a nearby gorse bush, I saw a tiny, dusty, furry thing, holding itself as still as a stone. Perhaps it had myxomatosis, which is why it hadn't run away, but it seemed far too young to experience that evil virus. Carefully shrugging out of my backpack and setting it down on the side of the path, I slowly reached out and picked up the tiny rabbit, cradling it with both my hands. It didn't panic or move at all, but simply allowed me to hold it, gently turning it so I could check its eyes for signs of illness or blindness (birds of multiple species are known to peck out the eyes of young rabbits, something I'd unfortunately encountered in the past). It seemed fine, eyes black and bright. With a soft breath, I blew the dust out of its fur and set it down next to the line of foliage on the edge of the path. As soon as its feet touched the ground, it shot off into the safety of the undergrowth. Putting my backpack on, I said an apology to the crow, that was eye-balling me balefully from its nearby perch, for buggering up his lunch reservation and continued on my way.

It was one o'clock in the afternoon when I arrived at the tiny village of Porlock Weir, which consists of one hotel, a couple of gift shops, a small art gallery and a harbour. According to the guidebook, this was me done for the day, unless I carried on and completed the next stage of the walk, which was Porlock Weir to Lynton, and another twelve miles. Unsure what to do with myself, I had a look around the gift shops – perhaps I'd buy myself a token of some sort to commemorate the start of the walk. But as soon as the thought entered my head, I purposefully extinguished it.

Buying crap, especially when I felt unsettled, was one of my default settings, a learnt behaviour to self-medicate for anxiety that I had no desire to perpetuate. Still, I could have a look for nothing.

One of the gift shops was set slightly back from the harbour, not far from the hotel. As I entered, I heard the worrying sound of tinkling glass, and realised that my huge rucksack had disturbed a plethora of window chimes and light catchers that were all made out of that fragile material. In fact, nearly everything being sold in the shop was made of glass in some form or other, but I was already too deep within the narrow shelving to consider taking off my rucksack. As I gingerly made my way around, marvelling at the hitherto unknown creative possibilities of glass, the lady behind the counter called out, 'Are you walking the South West Coast Path then?' Oh fuck. I'd been caught out. She'd seen the cheap rucksack, the brand-new shiny shoes of an unknown brand, the comedy shorts, and immediately realised that I had no idea what I was doing; that I was nothing but a colour-coordinated hiking imposter. 'Well,' I replied, with a wry smile, 'I'm going to give it a damn good go!' She laughed and said, 'You're so brave, I wish I had the courage to do something like that.'

Her friendly, open demeanour put me at ease and, when I replied, it was completely without guise, 'I don't know about that . . . I reckon it takes more courage and bravery to try to exist within a system that does nothing but repress us and keep us all in poverty than it does to pack a bag and say "bollocks to it all, I'm off".' She laughed, a lovely, bright sound, like the tinkling of the glass she sold, and then her face became more serious. 'You're so very right. It makes me feel good knowing that there are people like you who say no to it all.' She bent down to rummage under the counter and, when she straightened, she held out a small, circular badge – it was an acid-yellow smiley face. 'Take this and put it on your rucksack, then when things get tough, you'll remember that you're not just walking for yourself, but for those of us who can't.' I took the proffered badge, a lump in my throat forming at the unexpected kindness. Thanking her profusely, I wished her well and then got out of there before I burst into tears. Once back outside, I sent a silent prayer into the ether that this lovely woman would win the lottery the next time she played.

Sitting on a bench outside the hotel in the early afternoon sunshine, I consulted the guidebook. The next stage of the walk, Porlock Weir to Lynton, was described as twelve miles of arduous ascents and descents through remote, wooded valleys. At the bottom of the page, a few sentences in a smaller type detailed that 'unless you are an experienced hiker, with a good level of fitness, do not attempt to walk both sections in a day – Minehead, to Porlock Weir, then to Lynton'. It felt like a challenge, rather than a warning, and I was too energised, too excited, to stop walking now.

It would be the first night in a long time that I had slept out of reach of my campervan, which was the comforting sun that my planet gravitated around. I could feel low-level panic simmering away at the thought that I was out in the world without my getaway vehicle accessible. Sod it, I'll keep my mind and body busy by continuing the walk. If I got tired, I'd pitch my tent – surely that was the whole point of carrying my home on my back? It was early September and there was still plenty of daylight left. I could do this.

Off I went, my rucksack feeling heavier than it did before, and my new walking shoes starting to pinch a little at my heels. The guidebook hadn't exaggerated the difficulty of the terrain. It was exhaustingly relentless. If I wasn't going up, I was going down. The geography of the landscape had decided to forgo the courtesy of having a flat bit in between for a weary traveller to catch their breath. I didn't see anyone else walking, and I felt quite vulnerable being alone in such a remote area. The only evidence of other people was the occasional silent farmhouse. The sun was no longer visible, covered over by the shadowed darkness of the forest. In my physically tired but wired state, the steep, woodland paths had a sinister feel, the trees seeming to lean in menacingly. My left heel was really hurting now – the new walking shoes that I hadn't bothered to break in prior to wearing them were protesting against my lack of preparation by breaking me. Stupidly, I didn't bother to take them off and check my feet for blisters, despite carrying the weight of a substantial first aid kit. In my head, any pause would shatter my momentum, so I just gritted my teeth and carried on.

At regular intervals, I would come across carved signs by the side of the path proclaiming the distance that I still had left to walk. 'Lynton – six miles' said one. Then I'd trudge along for another hour and come across another sign . . . 'Lynton – eight miles'. Is someone playing silly buggers or what? How could it possibly be eight miles when it was frigging six an hour ago? I looked around with accusing eyes, searching for the bored farmer who was likely sitting watching me from behind a wall, laughing at my angry confusion. If pissing about with signage was how folk got their kicks around here, then fair enough, but surely there were better ways to have a laugh than discombobulating knackered hikers, like playing charades, shoplifting or swinging, or whatever.

The path finally left the vertical-sided wooded valley and opened out on to an altogether different terrain. As I emerged from the trees on to the exposed cliff side, taking in this new vista, a little wave of vertigo washed through me and I swayed slightly. The sea was a sheer drop mere yards to my right; the narrow path I was on snaking across the steep cliff side, barely big enough for two feet. Bring back the trees, I thought – at least then I wouldn't have had such a good view of my imminent death. The weight of the rucksack was becoming almost unbearable, my heel was a red-hot, burning area of pain, I was feeling pretty knackered and my knee was starting to hurt. Drastic steps were required. A little way up the hillside, I spotted a farmers' gate. The field beyond the gate was still heavily sloping, but it was the flattest area around and, comfortingly, some distance from the cliff edge. I hauled my pack over the gate and climbed into the field. I checked my phone for signal. Of course there wasn't any, but the screen told me that I had about three hours left until sunset. I had no idea how many miles away from Lynton I was, but I knew that I'd move faster if I released some ballast and strapped up my heel. It was time to reorganise.

Emptying my pack completely, I spread it out over the sun-dried grass and critically surveyed the contents with my new, more experienced eyes (seven hours on *that* terrain was plenty of experience, thank you very much). What had I actually been thinking when I packed this thing? A book of sodding poetry? It would have to go. Body wash, a bar of soap, shampoo *and* conditioner? What was this, a Premier Inn in a backpack? There was nothing for it – I'd keep the shampoo, use that for everything, and get rid of the rest. Three pairs of animal print leggings? The vanity of style was weighing me down, literally. Two pairs would have to go. By the time I'd finished my merciless cull of crap, I nearly had a full carrier bag of stuff that I simply didn't need. What could I do with it? I was in the middle of nowhere. Pulling out a few more carrier bags, I wrapped up my parcel so that it was completely watertight and stashed it in a secure place next to the gate post. Marking the location as accurately as possible in my guidebook, I resolved to come back for it. (I never did, so if anyone finds it, can you please contact my agent – I really liked those leggings.) That was the best I could do and, although I felt guilty about leaving it, at this stage, it was about survival. Sitting down, I gingerly peeled off my hiking shoes. The heel on my left foot was literally a huge, pus-filled blister. I stuck some plasters over it, threw a bit of clinical tape on and put on an extra pair of socks. That would have to do. I considered pitching my tent and sleeping there, but it was too remote, too close to the edge of things for me to feel okay. I had three hours of daylight to cover an unknown amount of miles. I was scared but determined.

Following the slim path across the wind-torn cliff side, I continued on. Fear of being alone out there in the dark sharpened my focus and gave me renewed energy, energy borrowed from adrenaline reserves rather than taken from food, as, in my frenetic state, I'd completely forgotten to eat.

The sky was noticeably getting darker, the landscape around me subtly changing colour as the light receded. For a time, the path took me away from the cliff edge, continuing up a hillside towards a small, stone-built church. Once at the church, the path disappeared into the long grass surrounding worn, lichen-covered gravestones. Consulting the guidebook, it wasn't clear, either in the description for the walk or on the map depicted, which way I went from there.

A car pulled into a gravel-strewn patch of ground next to the church, tyres crunching, and I watched a man with a young boy get out. They walked over, near to where I was standing, taking in the same view that the gravestones had, facing out towards a darkening sea. Perhaps the man was local and had some knowledge of the area – he might know where the path continued. 'Hi,' I said, smiling as I approached, 'I'm trying to work out where the South West Coast Path continues from here. Do you know the area by any chance? I'm struggling to read the map in my guidebook.' I think the man could tell that I was reaching the end of my energy reserves. Even though I'd tried to come across as calm and friendly, I probably had a slight edge of frantic panic. 'I'm on holiday,' he said, 'but let's have a look at the guidebook. I'm actually from Poland, but I've done lots of long-distance hiking in Scotland and

Europe, I reckon we'll be able to work it out,' he smiled reassuringly as I handed over the guidebook for his consideration. After some deliberation over the guidebook, he then pulled out his phone and brought up an OS Maps application. 'Well, I think the path continues over there and, by the looks of it, the village is just at the bottom of the hill,' he pointed to an area across to the right. 'I tell you what, we'll walk with you for a little way just to make sure.' I could have cried with relief. What an absolute legend of a human being. We walked together for a time while the lovely man regaled me with some of his hiking stories. Before the sun had completely left the sky, he wished me well on my travels and turned back to return to the church, and his car. I thanked him profusely for his help and for taking the time to walk with me.

As true night rolled in, I arrived in Lynmouth, a cluster of cafés and hotels on the river estuary set below the village of Lynton. It was nine o'clock in the evening. Crossing the bridge over the river, I made my way to the public conveniences. As soon as I had extricated myself from my rucksack and sat down on a low wall nearby, a wave of dizzy nausea washed over me and I nearly passed out. Woah. What was that all about? From my seat on the wall, I shakily lowered myself to the ground so that I was sitting on the pavement. I put my head between my knees and took some deep, slow breaths. Walking twenty-one miles over extreme terrain while wearing brand-new shoes and carrying an incredibly heavy rucksack had not been a good idea. Especially not on my first day. I was so exhausted now that I could barely move. Forcing myself to eat a flapjack helped enormously, realising that I'd expended energy without putting any back in.

It was late, and I hadn't planned on where I would sleep once I arrived in Lynton. Googling a few campsites, I rang them, apologising for the lateness of my call, but every single one was fully booked. When I arrived in town, I walked past a children's park, which had a large grassy area near a set of swings. Dragging my rucksack back on, I stumbled my way over, my knee barely holding my weight. I pitched my tent in a dark corner of the grassy area, figuring that I'd be awake at first light and gone before anyone even knew I was there. Sliding into my sleeping bag fully dressed, with my shoes still on, too tired to do anything else, I tried to sleep, but even though I was physically exhausted, my mind was racing. Sleep came and went in fitful patches, until light flooded the tent indicating that it was once again daytime.

Upon waking, I fought my way out of the sleeping bag and tried to exit the tent in a dignified manner (which hadn't worked, according to the shocked facial expression of a passing dog walker). It became immediately apparent that I had severely damaged my knee. The pain was so great, I could barely stand. What a complete nob I was. The grand adventure was over before it had even begun. Taking down my tent, being careful not to put weight on my knackered knee, I packed my rucksack and limped over to the only café that was open at such an early hour. Drinking a lukewarm bitter cappuccino, I considered my options. I wasn't going to give up yet. I probably needed to rest my knee for a few days and then re-evaluate things. The campervan was in Newquay with friends, which meant that I'd have to spend some money on a hotel for a couple of nights.

After ringing Mum to have a cry and for some moral support, we both then rang around to try and find a hotel. It seemed that there was only one hotel in either Lynton or Lynmouth which had any vacancies. I booked two nights and proceeded to drag both myself and my rucksack to the hotel, and then up to the single first-floor room they'd allocated me. To my amazement, the little room had a bath. Even though it was barely ten o'clock in the morning, I put the plug in, stuck the taps on and started to strip off – shoes first, which had practically welded themselves to my feet, then socks, which had done something similar. As I took off my socks, I felt warm liquid trickle down the underside of my left foot. That can't be good. Looking down, I saw that the blister, which was more or less my entire heel, seemed to have popped, and the skin that had covered it was now attached to my sock. My heel, without the protective barrier of the blistered skin, was just red, raw tissue. I could actually see the mottled white of muscle, now completely exposed. Bugger.

After a careful soak in the bath, I threw on some clothes, strapped on my sandals and headed out, slowly, to the small doctor's surgery in the village. Once there, I explained my foot situation to the receptionist. She took one look at it, eyes widening in shock, and sent me straight through to the nurse. 'Oh my days!' the nurse exclaimed. 'That's the worst blister I've seen in a long time! Let's get you sorted out love, you won't be walking very far on that for a while! New shoes ey? You should have broken 'em in first!' She cleaned up my heel and covered it over with a hydro-colloid dressing, a type of plaster designed to act as a second skin. While she worked, she told me how to take care of it and how to redress it in a few days' time. She also gave me a special shoe to walk back to the hotel in. I looked like a right plonker, but I was so grateful to be the recipient of her care and kindness.

Nurses, and people who deliver care, truly are the best. There's something inherently wrong with a world that is happy to pay footballers almost incomprehensible amounts of money, while nurses, paramedics and care workers, especially care workers, are at the bottom of the pay scale.

With the wound on my foot and my knackered knee, I decided that the best course of action would be to travel down to Newquay (it took two buses, three trains and five hours), collect my van, drive back to Lynton (or somewhere near) and book in with a physiotherapist. The universe, via my poor choices, complete fuck-ups and inexperience, had obviously decided that I needed to learn a lesson. Which was fair enough, but the dream wasn't over; it was still only just beginning.

Chapter Twenty
Car Park Warren

The sun warmed my bare skin like gently heated oil poured across my back. I smiled to myself in contentment as I curled my bare toes into the sand. The sea in front of me was as still as a pond, shimmering turquoise and clear in the midday September sun. This beautiful cove, little Hele Bay on the outskirts of Ilfracombe, was the perfect place to convalesce. High, stepped cliffs sheltered a perfect rectangle of ocean, small enough to swim from one side to the other. It wasn't busy; schools had returned after their long summer break, leaving adult couples and retirees to enjoy the quieter, more languorous energy of early autumn.

At the beach, I was taking full advantage of my forced period of rest having returned from a morning appointment with a physiotherapist in Barnstaple, half an hour's drive from where I was. The physiotherapist had diagnosed the damage that I'd done to my knee during the frantic and ill-judged first day of my South West Coast Path hike as being severe ligament strain. Rest and sports massage was the prescription given, with two to six weeks' healing time. The physiotherapist, after I questioned her, advised that walking on the knee before it had fully healed would not increase the damage, but would be painful. With that news, I decided to rest for the minimum amount of time recommended, which was two weeks, before continuing my walk. My campervan was parked in a clifftop layby above the little cove, which had truly stunning sunset views across the ocean. There were public toilets and a small convenience store at the mouth of the cove. I'd been living in the car park for four days so far without issue. There were no parking restrictions signposted and, every morning that I was there, a local dog walker had come past exchanging morning greetings in a warm and friendly manner. For once, it would seem that being in a campervan in a car park wasn't a problem. I spent my time reading, resting my knee, floating in the sea and sunbathing on the beach. It was truly wonderful to do nothing but exist and take in the beauty around me.

After the complete chaos that was my first day hiking, I'd decided to finish the walk using my campervan as a base, rather than using a tent. The traumatic debacle of the impromptu playground 'campsite' had left its mark. It would be logistically difficult to use the van, but not impossible. My plan was to walk a stage of the hike, then get the bus back to the campervan, before driving to the end of that stage, parking up, sleeping over and doing it all again the next day. The only issue would be that the buses in the southwest are infrequent and often unreliable; occasionally, for no fathomable reason, a scheduled bus simply doesn't turn up. But if that happened, I was sure that I could hitchhike or thumb a lift, even if the prospect of doing so put me out of my comfort zone.

The clifftop car park was frequently full of other campervans – people who were either on holiday or perhaps lived in their vans full-time, like I now did. Some would stay a day, or a night, before moving on. Beyond saying an amiable hello in the morning, we didn't have any prolonged conversation; everyone was so busy making the most of the sunshine to stay in one place for too long. One evening, as the sun was setting, illuminating the cliffs with radiant orange splendour, a medium-sized white van pulled into the car park. It was only remarkable in that it clearly wasn't a campervan, with no external indicators or extra windows to proclaim it as being a vehicle designed for habitation.

The sunsets from the car park had been spectacular nearly every evening and, at these times, the car park would fill up suddenly and people of all ages, backgrounds and ethnicities would gather at the edge, camera phones at the ready. As soon as the sun had set and the orange tones transformed into deep lilacs, vivid pinks and dusky purples, the car park would empty as suddenly as it had filled. Perhaps whoever was in the white van had come to watch the sunset. As I got ready for bed, closing the curtains in my van, I didn't give it much more thought. I brushed my teeth, wiped my face clean and dutifully applied the cheap wrinkle cream that clearly didn't work. Undressing and slipping under the single cotton sheet covering my soft, foam bed, I could still feel the comforting warmth of the sun lingering on my salt-kissed skin.

The next morning, I noticed that the white van was still in the car park. Whoever was in there must have slept over. The air was already warm, even though the sun hadn't been up long. I opened the side door of my van to allow the air to circulate and to prevent myself from overheating as I boiled the kettle on my little gas stove for a cup of tea. Taking a bowl out of the cupboard, I threw in some granola, sliced banana, a dollop of peanut butter and some oat milk. As I sat down on my bed, my breakfast perched on a little table in front of me, I saw the side door on the white van slide open . . .

A slim, middle-aged man stepped out. He was wearing khaki combat trousers, a black T-shirt and an army-green peaked train driver's hat. As I ate, I watched him fold out a little aluminium camping table, which he stood on the ground, before he reached back into his van for a portable stove, which he placed on top of the table. He proceeded to make a brew by boiling water in a small, stovetop kettle and, when that was done, he set the kettle down and pulled out a frying pan to cook bacon. If he's cooking, I thought, then maybe he's staying in his van, but the glimpse I'd had of the inside through his sliding door had just showed bare metal, rather than the fixtures and fittings of even a home-built campervan. I'd say hello, I decided; it might be useful for him to know where the public toilets are and that I'd stayed in this car park for a good few days with no trouble.

'Morning!' I said, with a smile. 'Your breakfast certainly smells better than mine!' I'd washed up my breakfast bowl, made another cup of tea and was now perched in the side doorway of my van, facing in the direction of where the man now sat in a foldout camping chair. 'All right.' He acknowledged my greeting in a matter-of-fact West Country accent, without a smile, raising the cup in his hand slightly as a substitute. 'I reckon bacon tastes better when it's cooked outside. Are you living in that then?' He nodded to my van. He obviously wasn't bothered about wasting time with small talk, which was fair enough, in which case, I wouldn't give him a small talk answer. 'Yeah, I'm living in it full-time now. I got sick of paying the bank for the privilege of borrowing money, they repossessed my home anyway, and I decided that there were better things to do in life than work forty hours a week in a soul-destroying job just to exist.' I think my honesty took him aback and it was a moment or two before he responded. 'Fair enough,' he replied, 'I'm feeling the same way myself. I'm Warren, by the way.' He stood up and walked over, holding out his hand. I shook it, 'I'm Charlotte, pleased to meet you.'

Pulling out a deckchair from under the bed in my van, I set it up so that I could sunbathe while we chatted. I sensed that Warren wasn't ready to be asked why he was here, in his van in the car park, so I built up a rapport by regaling him with my recent misadventures. I told him how I'd completely fucked up the first day of my South West Coast Path walk, overpacking a too-heavy rucksack, purchased because it matched my shorts, which made him laugh, wrecking my knee and savaging my heel. I proudly showed him the still-healing wound from walking twenty-one miles in brand-new shoes, and he satisfyingly exclaimed how sore it looked.

He told me how he liked to wild camp using a lightweight tarp and a bivvy bag as a shelter, and how he was learning bushcraft skills via YouTube videos. I showed him my campervan and he commented on how homely the interior felt and on the efficient use of space for the layout. He showed me his van, which he said was a recent purchase. The back of it was completely empty, bare metal on every surface apart from the floor, which was ply board. There was no bed, no curtains, nothing. It was empty, apart from a plastic container, which had a few cooking implements in it, and a rucksack.

'Where are you sleeping?' I asked. He replied, 'I have a lightweight inflatable camping mattress, which I use for wild camping, and a lightweight sleeping bag. I just roll it out on the floor.' The look on my face must have communicated my thoughts, as he added, 'It's okay – it's comfy enough. I plan on doing a proper conversion at some point in the future.' I desperately wanted to know what he was doing, roughing it in the back of an empty van in a car park, in part, because I was concerned for him and also, if I'm honest, because my paranoid, fear-filled mum had brought me up to think that everyone was a perverted serial killer. There was nothing for it, I'd just have to come right out and ask him.

'Are you living full-time in the van then Warren, what's the deal?' He looked at the ground for a moment or two, perhaps deciding how to answer or what to say. When he looked back up and his eyes met mine, I could see the turmoil there. 'I couldn't do it anymore, Charlotte.' He paused, looking out at some distant point that I couldn't see. 'I've been an engineer all my life, spannering and fixing, pissing about with cold metal and machinery. Last week, my boss asked me to do a job, which I knew was going to be complicated and messy. Normally that wouldn't have bothered me. I'd have just cracked on and got it done. But that day, I just couldn't. I don't know why. I put down my tools and told my boss that I was leaving. He convinced me to finish the job that I was doing, which I did, and then told me to have a few days off to get my head straight. He's asked me to give him a call at some point to let him know what's happening. I threw a few things into the van, I wasn't really thinking straight – I didn't even pack any spare clothes – and I buggered off, with no idea where I was going. And here I am. In this car park, chatting to you.'

Woah. How would I reply to that? With honesty, as always . . . 'Warren, that's awesome mate! Good for you!' I don't think he expected all-out support as my response. It was clear that he was suffering because of the decision he'd made, and I wanted him to know that walking out of a job which was causing him to feel distressed wasn't a bad thing – it was an act of self-love. Even though his boss was clearly compassionate and understanding, it didn't mean that Warren owed him anything. I said as much as we talked. 'I don't know what to do though, Charlotte. Do I have myself a little holiday then go back? The thought of going back makes me feel sick. My head is a mess.'

'Well,' I said, 'first things first. I've got some spare kit in my van that you can have just to make things a little easier for now. And I was in a charity shop in Barnstaple the other day, near my physiotherapist's place, and I saw a single wooden futon in there, with a mattress. It'll fit perfectly in your van and be so much better than sleeping on the floor. I've got some curtain wire and fittings, and a drill, so we can rig you up a curtain for your back window. And there's always Primark for extra pants, socks and T-shirts. The thing is, you don't need to know what to do. Just be. Go with the flow. With everything that happens in the world, leaving a job, even if your boss is awesome, just doesn't really matter. People walk out of jobs every day and the world keeps turning. There are always other jobs, with other awesome bosses. I don't know about you, but I need a wash. Do you fancy a swim?'

It was amazing how much crap I had in my van – too much, if I'm honest. I was able to give Warren a towel, a griddle pan, a knife, fork and spoon, a bowl, a plate and a contraption called a Bright Spark, which made it possible to toast bread and crumpets on a single hob stove (being able to toast things is a game changer when it comes to standards of living in a van). Using my drill, we fitted the curtain wire on his back window, ready for when we found a curtain, and agreed to go to Barnstaple the next day to see if the single futon was still in the charity shop. Now that he had a towel, there was no excuse for not going for a swim, although he did take some convincing . . . 'It's going to be fucking freezing!' he moaned. 'Don't be such a wet flannel, man! You've got to wash your balls somehow!' I replied. So, off we went, down to the little cove below the car park, claiming our spots on the pristine beach with our towels. 'Are you ready?' I asked. 'It's best to get undressed quickly, then run into the water – you don't have time to think about it then. Let's go! Woohoo!' We both threw off our clothes – I had my bikini on underneath, he was swimming in his boxer shorts on account of having no swimwear (or any wear, really) – and ran into the sea. As soon as he hit the water, Warren screamed hysterically, like he was being attacked by a pack of rabid dogs, or rabid fish. The other people on the beach were looking over, clearly alarmed at this unreserved display, but I was laughing so hard that I nearly drowned. Once he'd acclimatised, and stopped screaming, he swam, floated and played in the beautiful turquoise sea.

There is nothing more effective than cold-water bathing, in a natural environment, to instantly quieten a worried or anxious mind. The release of tension that Warren was carrying was visible: his forehead was no longer furrowed, the tightness had left the area around his eyes and he was smiling at the pure joy of being in the water. As we swam together, the surface of the water in the space between us suddenly erupted, and a large, silver fish leapt out, its scales flashing as it twisted its body in the air, before diving back down again into its azure home. 'Wow! I've never seen that happen before! That was amazing!' I exclaimed, astonished by the slim chances of such an encounter occurring, right then, in that moment. 'You know why he's jumped out of the water don't you?' said Warren, in his matter-of-fact West Country drawl, while he was treading water. 'It's because an even bigger fish was chasing him.' A little shiver of fear went through me as I tried to look into the water, my imagination taking over. The dark shapes rippling beneath the surface, likely shadows caused by the sun filtering through the gently rolling waves, became instead bloodthirsty pollack with a taste for human flesh. 'On that note, Mr Warren, I think it's time to get out!'

We left the water and headed back to where we'd laid out our towels on the beach. As we began to dry ourselves, I could hear Warren's teeth audibly chattering. Unused to cold-water swimming, he was taking too long to dry himself, leaving his wet skin exposed to the cool breeze that was coming in off the sea. 'Faster lad! The quicker you dry yourself and get your clothes on, the faster you'll warm up.' As I bent down to dry my feet, I couldn't help but notice a series of dark purple-coloured scars on the bottom of Warren's legs. The scars were heavy indentations, like bullet holes that had healed; the veins around them raised and angry looking – blue, purple and red – spidering their way around his ankle. I glanced up, worried that he may have seen me looking. He had; bugger. The last thing I'd want would be to make him feel uncomfortable in any way. I immediately struck up a conversation, and the moment passed.

'That's the first time I've been swimming in twenty-five years, you know,' Warren remarked, as we headed back up to our clifftop car park hang out. 'No waaaay. That can't be true! Do you mean swimming in the sea or swimming in general?' I replied. 'Just swimming. Anywhere. I'd forgotten how good it feels to float in water. Thanks for making me go in, even if I'm probably a eunuch now.' 'No worries man, anytime. At least if you don't have balls, you don't need to worry too much about washing them, right?'

The next day, we took a trip into Barnstaple. We were on a mission to buy the single futon that I'd seen in a charity shop, some curtains and some extra clothes, and for me to attend a physiotherapy appointment. I still had another five days to rest my knee before I continued my South West Coast Path hike, but I wanted to make sure I had everything I might need should it become aggravated again. We drove in Warren's van and left my van in the car park. Considering I'd only known him for two days, I felt very comfortable and safe in his company. Effectively, he was still very much a stranger, but then I guess everyone is at first.

Unbelievably, the futon bed was still in the charity shop when we arrived, and it fitted into Warren's van perfectly, with plenty of room to spare. It would be luxury compared to his previous 'mat on the floor' effort. We found some blue curtains that covered his back window, which would give him some privacy and make the van seem a little more homely. He bought himself some extra clothes and swimming shorts (on my insistence) from Primark and allowed me to drag him around the charity shops. Surprisingly, given his engineering background and stoic, West Country farmer demeanour, he had an eye for fashion that was frankly mind-blowing . . . 'If you're opting for that high-waisted, block-colour skirt, young 'un, then I'd probably team it with a patterned crop top. Sleeveless. And maybe some low-heel ankle boots in a shade of tan.' What? Where did that come from? 'What do you know about fashion? Do you call yourself Warrenella on a Tuesday night or what?' I teased, in a very politically incorrect way. He laughed, 'I apply engineering logic to the equation of fashion. I measure the angles and lines in a garment, by eye, and calculate the aesthetic success of a particular combination.' He delivered this in a deadpan voice, but the twinkle in his eye gave the joke away. Still, there was no denying that he knew what looked good – it was like going shopping with an understated, sarcastic, West Country version of Laurence Llewelyn-Bowen.

It was late afternoon when we arrived back at the car park, where each of us retreated to our vans to cook some dinner and have a bit of down time (shopping is more tiring than hiking twenty-one miles) before agreeing to meet later for a brew. At the allocated time, Warren tapped on my van window and I invited him inside. We talked about campervan conversions, sea-swimming, the hike that I would soon be completing, bushcraft techniques and our favourite Wetherspoons. There was a pause in the conversation, which Warren filled with, 'I saw you notice the scars on my legs . . .' Oh fuckery. 'Yeah, I saw them. I hope I wasn't staring! I'm sorry. I didn't want you to feel uncomfortable, I'm sorry if you did.' He laughed, 'Don't be silly young 'un, you can look all you like, it doesn't bother me. The scars are from using.' My naivety was embarrassing . . . 'err, using what . . . ?'

'Heroin. I used to inject it into my legs. I was a functioning addict for nearly ten years. I went to work, I paid a mortgage, but most of my money went on gear.' The only other contact I'd had with anyone who had used heroin was someone who had previously rented a room at my house, before it got repossessed. Even then, I wouldn't have known, he was such a bright, lovely man, but when the teaspoons started going missing, and then my drill, and, finally, the lodger himself (after not paying his rent for three months), it became clear that he was an addict. I asked the first question that came to my mind: 'How did you get off it?'

'I went to prison for seven years.' Oh right, well that would certainly do it. My mum's voice suddenly filled my head: 'See, I told you not to talk to strangers. Now look what's happened – you're in a car park on your own with an ex-convict heroin addict!' Give it a rest Mum, will you! I had stern words with my inner Mum, recognising how privileged I was, even if I was a little bit scared at these new developments, that Warren felt comfortable enough to share some of his life experience with me. 'Well,' I said, 'I suppose my next question is why did you go to prison? If it's uncomfortable to talk about, please don't feel that you need to.'

Warren shared with me that he'd sold a firearm to the wrong person – someone who didn't have a gun licence, like he had – and an undercover police officer had been involved in the exchange. He explained that he'd always had a passion for guns, something which ran in his family, but, on this occasion, his addiction had dictated his actions and he'd sold it for the money. He'd been sentenced to fourteen years in prison and served seven of those before he was released. After his release, he returned to work in the same industry that he'd been in prior to his jail sentence, which was metal work and engineering. He'd been out for two years. I couldn't even begin to comprehend his experience – seven years in one cell, in one place. It was no wonder he wanted more from life, at this point, than working forty hours a week in a different kind of prison.

'Thank you so much for sharing this with me. I can't begin to know what it was like for you. From the outside looking in, it would seem that, if you hadn't gone to prison, you would still be doing heroin, and it's highly unlikely that you'd be swimming in the sea or hanging out on the beach, like you did yesterday, on this beautiful Devon coastline.'

'You're absolutely right,' he replied, deadpan, as usual, 'if I hadn't gone to prison, I'd be dead now.'

The next day, we swam in the sea again and spent some time on the beach. At the point when his thighs entered the water, Warren still screamed like a man having his leg sawn off without anaesthetic, but I was used to that now, even if the other beach-goers weren't. He mentioned that he was going to call his boss later that day to advise him that he wouldn't be returning to work.

I could tell that he was worried about the exchange, so I offered to sit with him while he made the call. Once we were back at the park-up, Warren made his usual strong coffee on his camp stove (three teaspoons of coffee, four teaspoons of sugar – you could stand a spoon in it) and brought it over to my van. He sat in the front passenger seat, with me in the driver's seat, ready to make the call. He dialled the number, and I heard his boss pick up at the other end.

Warren started the call by saying that he wouldn't be returning to work, and how sorry he was to let everyone down. I heard Warren's boss offer him reduced hours, an increase in pay, more responsibility, less responsibility, more holiday, the opportunity to pick and choose what jobs he took on . . . I was waiting for the offer of a yacht and an all-inclusive two-week holiday to Mexico and thinking, 'Fuck me, this guy must be an *incredible* engineer', when Warren said to his boss, 'I really appreciate everything you're offering me, but I'm tired of spannering and I need a break.'

Warren's boss said that he completely understood how he was feeling, thanked Warren for all his hard work and made it clear that if Warren ever wanted a job in the future, he would always have one at his company. Tears rolled down Warren's cheeks, seemingly overwhelmed by his boss's kindness and compassion. I was nearly crying myself. Human beings truly are awesome. The phone call ended, and I gave Warren some space to regain his composure, climbing into the back of my van to put the kettle on. 'So lad, what now?' I asked.

'I was thinking Char, how would you feel about me walking the South West Coast Path with you?'

The universe works in very strange and wonderful ways, and sometimes, well, always, it's best to hold any judgement and just go with the flow. I'd known Warren for three days. All I really knew about him was his previous heroin addiction and his arms-dealing conviction.

Did I want to walk six hundred and nine miles with this person? I wasn't sure. But the universe had brought us together for a reason, so I replied, 'Yeah, fuck it, why not?'

Warren's real name isn't Warren. I thought you might like to know that he chose that name himself on account of the joke 'what do you call a man with a hundred rabbits up his arse?'

Chapter Twenty-One

Fear

'Ooo no, I wouldn't go there if I was you – you'll get kidnapped, raped or murdered; in fact, probably all three. They've got them . . . what do you call 'em? Guerrillas, that's it, running around everywhere, kidnapping folk left, right and blummin' centre. You'll be dead within ten minutes of stepping off the plane, I'm telling you. And if you're not dead from them guerrillas, then you'll wish you were after drinking the water out there, it's got bugs in it that will have you on the toilet for two weeks solid. Why don't I have a look at a static caravan for a week in Scarborough for you love, ey, if you want a nice holiday on your own?', was my mum's response when I brought up my intention to arrange a month away in Costa Rica in order to help with sea turtle conservation. I was twenty-four years old, desperate to see the world and mindful that I needed to find a way to distance myself from the toxic social circles that I moved in, which all focused on substance abuse. Needless to say, with those dire warnings, I didn't go to Costa Rica. If I'm completely honest, I haven't been anywhere further than Malta, which was over twenty years ago. My lack of travel experience is something which I hope to change in the coming years.

Scaremongering has always been my mum's default response to most things, even now. Everything my brother and I do, or plan on doing, comes with a warning or a frightening tale of caution:

'Mum, I'm going on the longest zip wire in Europe, it's in North Wales,' said my forty-one-year-old brother. 'Ooo, well I remember your cousins' friends' Uncle Jimmy's daughter going on one of them things once, and she ended up in a coma for seventeen years, woke up unemployed, overweight and single in her forties, and her favourite guinea pig Fuddles died while she was unconscious, the poor love. I'm just saying . . .' With these dire warnings preached for everything – from getting a bus to Leeds when I was fourteen years old ('You'll get lost in Leeds, it's a big city, and it's full of weirdos'), to walking the South West Coast Path when I was thirty-seven years old ('You'll probably break your leg and die, fall off a cliff and die, or fall in the sea and die. I'm just saying, but it's up to you love, go if you want') – it's an absolute miracle that I even left the house.

All the cautions and warnings come from a place of love and care, but over the years, especially while I was growing up, my mum's projected fear became my fear, topping up my own reserves of fear, and my internal dialogue was always, 'I can't' and 'I'm too scared', rather than 'I can' or 'I will'. I already had an incredibly low opinion of myself and what I could achieve in my life, with the contributing factors for that opinion consisting of a complex array of several different issues: my class, my education, the way that I spoke, my turbulent upbringing, my place of birth, my sex, the mental health issues that I struggled with and the core belief that I was inherently without value. How could someone like me – a sweary, rough-speaking, northern, uneducated, working-class female with a history of domestic violence and drug abuse, low self-esteem and anxiety issues – ever be so ridiculous as to think that they could travel the world or write a book? How utterly preposterous.

As I grew, both in years and self-awareness, it became clear that I would always feel fear of some description. Feeling fear, for me, seemed to be part of living as a human being on this planet. In my opinion, the generalised fear that I experience is either learnt, developed via social conditioning, from my upbringing, or simply an aspect of my personality type, although the reasons why are almost irrelevant.

There are so many aspects of human life where fear plays a part – these are just a few which I have felt, and continue to feel, sometimes every day: fear of being alone, fear of being rejected, fear of being unloved, fear of not being accepted, fear of saying the wrong thing, fear of what happens next, fear of the judgement of others, fear that I'm not enough, fear that I'm wasting my life, fear that I'll fail if I try, fear that things will change, fear that things will stay the same, fear of death, fear of pain, fear of suffering, fear of violence, fear of myself, fear of the fear, fear of who I might be without the barriers of that fear.

Fear can dictate so much, and often we have no self-awareness of it, nor how its existence within us can affect the decisions that we make. This is highlighted by a recent conversation I had with a friend. We were initially chatting about her childhood, which was very different to my own in that her family had never struggled for money. The conversation progressed to discussing how we choose to spend our time outside of work, and she confessed that she dislikes socialising and engaging with other people, preferring instead to spend her time solely in the company of her partner. She expressed how happy she is with her life, existing within her small social sphere, and how she has no need, and no desire, for any further social interactions. I explained that, in my opinion, it's only through connection and communication with others that we truly grow as people and that, by disengaging from that, she was potentially excluding herself from wonderful experiences and new opportunities. She wasn't convinced.

The conversation turned to politics, as conversations often do, and she went on to say that her family has always encouraged her to vote selfishly (her words), in favour of maintaining her current lifestyle. She revealed that if a certain political party had come to power at a particular time in her life, she would have lost £200,000 of her inheritance due to a proposed increase in inheritance tax by the opposing party. I questioned her on the longevity of her voting stance, on how voting to maintain her immediate lifestyle could have a negative impact on her children's future, on the future of the planet, through climate change, and on the ever-increasing gap between the wealthy and the poor. She agreed that voting primarily to maintain, or increase, her wealth could indeed have long-term negative results but made it clear that she wouldn't be changing how she votes.

From the conversation that we had, which was amicable, open and honest, I came to the realisation that, on many levels, she was afraid – that she was reluctant to interact, connect and engage with other people, in case, by doing so, the carefully controlled status quo of her life, her opinions and her judgements were compromised or changed in some way. Even if someone is so far removed from poverty that they are unable to relate to the people experiencing it, that person can still have empathy and compassion, but in order to feel those emotions, there must be a willingness to connect, a desire to try to understand and, most importantly, the inclination to care. Closing ourselves off from the suffering of others doesn't make it go away, it only widens the gap between us all.

It can be hard work, this life business. But it doesn't have to be so full of fear. Yours might not be; if it isn't, that's fucking awesome – roll two dice and skip to the next chapter indicated . . . just kidding. The only sentient being reading this who hasn't felt fear is the AI currently poised to take over the planet. Maybe if we all said, 'Alexa, tell these billionaire fuckwits to quit dicking about trying to get to Mars and use their money instead to eradicate world poverty and starvation, alongside reversing global warming,' something truly wonderful might happen.

Though I made external changes to my life to alleviate some of my fears, like choosing to live in a van, therefore reducing my financial outgoings and stress levels, it was the changes that I made inside that had the greatest impact, not just for me, but for the people around me too.

Throughout my life, at different points, I've received counselling which employed various techniques and approaches. I found that the most beneficial method was a blend of cognitive behavioural therapy (CBT) and mindfulness, which taught me how to observe my thoughts and my behaviours, and to reflect on how they were connected. I discovered that, when I felt angry, it was almost always because I was afraid, even if that fear was perhaps irrational or illogical. An example of this would be how I previously felt (and sometimes still feel) regarding using trains as transport. For most people, getting on a train is a normal part of everyday life, but for me, being trapped in a metal box which I'm not in control of, that's flying down a track at wild speeds, prompted severe anxiety, which then became fear, which then manifested as anger. I failed three car theory tests, not because I'd actually attended, but because I'd had a panic attack on the train en route to the test centre, got off at a stop nowhere near it and walked home. I think I was seventeen or eighteen at the time. My mum, once she found out, was quite rightly pissed off as she'd paid for at least two of the theory tests, but when she became angry with me, I was just as angry at her. At the time, I blamed her for forcing me to get on a train, and for the panic attacks that had occurred as a result. Looking back, it's clear that the anger I directed at my mum was actually anger at myself for having the panic attacks in the first place, for judging myself to be pathetic and useless because I couldn't even get on a sodding train.

CBT and mindfulness taught me to accept how I was feeling, rather than distract myself from it, even if those feelings were uncomfortable, like fear or anxiety can be. The techniques I learnt focused on consciously being non-judgemental and applying compassionate acceptance to anything that I might be feeling. Yes, I might be feeling scared, but that's okay. Feeling scared or anxious isn't a 'bad' feeling, it's just a sensation. By acknowledging my fears, by allowing them to exist within me, observing them, rather than reacting to them, they slowly reduced. Mindfulness practice gave me the knowledge that how I reacted to my fears and anxieties was a choice that was within my power, rather than an inevitability.

I know that there will always be occasions when I think that I'm not good enough, when my anxiety influences my behaviour, moments when I'm of the opinion that, because of my class, lack of wealth and upbringing, some things simply aren't for me. But rather than allowing those fears, or those inaccurate beliefs, to negatively dictate my decisions, prevent me from taking action or from experiencing wonderful things, they are now my motivation, the fuel for my fire. Instead of thinking, 'That's not for the likes of me' or 'I can't do that', instead, I consciously acknowledge those thoughts and feelings of self-doubt (hey, thanks for popping up and telling me that you're worried, I appreciate it, taa), and do the thing that I told myself I couldn't do anyway (or try to).

Many of the choices that I've made in my life have been influenced by my fear: staying in jobs that made me ill because I was too scared to leave, continuing in relationships that were toxic because I was frightened of being alone, not daring to pursue my creative ideas in case I failed, missing out on opportunities, like being accepted at Aberdeen University to study animal ecology, but not attending because I didn't think I was good enough and it was too far away from home. When I hit rock bottom and lost everything that I'd been told was essential to be a successful human being, the hold that my fears and anxieties had over me fell away. I realised how little it truly mattered, and that should I find myself lying on my deathbed one day, which of course I will,

I wouldn't be congratulating myself on working forty hours a week for however many years, nor would I find any solace in how new my car was or the size of my house. Instead, I would derive comfort remembering the time I swam naked in the piercing cold and crystal-clear fairy pools on the Isle of Skye, watched playful otters catch their dinner off the Isle of Arran or connected with friends, new and old, over a meal cooked on an outdoor stove on a Cornish beach.

The clarity I experienced regarding how I wanted to live versus how I was currently living was like the light and heat of the sun dispersing heavy, morning mist. It was counterproductive to focus my attention on being *seen* as successful, to anyone who cared to look, if I was desperately unhappy. I realised that I didn't owe anyone anything, especially not a society which kept me mired in debt and despair, but, with only one life to live, I owed it to myself to do the things that made me feel good, that gave me a sense of purpose, of belonging, even if doing those things meant confronting my fears.

Chapter Twenty-Two

The Path of Glory

The rain was relentless – it poured out of the sky in a continuous heavy downpour that no amount of Gore-Tex could withstand. Everything was wet, right down to underwear levels, as we squelched along in walking boots overflowing with water. As I looked out at the blue-grey sea a hundred yards away from our feet, waves lapping level with the footpath, I figured it would have been easier, and probably drier, to swim this section of the coast path.

'Get a move on fat arse, there's chocolate milkshake and cake at the end, and if *that* doesn't get your little legs going, nothin' will . . . only another two hundred and twenty miles to go.' Warren.

'You could do with eating more cake, you bandy-legged streak of piss, then you could carry a heavier rucksack . . . with cake in it, obviously.' Me.

Warren and I had settled into a rhythm of friendly banter, his acerbic wit and deadpan sarcasm had both of us frequently in stiches as we navigated the ever-changing landscape of the South West Coast Path. We were evenly matched in our pace of walking: I would always start slow, speeding up as we neared the end of a stage, motivated by the thought of cake, milkshakes and a stroll around the shops, and Warren would always start fast, slowing down as his morning dose of three heaped teaspoons of Nescafé Azera wore off.

As we trudged along in the inclement weather, the path slowly led away from the shoreline, moving towards a rocky crag wreathed in mist, which had a small, white lighthouse perched precariously on its summit. The footpath widened as we neared, becoming an old cart track, where rounded pebbles, of all shapes and sizes, had been used as cobbles. Two older ladies, trussed up in ankle-length rain macs, white hair tucked under their hoods framing crinkled, wind-chapped faces, were approaching. They were clearly struggling on the uneven surface of the cart track, with the smooth, rounded edges of the wet pebbles offering no traction at all. Warren, on top form, even in the miserable weather, offered a greeting: 'Good morning ladies! The roads around here are shocking, I'd be having a word with the council if I was you.' I'm not sure that they understood the joke, or perhaps the rain had robbed them of their humour as they battled both the weather and the slippery road. They didn't laugh at all and, instead, gave a terse 'good morning' before staggering past, but I was laughing on and off for the next four miles.

The two of us walking the South West Coast Path, with two campervans, was a logistical success, and far more reliable than public transport. Not only were our rucksacks lighter as we didn't require tents, sleeping bags and cooking equipment, but it meant that, after a long hike in the pissing down rain, we each had a functional space to dry our clothes and warm up. Even though Warren's van wasn't kitted out to be a campervan, with its new single futon bed liberated (legally) from a charity shop, it offered more comfort than a damp one-man tent and a flaccid inflatable camping mat. We drove/hiked in a relay system: one van would be parked at the start of a stage, we would then drive a van to the end of a stage, hike back to the start, collect the van that we'd left there, before driving back to the van which we'd left at the end, and do it all again the next day. In an ideal world, both of our vans would have been electric, negating the impact that we had on the environment. As it was, on days when our hiking end destinations were more accessible, we would minimise our impact by using public transport.

Warren, applying his engineering logic to everything, maintains that every step he takes is perfectly calculated, taking into account weight distribution, centre of gravity and the structural integrity of his bone, muscle and sinew. This unconventional approach often results in rather strange, but compelling, little dances as Warren descends steps and hills or navigates rocky terrain on the coast path. He also applies his engineering logic to our energy consumption by allowing us to only fill our vehicles with one-third of a tank of fuel at any time. One litre of fuel roughly equates to one kilo of weight; therefore, by implementing weight carrying capacities to fuel usage ratios (Warren's own words), we can reduce the amount of fuel we consume by reducing the weight that we carry. This helps to mitigate our resource use and environmental impact. Warren can often be seen reading the weight of every item he puts in his shopping basket at the supermarket, particularly avoiding wet foods and glass jars as he maintains that they weigh too much. I ceased making dinner suggestions after he told me that pasta and pesto was too heavy and wasn't in line with the strict mechanical sympathy that he maintains is necessary for the longevity of his van (although I'm pretty sure he didn't check the weight of the fishing rod and tackle box he bought the other day).

There's no right or wrong way to walk the South West Coast Path and, indeed, there are those who insist it should be done using only a tent and the power of two legs. And they can insist all they like, especially while they are trying to wipe their arses in prolonged heavy rain after defecating in a rather spikey bush. I'll stick to my sandcastle bucket in the back of my warm and dry van, thank you very much. The people who we met along the way were all approaching the walk differently; some were doing day hikes of sections and ticking them off on a map at home, others were hiking for longer periods and staying in hotels. Very few people were hiking the entire trail of six hundred and thirty miles, but we did meet some. From chatting with those we met, it seemed that, for many, financial obligations and work commitments were the main barrier to completing the walk in its entirety.

It was initially nerve-wracking, and surreal, to spend all day every day with someone who was essentially a stranger, but as anyone who has attended a corporate team-building day will know – where you are tasked to build a bridge over a 'stream' (sewage run-off) in some hole of an industrial estate somewhere using nothing but a box of tampons, chewing gum, an old shoe and some twigs – it doesn't take long before you are blood brothers with Abdul from Accounts, have forgiven Steve from IT for ignoring your email and are desperately in love with Angela from HR.

Warren would regale me, as we walked, with tales and stories from his days in prison, a world that I had no previous insight into. I marvelled at the range, and size, of various objects and substances that seemed to be inserted, as a matter of course, into the lower orifice of the alimentary canal – or, in other words, up someone's bum. It was the only way to get things into, and out of, prison, without being detected. But even then, he advised, searches of anal cavities were a regular occurrence, often conducted without the comforting softness of lube.

He told me how he would make hooch – an alcoholic drink distilled from fresh orange juice, sugar and water – in his prison cell, and trade it with other inmates for luxury items, like freshly ground coffee and heady, dark chocolate. The process to make hooch was chemically complex and, if a batch went wrong, it would blow up, covering everything in the prison cell, including its occupant, with sticky fermented orange.

He read nearly every book in the prison library and attended any course that was on offer, from electrical installation to barista training. He explained that it was possible to earn money in prison, even though the rate of pay was nominal, but he topped up his bank account by keeping himself busy either gardening in the prison allotment or undertaking maintenance work on the prison wings. During his time there, he turned his wonderfully creative and technical mind to sculpture. As art materials were in limited supply in prison, he started with what he immediately had to hand, which was standard-issue glycerine soap. Warren would save up his soap blocks, and trade other inmates for theirs, until he had several blocks of soap, which he would then melt together and pour into a mould (a mess tin lined with greaseproof paper), giving him a larger area than one block alone to work with. Using tools that he'd crafted himself, he carved intricate three-dimensional landscapes into the soap bars, with trees, mountains, rivers and antlered fallow deer.

The success of his soap sculptures motivated him to attempt something larger, made of material with more longevity than soap, and he began a life-sized model of a golden eagle, with its wings furled and head held regally aloft. It had an internal frame of steel wire (which he'd begged, borrowed and traded to obtain), with the outer material consisting of painstakingly, meticulously layered copper wire (again, which he'd begged, borrowed and traded to obtain). Even the prison wardens, once they'd seen Warren's soap sculptures and the beginning of his golden eagle, would occasionally arrange for some copper wire to appear, as if by magic, in his cell when he was out. With the limited supplies and time-consuming nature of its construction, the sculpture took two years to complete, but, once it was done, it was truly amazing – a feat of art, engineering, ingenuity and tenacity. The sculpture was so well-received, and Warren's talent and character so well-liked and respected, that, on his release, the wardens insisted that he was allowed to take it with him, despite the reasonably high monetary worth of all the copper wire.

Our hiking duo, with our twelve-year age gap (I was thirty-seven and Warren was forty-nine), alongside our very different characters – me, with my 'eighties aerobics instructor' look, and Warren, with his 'gamekeeper about to go trout fishing' look – made for a very unusual combination. He would often remark, with some amusement, how the people we met and chatted to while walking clearly found it difficult to place us, with most adhering to the rules of social convention and refraining from asking outright the questions they had in their heads: were they boyfriend and girlfriend? Husband and wife? Father and daughter? Rich Somerset landowner with middle-aged, outdoor pursuits-orientated, rough and ready Yorkshire escort? God knows what they were thinking. But it was wonderful to watch any judgements that they may have had fly out of the window in the face of our good-natured humour, amiable dispositions, ridiculously strong accents and genuinely attentive curiosity.

We chatted to everyone we met, both on the walk and in the various towns and villages that we explored after our hiking was done for the day. I have always gone out of my way to be vocal in my praise of someone's style, fashion sense, their boldness in being visually unique or their creativity. If I have a positive thought about anyone in my vicinity, I'll tell them, if it's appropriate and constructive to do so – compliments, delivered with authenticity, have an undervalued capacity for positive change. Unspoken, Warren came on board with my mission to make as many people feel good as possible, without outright lying (it never works if a compliment isn't one hundred per cent genuine) and we moved through our hiking adventure leaving happy people (both of us) and swooning ladies (Warren) behind us.

Warren always referred to the South West Coast Path as 'the path of glory'. We would sing those words, frequently and loudly, as we walked along, to the tune of 'Eye of the Tiger' by Survivor. It became our anthem, and we would make up new verses as the mood took us:

> Warren and Char, back on the path,
> we swapped the concrete for dirt and grass,
> what's the difference now we're back on the path,
> Warren and Char gonna climb to the stars,
>
> so many times Char needs a piss,
> on the path of glory . . .

One particular day, we were belting out an expressively powerful rendition, when we heard the distant sound of other voices raised in song. Exchanging a glance, we stopped singing and listened. There was no one in front of us or behind us. We were coming up to the corner of a headland, so whoever was singing must have been behind it. After a few minutes of walking, we could see two figures heading towards us; they hadn't seen us yet and were still engaged in what could only be referred to as coast path karaoke. The song they were singing was 'I'm Gonna Be' by The Proclaimers. Without conferring, Warren and I automatically joined in – it seemed the only reasonable thing to do.

The two strangers seemed delighted to become a quartet, if only for a chorus, and that's how we met Joe and Joanna. They were a lovely young couple in their late twenties who had taken time off work specifically to walk the entire six hundred and thirty miles of the coast path. For every place they visited, they made it their mission to include the name of the village, or town, in a song. Joe always wore a wide-brimmed safari hat and became known as Indiana Joe. Because of his hat, we could see them coming from miles away. They were great fun, and we came across them on several days over the course of our walk (they were walking straight down the coast from Minehead, but because Warren and I were doing the relay with our two vehicles, it meant that we were walking in the opposite direction on each section of the walk).

We met so many amazing and wonderful people during our hiking adventure, it would be almost impossible to mention them all. Some, we have stayed firm friends with, like Barefoot Ben, the intrepid meditating hiker who was walking the coast path in bare feet in order to raise money for refugees. The second day that we'd known Ben, he stood in a dog poo, cut his foot on glass and had his toe stung by a bee . . . if that doesn't deserve a donation, then I'm not sure what does. Through Ben, we met Lorraine, the wonderful lady who lives off-grid in a cabin on her own land and makes stunning clothes from fabric that she's printed herself. Then there was Orisa, who we thought was a secret Nigerian princess. She literally had an entire camping shop's worth of equipment in a backpack that towered over her petite body. And Camille, a lovely French girl who lived in her van in Brighton and worked on an organic farm. We also met Jade, an amazing woman who we were all in awe of: she'd solo-hiked the Pacific Crest Trail in America (nearly three thousand miles) and undertaken hikes in extreme environments where her survival had relied on other people burying water for her at various points across deserts. Through circumstance and chance, some of us ended up camping together for a night in Bude. We all had an impromptu holiday from hiking and spent the next day sea-swimming, eating ice cream and sunbathing. Despite, or perhaps because of, the fact that we were all practically strangers, it was a most memorable and wonderful day.

'You're doing it the right way, you know,' commented Warren, one evening, as we were winding down with a brew in my campervan after a particularly strenuous day of hiking. 'Doing what?' I asked. 'Living,' he said, gesturing with his cup to the interior of my campervan. 'You don't have to worry about bills, you're not handing money over to banks or landlords, you can live wherever you want, you don't need to work as much because your expenses are minimal, you could do anything . . . I'm going to do it, you know. I've been watching van conversion videos on YouTube. I'm going to sell my current van, buy a bigger one and spend this winter converting it myself.'

I was absolutely thrilled to have inspired Warren to start his own journey towards living alternatively.

Living in a van may cost considerably less than living in a house, but there are still financial obligations: food, fuel, tax, insurance, phone bills, unexpectedly buggered laptop, rucksack-buying addiction. It doesn't help that my van is relatively old and has now reached the point where things are breaking and expensive parts need replacing, like clutches and top struts (whatever they are). Welding is also now a major expense as age, sea salt and the damp British weather slowly corrode the metal of my little home like Cornish clotted cream ice cream melting on a summer's day. However, there are houses to rent in Cornwall, and indeed, across the entire UK, where one month's rent alone is £1,500 (in my opinion, those prices are not justifiable). In comparison to that, the cost of my vehicle upkeep is still incredibly minimal.

While I was walking with Warren, the small amount of savings from my job with the NHS reduced bit by bit – the ice creams, pasties, hot chocolates and cakes soon added up and, as we neared the halfway point of the walk, a place called Porthallow, it became clear that I wouldn't have enough money to finish the walk. It was October now, and the weather was slowly turning, with grey, rainy days becoming more frequent. We agreed to put the walk on hold (we'd covered three hundred and fifteen miles, which was exactly half of the distance) and return to finish it the following spring. I would work in Cornwall through the winter to save up some money, and Warren would commence his campervan conversion project in his hometown of Bath.

Warren did exactly what he said he would and bought a larger van, which he then spent the winter months meticulously converting into a functional home. He rented a unit on a farm to ensure that he had the space he needed to complete the conversion. Randomly, and hugely in his favour, two lovely lads, who had the unit next to his, were running a successful business converting vans into high-end campers: Eyesopen Vanlife Workshop. Not only did the lovely Daryl from Eyesopen help Warren and offer advice on his conversion, but they soon became firm friends.

Warren was very close-mouthed about his conversion while he was doing it, and I only saw the new van once, when it was empty. He refused to send progress pictures and, instead, wanted the grand reveal after he had finished. We had agreed to continue the walk in June, and I drove over to Bath to meet Warren a few days before we once again set out on 'the path of glory'. I knew Warren's conversion would be good, with his engineering skills and practical mind, but when I finally saw the completed van, it was, and is, spectacular. No expense had been spared, every detail, right down to the smallest screw, carefully considered. It is a true home, far more luxurious than any van I've ever lived in: hot running water, shower, oven, grill, multiple hobs, a heater (that works, unlike my temperamental piece of crap), a deep sink and polished oak worktops. Warren's talent in all things, from electrical installation to precise cabinetmaking, is an absolute wonder to behold.

Making the move from conventional living – surrounded by stuff, weighed down with bills, debt and stress – to a different way of living has been life-changing for Warren. With reduced financial obligations, he now has more free time and more head-space. He can pick and choose how frequently he works and what job he does. Warren maintains that choosing to live in a van has been one of the best decisions he's ever made. He adores his little home on wheels. It's a home that he owns outright, that he built himself, a home that the bank can't repossess, and a home that he can take anywhere that the road allows and his heart desires.

Chapter Twenty-Three
Pirate of the Tarmac Sea

I wake up in a slight panic, feeling a little disorientated. Seagulls are screeching above me, the tell-tale thumps on the van roof indicating their morning bowel movements and the reduction in capacity of my shit-splattered solar panels. Where am I? I struggle to remember which town I've parked in and where. Then a profound realisation comes over me, completely silencing the hazy anxiety that I've woken up with . . . it doesn't matter. It doesn't matter one bit where I am, because I am home – safe and sound in my campervan, with everything I could possibly need no more than two metres away. A wave of pure contentment washes over me, bringing a half smile to my sleep-creased face, and I snuggle back into bed, the only worry occupying my mind being the pressure of my full bladder threatening to force me out of my cosy, blanketed state.

I can hear the sounds of waves breaking gently on the soft, sandy beach outside my van window, the whoosh and rush of their lazy push and pull a morning lullaby as I drift in and out of sleep. Wherever I am, I must have parked next to the sea, which is my preferred place to be, except in winter. The colder months blow in fierce Cornish storms that rock my little home as if three tonnes of metal weighs nothing more than a pebble on a wind-swept shore. The ever-changing mood of the ocean, on the days when I park with its wide expanse in view, never ceases to move me, my heart and mind taking on the energy of what my eyes can see and what my heart can feel.

Some days, the ocean is as still as the air on a hot and heavy midsummer's day. Languid and sultry, the clear turquoise water will barely move; slow tides, without waves, gently tease the shore. On other days, the beguiling turquoise changes to a deep, carnal cobalt blue, breakers rising and raging in angry, white-capped curves, before crashing down in an ear-splitting, rushing chaos of spitting foam. When measured against such wild and untamed energy, anxieties and worries about most things fade into unimportant mundanity: how could anything be more important, or have more power to command attention, than nature, with all its overwhelming complexity and implacable simplicity?

Choosing to live a nomadic life opened doors for me that I didn't even know existed, doors that would have remained closed had I still been living in a fixed abode, in one town, in one area. Making the transition from a stationary existence to one of movement and fluidity, offered more opportunities and choice than I could have ever imagined. Potential employment was no longer restricted to how long and how far I was willing to travel from home to work, because I could move my home, and therefore any job, in any area, could be considered. I was the captain of my ship.

The sense of 'home', and of safety, that I feel when I have my campervan with me is the same feeling that I had when my home was a conventional stone building. One of the most important and freeing statements that I have ever been privileged to hear in my life was from my good friend Andrew Varley. I was having a mental health crisis, feeling adrift and unstable, which wasn't unusual in my earlier life, and Andrew, who has spent more time on the earth than me, and who has also done a considerable amount of inner work, gave me the following gift: he said 'home is not a place, it is a feeling. We carry our home within us wherever we go. Anytime that we feel unsafe, unsure or afraid, we can access that sense of home by simply focusing our attention within.' And I believe he is right.

Home is the self-assurance and groundedness that come from accepting ourselves fully, from loving ourselves, and each other, completely; from being courageous enough to show our humanity, our vulnerability and the fallible nature of being human to the world. By letting go of the fixed, immovable concept of home, regardless of where and how we live, there is an increased capacity to live more fully, to fill the mind with the expansiveness and creativity of adventure, to turn uncertainty and worry into curiosity, anticipation and excitement. I know that wherever I am in the world, I am home and, with that knowledge, I can let go of fear and step into the wide, open expanse that is the future (or give it my best shot, anyway).

With our hike of the South West Coast Path paused halfway, due to a lack of funds, the next course of action was to find a job. I had no desire to return to West Yorkshire. The rolling beauty of the Yorkshire Dales and the striking drama of the Lake District nearby certainly had their own unique appeal, but for me, nothing compares to the rugged magnificence of the Cornish coast. Cornwall has always been the home of my soul, if not my birth.

Because I had no mortgage, no rent and minimal living costs, I found myself applying for roles which I would not have applied for previously, had I still been weighed down by the immense financial obligations of running a house. I could take more risks, safe in the knowledge that I wouldn't have utility providers or banks sending me urgent demands for owed money or missed payments in official, letter-headed, red-stamped envelopes. It didn't matter whether I got the job I'd applied for or not, I would still have a roof over my head and money to buy food. Liberated from financial pressure, my confidence and self-assuredness went from strength to strength.

Interviews, like most of the ones that I'd had when I lived in a house and paid a mortgage, were no longer a desperate, frantic, contrived and anxious affair, with the focus being on simply getting some money into the bank as soon as possible. I no longer had to bend over backwards and put on a facade so that I would be employed. I now had the freedom to be my authentic self (well, as authentic as possible, there are limits; when asked if I have any criminal convictions, of course I say no, but we all know by now that I'm a crazed fly-tipper), and if that wasn't right for my potential employer, then it wasn't right for me either. Empowered by the financial and psychological freedom that living in a van had allowed me, I began to comprehend and appreciate my value and worth; interviews became more about what the employer could do for me, rather than what I could for them.

The first interview I had was for a role as a customer service representative for a property management company that was based inland, half an hour's drive from the sea. It took me an hour to find the main office, which was hidden away at the back of a small industrial estate. The lady who interviewed me was an interesting character – forthright and chatty, she was a rental property manager by day and a scientist researching cures for diabetes by night. As the interview progressed, she mentioned that she loved my singing voice. Bemused, as I definitely hadn't burst into song during the interview, I thanked her and asked her how she knew that I used to be a singer. She went on to admit that she'd googled me prior to the interview, actually singing a couple of lines from one of my original songs. Which was worrying, on several levels.

If she'd googled me extensively enough to learn my song, then she would have also come across the incriminating newspaper article detailing my fly-tipping conviction, alongside some incredibly dodgy YouTube music videos, the most cringeworthy of which was from a gig I did years ago at a workingmen's club in Queensbury, Bradford. Apart from a few wobbly bars of a Blondie number (I'd have been on the brandy for sure, back then), the video predominantly features me arguing with a group of grizzled, disgruntled old men for having the audacity to interrupt the darts tournament that they were watching on the pub TV with a gig. Skimpily clad lass with reasonably sized, err, assets, versus darts – they chose the darts, as any Yorkshire man worth his pint of Timothy Taylor's should. I didn't take the role when it was offered, not because the interviewer had heavily stalked me online, but because the job seemed to consist mainly of dealing with disgruntled tenants, which sounded like too much stress for not enough money to me (admittedly, the same as most jobs).

The role that I *did* end up taking was a position that I'd applied for, and interviewed for, to be a spa host at a high-end hotel near Newquay. When I applied for the job, I had no idea what being a spa host entailed, but I figured that there would be showers in the spa (I'd have been worried if there weren't) which I would need.

My role as a spa host was a vanlifer's dream job. In fact, it was a pretty fantastic job for anyone. The hotel – the Bedruthan – is located on a clifftop which overlooks the rugged Cornish coastline. The cleverly tiered architecture of the hotel rooms, restaurants, gym and spa means that each space has views of the sea and the dramatic, life-affirming sunsets which set the sky aflame nearly every night.

Through the day, while at work, I would park in the hotel car park, which was free for staff members, but at night, I would drive down to sleep over in a large privately owned car park located behind a row of shops in the bottom of the valley (which was free for overnight parking, and parking out of season). I don't think the hotel would have minded had I slept over in their car park, but having tried it for a few nights, it became clear that their beautiful clifftop location meant increased exposure to the elements, resulting in a lack of sleep due to the van being hefted this way and that by the wind.

I was responsible for hosting and curating the well-being journey for guests booked in at an outdoor experience, which is entirely unique to the spa. Clients would arrive, in all weathers, wearing their swimming kit and spa robes, and I would guide them through the journey, which began with a dry body scrub made out of oats, essential oils and herbs, followed by a shower, a sauna, a cold-water drench, hot tub, an oil-based scrub infused with twelve essential oils and, finally, a hot herbal tea enjoyed while seated around a warming, aromatic fire.

It was difficult work at times, with long shifts synonymous with the hospitality industry, and it could be exhausting, engaging with so many different people every single day. On busy days, new clients would arrive every fifteen minutes. The hardest part of the role, and the most rewarding, was being able to hold the space for clients at the end of their experience, when their tension or stress had finally reached the point of surrender. They would sit with their herbal tea by the fire, tucked up in blankets, surrounded by scented plants, and speak about their worries, their difficulties and their lives. I met some truly wonderful people while I worked there. Two clients who stand out, and whose life journey aligns with mine, are John and Trudy.

John was a paramedic and Trudy was a care assistant, and they'd been living in Ilfracombe and renting the same house for the last six years. During the period of time when the country was released from lockdown, but still unable to holiday abroad, John and Trudy's landlord abruptly evicted them in order to rent out the property on Airbnb, which was more financially lucrative, at that time, than long-term letting.

Unfortunately, all the other landlords in the southwest were doing the same, which meant that John and Trudy were unable to find anywhere to live. Neither of them wanted to leave their jobs and relocate completely, so with no further housing options available, they decided to convert a van to live in.

They admitted that they were initially worried about the challenges of living full-time in a van, but, once they'd made the transition, both Trudy and John said it was the best thing they'd ever done. Due to the dramatic reduction in their outgoings, they were both able to reduce their working hours and now had more time, *and* more money, to engage in vital well-being experiences, like having a day out at a spa. The greed of their former landlord and the trauma of being evicted from their long-term home turned out to be a gift, which, from my experience, is often the case when shit things happen in life.

Working at the spa meant that I was able to use all the facilities there. I would go into work early every shift in order to complete a thirty-minute yoga routine in the hotel gym, a truly beautiful space that had sea views. When my shift was over, I would release the tension of the day and watch the sun set as I floated around in their heated hydrotherapy pool. On my lunch break, I would head back to the van in the staff car park, grab my empty water bottles and fill them up at the hotel. I made full use of their showers, complete with free toiletries, and one time I even washed my clothes (including a rug) in one of the outdoor hot tubs, before I emptied it, cleaned it and refilled it.

Occasionally, a therapist would need a model to train a new staff member in a particular massage technique, which meant that I was also, occasionally, the recipient of free massages. People pay thousands to experience what I had access to every day, and I was so grateful to be there, especially as it made living in my campervan even easier than it already was. If I'd have worked at the hotel for a year, I'd have been gifted with a free stay, complete with an evening meal, breakfast and use of the spa. As it was, my time there was simply to save up enough money in order to take the summer off and complete the South West Coast Path hike. Which is exactly what I did.

After seven months of working at the hotel and staying in one place, both my little home on wheels and I were ready to set sail again on the tarmac seas.

Chapter Twenty-Four
Thank You for Bringing Me Here

The side door of the van is open, distorting the line between outside and in. I'm lying on my bed, head propped up by a pillow, taking in the view beyond. The warm, gentle breeze, imbued with the heady scent of honeysuckle, intermittently finds its way in through the open door, scenting the air, rippling my curtains and caressing my skin. The colour blue, in its various manifestations of shade, tone and intensity, fills my eyes, the sea and sky merging together, with white-tipped breakers reflecting the ivory clouds strewn above. I lazily entertain the idea of going for a swim, idly calculating the effort that it would take to get changed into my swimwear and walk the few hundred yards from my van to the ocean's edge. I imagine the buzz and tingle of my skin as the heat of me is immersed in the cool, gritty water. And although I know that I would feel amazing afterwards, in my sun-saturated, warm and languid state, I consider the effort to be too great. I am happy to rest my mind and body, and watch nature unfold, feeling connected to the natural world.

Closing my eyes, I focus my attention on my breath, consciously measuring my inhales to a count of four, before pausing and holding my breath for another four seconds, then slowly exhaling, again, to a count of four. Measured breathing, box breathing or equal breathing helps to anchor my mind in the present moment. It slows my heart rate, reduces any feelings of anxiety that I may have and supports the connection between my mind and body. When I pay conscious attention to my breath, I inhabit the present moment, and any worries about the past or the future fade. Mindfulness practice teaches that neither the past, nor the future, exist; there is only the now.

After several rounds of measured breathing, I expand my attention from my breath to the sensations that I can feel in my body. Thoughts enter my head in a constant stream of internal chatter, but rather than pushing them away, I allow them in. My acceptance and acknowledgement of each thought, without judgement, regardless of its nature, takes away any power that they might have to hold my attention. Once I have acknowledged them, they gently float back out of my mind as quickly as they entered.

From my body, I move my attention to the sensation of the breeze swirling in through the open van door, lightly pushing and pulling, rippling over the bare skin of my face, hands and arms. I have heard this technique referred to as breeze bathing, which I think is a wonderful concept. Sometimes, if my anxiety is particularly elevated, I'm unable to focus my attention on my breath . . . it freaks me out and I start to have panicked thoughts like, 'What if I stop breathing?' or 'I don't think I'm breathing right. Am I breathing right? It feels weird, why does my breathing feel weird, oh fuck, I'm probably dying', which isn't helpful. On these occasions, rather than focusing on my breath, I'll instead focus on the sensations that I can feel in my body as an anchor for my attention.

Sound is also an effective alternative to help focus my mind. Keeping my eyes closed, the warmth and light of the sunshine filtering in through the delicate skin of my eyelids, I move my attention to any sounds that I can hear in the space around me, alternating between the sounds which seem the furthest away and those that I can hear which are the closest. Irate seagulls, wheeling and diving in the sky above, their shrill calls filling both the air and my mind, ground me in the present moment.

Mindfulness, as a practice, was first introduced to me when I was twenty-six. I'd finally reached a point in my life when I felt like I had no choice but to get professional help. My anxiety and PTSD were out of control and, even though I'd stopped taking drugs and drinking alcohol, I was still struggling to function. I desperately wanted to take a pill that would somehow cure me of my malady, that would make me sane and normal. But pills like that don't exist, in the same way that 'sanity' and 'normality', as concepts, don't exist.

My GP referred to me to a counselling centre in the next town. It took months before an appointment date came through. I was offered anti-anxiety tablets and antidepressants – prescriptions which I collected, but didn't take. After reading the side effects leaflets and doing my own research online, I was too scared. Most of the tablets that I was prescribed often detailed that they made symptoms worse before they improved. In my logic, if my symptoms worsened, it would equate to outright death, which seemed somewhat contradictory. The interim period, between visiting the GP and my initial counselling appointment, was a torturous time of uncontrollable anxiety, panic attacks and breakdowns, but in my head, all I had to do was get to that appointment and then everything would be okay.

Terror consumed me as I waited to be called in by the counsellor. The Bingley surgery where the therapy rooms were based was seemingly designed and decorated to look like a ship out of a *Star Trek* movie – modern lines and sharp edges, chrome details on every white painted surface, dimly lit with eerie blue and green lights. Its alien design did nothing at all to comfort me. In my head, this was my last moment of freedom. I honestly believed that, after my first counselling session, I would be sectioned and placed on a secure ward in a mental hospital somewhere. Which, in a way, I was half looking forward to; being on a secure ward would mean that someone else would have to deal with it all. It would be like a holiday – I wouldn't have to worry about paying bills, or a mortgage, or indeed anything, if I was drugged up with happy pills and being fed three meals a day in a space with central heating and lovely clean white sheets.

'Charlotte Bradman?' My name was called, jolting my attention out of my head and into the space around me. A handsome, middle-aged woman, with long brown hair, stood at an open door, looking at me expectantly. 'Yes, that's me,' I mumbled, standing up. Shakily, I walked towards her, trying not to make eye contact in case she could tell how mentally unwell I was just by looking into my eyes. She led me to a small, brightly lit room at the end of a dim corridor. Comfy chairs were arranged in a neat semicircle around a table adorned with a clear glass vase of freshly cut daffodils. She asked me to sit down, which I did, keeping my rucksack close in case I needed to leave in a hurry. We went through a questionnaire, something which she said would have to be done at the beginning of every session in order to determine whether my illness was at a point where I had the potential to either hurt myself or others. I think the questionnaire, and the level of illness it indicated was possible in a person, was the most terrifying part of the counselling, hitting home just how powerful the mind can be.

Using a blend of CBT and mindfulness, over the course of a twelve-week programme, with one hourly session per week, my counsellor taught me that I wasn't mad, bad, dangerous, insane or broken; that I was, instead, completely and utterly normal. She taught me that the thoughts I had were separate to who I was as a person, and that they weren't facts, nor were they an indication of my character. She gave me the insight and the tools to manage my anxiety, alongside starting me on the journey to changing the damaging core beliefs that I'd developed over the years; essentially, that I was a massively shit, damaged person beyond any hope of redemption. Undoubtedly, she saved my life. And perhaps, by taking responsibility for my mental health and finding the courage to seek professional help, I saved my own life.

Mindfulness has helped me, and continues to help me, to be less reactive when it comes to anxious, distressing thoughts, difficult situations or emotionally charged exchanges. It has taught me to be objective and take a step back in order to observe my thoughts as something separate to myself, which they are.

Violence was so deeply inherent in my childhood that it became part of how I coped with difficulty in my teenage years and early adult life. Over time, with counselling, life experience and mindfulness practices, I learnt how unproductive violence is for any situation and the detrimental effect it had on my own well-being, as well as the well-being of the people around me (and not just because I may have punched them).

Mindfulness, as a practice, has helped me to recognise the cause of anxiety flare-ups and whether the way that I feel in a particular moment has more to do with previous trauma than what is actually unfolding in the here and now. Just as important as helping myself, mindfulness gave me the tools to help others, which is why, a few years ago, I completed a training course to become a mindfulness therapist.

I have always been good with people; determining their mood, their personality type, what they need to hear or when they need to be listened to. Even when I was very young, still at primary school, I made an effort to be inclusive of everyone, especially those who were shy or introverted. That's not to say that I wasn't an insensitive shitbag on occasion too, because I was – at ten years old that's inevitable (or at any age, to be honest).

Prior to having counselling, in my early twenties, I became known as a 'fixer' in my friendship group, which seemed absurd at the time as I clearly needed fixing myself. However, I found that when my mind was taken up by supporting others, I didn't have to think about my own problems. When I was twenty-two years old, a friend unexpectedly called around at my house one day. She had another girl in tow with her. I'd met the other girl once or twice before, but I didn't really know her. 'Hey Charlotte,' said my friend, 'this is Betty. She's split up with her boyfriend and can't cope. I said that you could help her. Betty, meet Charlotte, Charlotte, meet Betty. Right, cool, I can't stay, I'm off to work, so I'll leave Betty with you. Okay bye!'

And with that, my friend simply buggered off, leaving Betty standing in my doorway, staring at her feet, tears slowly starting to trickle down her face. Oh shit. What could I do? I couldn't turn her away, the girl was clearly suffering, so I put on my game face and got to work.

From the moment my friend dropped Betty off at my house, she moved in. It was surreal to begin with, sharing my home with a complete stranger, but as the weeks went by, it became the new normal. Initially, Betty was so deeply depressed that she didn't have the capacity or motivation to participate in self-care, from washing herself to feeding herself. I spent the first week she was with me focusing on the foundations of care: making sure that she ate, washing her clothes, running her baths and putting her to bed at a reasonable hour. I still had to work, so when I was out of the house, other friends would come round and take it in turns to keep her company. Taking care of Betty's physical needs provided the space to then address her emotional needs. For the next few weeks, I listened and comforted her while she talked, cried and sobbed her way through heartbreak. It would have been advisable, at that stage, to *slowly* encourage Betty to think about re-engaging with society. But I was only twenty-two, and Betty was twenty-one, so instead, I took her out to clubs and parties, where we got off our faces on sticky, sugar-sweet sambuca, danced until our bodies ached and snogged whoever was up for it. My unorthodox methods seemed to work and, with Betty on her way out of debilitating depression, she was able to move back to her own home.

Betty's parents owned and operated a supported housing project for vulnerable adults with mental health issues, something which I was completely unaware of during the time when I was supporting her. She must have spoken about me to them and her experience living at my home, as they requested to meet me, inviting me for dinner at their house one evening. During dinner, they thanked me for looking after their daughter and offered me a job, with training, as a mental health support worker at their project. They explained that they felt I had a capacity for care which they wanted to support me to develop. Even though I felt like an imposter, knowing full well that my own mental health was fucking terrible, I accepted their offer. It was an opportunity to help others, develop myself and, if I'm honest, get some cash in the bank – it would be the highest paid job that I'd had up to this point.

Working as a mental health support worker was, at times, fun, but it was also incredibly challenging, not least because I was supporting people while navigating my own mental health issues, something which I kept hidden in case I lost my job. The project consisted of several individual flats with a shared community space that all residents could access. Staff were always available in the shared space to offer support, if required, or assistance with benefits applications. We supported vulnerable adults from the age of eighteen to eighty, all with complex and varied mental health issues. On occasion, individuals would become so ill that we would have to liaise with medical professionals to get them sectioned in order to ensure both their safety and the safety of the people around them.

We had residents who would stride into the shared space in a blind rage and announce, 'I'm going to kill someone today!', which was always slightly worrying. Some staff members were so frightened by these outbursts from certain residents that they left the project, seeking employment elsewhere that didn't involve daily death threats. But I'd seen it all before when I was a child and my dad was drunk – I knew that it wasn't a serious threat, but a cry for help, an exclamation of discontent. Humour, as always, would defuse the situation in a heartbeat . . . I would respond with, 'Well, if you're going to kill someone, can it not be me? I've got a date tonight and I'm on for a promise.' Laughter changed the dynamic with immediate effect, which then allowed the space for me to provide support.

Two years of working at the project, of hiding my own mental health issues, alongside supporting others, was enough. One Friday night, I was locking up ready to go home when a resident tried to take his own life by slicing into his stomach with a knife. It was a surreal experience, like I was in a film, waiting for the ambulance and trying to keep him conscious as the paramedics had directed over the phone: 'Stay with me Gavin. Gavin open your eyes, that's it, keep them open, everything is going to be okay Gavin, Gavin, stay with me. What's your favourite song? Can you remember the words to your favourite song? Gavin, open your eyes, stay with me . . .' Even though Gavin was fine (after that incident, at least; he had a long history of suicide attempts), I left the project two weeks later. Overextending by giving my energy to others without giving any to myself had tipped the precarious balance that I'd worked so hard to maintain. Unable to hide my own mental health issues anymore, I ended my role as a mental health support worker, which was part of the catalyst of events which began my own healing journey.

All the things that have happened in my life – all the experiences I've had and the people I've met – have brought me here, to this moment. And I am incredibly grateful for all of it, even the experiences which I've found difficult, painful or traumatic. Without them, I wouldn't be who I am today, nor would I be living the life that I am. Growth is often painful, like the physical muscle ache and bone soreness of moving from a child into an adult. Inner growth is the same: whether it's referred to as psychological growth, spiritual growth or mental growth, it's the same process – a thing happens, it might hurt, it might not, and, as a result, we emerge from the thing changed in some way. Through my experience of change, I've learnt that even if something feels painful during the time that it's occurring, like when I experienced domestic violence in my childhood, when a relationship has broken down or when I lost my home, often the end result is unexpectedly wonderful. As just one example, my experience of domestic violence helped me hone the communication skills necessary for me to help others, and also to help myself.

My reality used to be working forty hours a week in a job that made me ill, being constantly hounded for money, disconnected from nature and disconnected from myself. I now know that it's possible to choose my own reality, that it's not compulsory to do what society expects or what is considered 'normal'. Possibilities and opportunities are only restricted by the barriers we put up in our own minds. The simple truth is that everyone has the power to do things differently, to change their lives, to change their own reality, if they choose to.

Chapter Twenty-Five
Council Says No

'Just a heads up love, we're putting the posts in now ...', announced the workman, clad in luminous yellow, like his counterparts the world over. He indicated a gaping hole at the side of the pavement, one that he'd recently, and expertly, drilled out (I should know, I'd watched and heard him from inside my van), 'but the fellas with the signs for the top will be along later today, so you'll have to park somewhere else from tonight.' He was friendly, clearly unperturbed by the fact that I lived in a campervan. The new road signs that he had been tasked with erecting outlined new parking restrictions which had recently come into effect on the road between Castle Beach and Gyllyngvase Beach in Falmouth, Cornwall. The signs would deliver the unhelpful message of 'no overnight parking between midnight and six am'.

In Cornwall, over the last few years, with the rising costs of living and the advent of Airbnb negatively impacting the availability and affordability of long-term lets, people have taken to living in various vehicles along Falmouth seafront (and indeed, in other locations throughout Cornwall and the rest of the UK). From large, expertly converted ex-horse boxes, to small, three-door cars, if you can sleep in it, you can live in it. For people who want to live in Falmouth, either for work or to study at the university there, living alternatively is, for some, their only viable option.

I'd been living on the seafront in Falmouth for about six months, splitting my week between Newquay (where my friends were) and Falmouth (where I worked for a well-established Cornish clothing brand, Seasalt). Four months prior to the council making the decision to implement the new parking restrictions, they had outlined their intention, via a local newspaper, to put together a working group in order to tackle the concerns raised by Falmouth residents regarding vanlifers. From the newspaper article, the concerns raised seemed to focus primarily on the aesthetics of having vehicles parked on the seafront.

I emailed the town councillor directly, who was the lead for the initiative, requesting to be part of the working group. As both a Falmouth resident (which is how I saw myself – I worked there, after all, and spent my money in the local shops and establishments) – and as someone who lived full-time in a campervan, I felt that I could contribute constructively, and with insight, to any meetings that were held. Eventually, after I'd sent several polite emails, the group lead replied. He said that he would be happy to have me as part of the Falmouth Town Council vanlife working group and advised me that he would be in touch to let me know when the next meeting was going ahead. I felt empowered. Having the confidence and sense of self-worth to put myself forward for an initiative of this nature was clear evidence of how much I'd grown as a person since living in a van. Perhaps I could really make a difference and be a positive voice in Falmouth for those of us who lived alternatively.

As the weeks and months went by, I heard nothing from Falmouth Town Council, expecting an email to come through any day with the date and time of the vanlife working group meeting. It never arrived. Via the local newspaper, I found out that the vanlife working group meeting had gone ahead without me and that the council had passed a motion to implement new 'no overnight parking' restrictions. Despite promising to look at alternative parking for vanlifers and other solutions to the problem, Falmouth Town Council had instead opted for the 'solution' with the least amount of responsibility.

I emailed the councillor in charge of the vanlife initiative, indicating various concerns that I had with the new parking restrictions and asking why they had not notified me of the meeting. The councillor apologised for neglecting to include me in the invite (too little, too late, in all honesty), but did not respond to my concerns.

The new restrictions would force the live-in vehicles, which had previously parked on the seafront, to now park further inland in more densely populated residential areas. This would, without a doubt, increase the number of complaints that the council received regarding vanlifers. Single people living in vans, like myself, would be pushed out to the fringes of the town, increasing our vulnerability and the risk to our safety. I asked the councillor how he expected to mitigate and manage the increased complaints and why he hadn't sourced alternative parking prior to putting the new restrictions in place. He didn't respond.

All the people who were living in vehicles on the seafront in Falmouth are employed in roles within the town itself. Many of them, like me, provide a service of some description to the more conventional residents of Falmouth, some of whom were undoubtedly the people who complained about the vans parking on the seafront in the first place. Without vanlifers, services in Falmouth, and indeed across Cornwall, would be negatively impacted.

It's that time of year when businesses are recruiting staff to work the summer season in Cornwall – every employment agency has posters up, covering their windows with a vast curtain of vacancies and outside every restaurant, café, pub and hotel is a board detailing 'staff wanted'. Who will fill these roles, when permanent housing is either non-existent or vastly unaffordable? It won't be the second homeowners or rich landlords changing sheets in hotel rooms, cleaning holiday lets, lifeguarding, waitressing or selling pasties to the masses during the summer season (or during any season). From having conversations with individuals who originally came to Cornwall fifteen years ago, living in their vans and filling essential vacancies, who are now permanent residents in houses and flats here, it's clear that, in the past, Cornwall council was more accepting of vanlife, recognising the value that this community had to their economy.

Now, everything seems to be dictated by the political voting system. Vanlifers, unless they know someone in the locality who will let them use their address, are unable to register to vote, which means that, even though there are councillors in Cornwall who recognise the economic value of this nomadic community, there's no motivation on their part to take any action in support of us as it won't garner any votes or increase their political standing. Yet another example of how narrow-minded, ineffective and vastly unfair the system is. Surely the fact that vanlifers fill essential vacancies and contribute significantly to the local economy, far more than any second homeowner, should be motivation enough to not only accept those of us who live this way, but welcome us with open arms.

Over the last few years, both the retail and hospitality industries in Cornwall have suffered from staff shortages due to the lack of affordable housing in the county. From my experience as both an employee and as a customer, the services provided to holidaymakers and residents alike have not met the quality standards that they should due to the lack of staff. There simply isn't anywhere realistically affordable for people in low-paid employment to live. Most of the houses to rent in Falmouth start at a minimum rental price of £1,000 per month. For someone in a minimum wage job, working thirty-eight hours per week, a rent of that size would leave them with only £600 to pay council tax, utilities, vehicle costs, a phone bill and internet, and to buy food. Oh, and have a life beyond simply putting a roof over their heads. It's simply not feasible.

Only a short while ago, perhaps fifty years, a household could be run entirely on a single wage. That is now an impossibility. How is that progress? Surely, after fifty years of advancement in technology, we should be working less, not more, and with an increased quality of life?

It's completely understandable that people who own multi-million-pound properties, purchased precisely for their sea views, would be slightly perturbed by those of us living in vans and enjoying those very same views for a fraction of the cost. Individuals and families who command the level of financial resource required to own exclusive seafront properties have either inherited them or have worked incredibly hard for the majority of their lives. Don't get me wrong, I'm all about working hard (ask any of my previous employers), but even if I worked full-time in a minimum wage job for fifty years, I still wouldn't be able to afford a beachfront property anywhere, unless it's a shed on the outer edges of the Orkney Islands. Does that mean that I should miss out? That I don't deserve to wake up to a view of the ocean? I wasn't born into wealth; does that mean, by default, that I haven't earned the right to experience the finer things in life?

Ingrained in society is the view that you don't get something for nothing, that there has to be some sort of compromise or suffering in order to justify material gains or positive changes. I no longer subscribe to that mentality. Life is far too short. Nature isn't owned by anyone. I make no apologies for desiring a sea view now, before my eyesight goes, thank you very much.

In the words of my good friend Chard, 'everything in our country, in our system, is being commodified. As soon as it's spotted that people are enjoying something for free, that freedom is taken away.' And he's absolutely right. Take the fact that, at the time of writing this book, Bristol Town Council has made the dubious decision to charge people £7 an hour to swim in the sea. The charge could be justified when taking into account the increased safety measures – lifeguards, water quality testing, and so on – but surely it's like charging people to walk on grass or to breathe air (which I'm sure are concepts that aren't too far ahead in the future, unless there are some dramatic changes in our society). No amount of water testing will change the fact that our seas and rivers are far from clean these days, with water companies pumping sewage into them without regulation. The managing directors of these companies are being paid obscene amounts of money, while they systematically destroy the environment, rather than reinvesting in order to update inadequate infrastructure designed for a much smaller population.

And then there's the issue of public toilets. Or should I say, the lack of public toilets, as so many of them are now closed. For me, it's a particularly interesting topic, one which accurately highlights the divide between the rich and poor alongside the lack of investment in public services. In the more affluent areas of Cornwall, like Falmouth and Padstow, public toilets are free to use. In my opinion, it would seem that the council is loath to inflict the indignity of paying for a piss on the wealthy visitors and residents of those areas. In Newquay, a much less affluent area, you have to pay. The working class and the less wealthy, who both holiday and live there, already suffer a multitude of indignities, from being vastly underpaid, forced into zero-hours contracts, contending with extortionate rents and increasing interest rates, trying to find the resources to cover the insurmountable rise in diesel, petrol, food and utilities, a perpetually increasing retirement age . . . what's one more indignity? What does it matter if an elderly lady suffers from distressing incontinence, simply because she didn't have a 20p piece or enough knowledge of advancing technology to tap her card on the contactless payment box?

The going rate for a wee is 50p in cash, which isn't particularly helpful in our near-cashless society. In some areas, namely Devon and Somerset, there are public toilets which charge more, conveniently offering a service where you can pay by debit card. In my opinion, paying for public services of this nature is yet another tax on the poor, like the National Lottery. Why do we pay taxes at all, if not for public services like toilets and water fountains?

In France, people who tour, or who live permanently in campervans or motorhomes, are welcomed. Their positive contribution to the economy is valued to the point that dedicated infrastructure has been implemented in order to accommodate their needs in the form of 'aires'. Aires are stopovers, park-ups and campsites which provide facilities such as chemical toilet disposal, wastewater disposal, showers, fresh water and a place to park for the night. Some are completely free to use, others may charge a nominal amount. There are over five thousand aires across France. In stark contrast, the UK ostracises travelling communities of any description, taking the view that by pretending they don't exist, the problem will go away. Car parks are frequently height-restricted with barriers, preventing vans or tall vehicles from entering, and more signs for 'no overnight parking' and 'no cooking' are being erected each week that goes by. Where are these people going to live? There's no housing for them, and the housing that is available isn't affordable.

It's clear that the amount of people living in vehicles, or living alternatively in different ways, is increasing, and will continue to do so, as a direct response to the rising costs of living and the lack of affordable housing. Rather than implementing parking restrictions that do nothing but exacerbate and displace the problem, Falmouth Town Council, and indeed every town council nationwide, needs to accept this growing community as a legitimate way of living and look at more constructive and permanent ways to support them and encourage positive engagement between them and the members of the community who live more conventionally.

What I find perplexing, in the case of the parking restrictions on the seafront in Falmouth, is that they were predominantly put in place so that the view of the sea for the individuals who live in the expensive flats wasn't compromised. Yet the restrictions detail no parking from midnight until six in the morning, which means that vans can park there all day, every day, and they do.

It would appear to me that some Falmouth residents have the uncanny ability to see in the dark.

Chapter Twenty-Six
Objects of Affection

'How many grannies have weed on that thing?' was Warren's questionable text message response to a photo I'd proudly sent him of my new quilt cover, recently purchased in a charity shop. Fair enough. It did, in the reduced light of my van spotlights, and viewed with a different gaze, look like it was straight out of an octogenarian's musty-smelling linen cupboard (a place it had likely previously inhabited). But to me, it was a thing of exquisite beauty. It showcased a stylised floral print in pastel colours, shades reminiscent of an eighties palette, with powdered lilacs, dusky pinks, sage greens and teals. You could clearly see the brushstrokes in each petal and the impressionistic, painterly outlines of the flowers. It had a sense of movement, of life, the energy of its composition lifting it from its cotton canvas, like the entire season of spring erupting in one moment. The quilt cover tied in well with the colour scheme and general design elements of the interior of my campervan, which didn't deviate from delicate, vintage florals (retro cupboard door handles) and varying shades of teal (everything else).

On a recent occasion, when I'd parked my van in a large layby that had views of the sea, I had received some impromptu feedback on my campervan interior design. It had been my plan to cook and consume my dinner with the rugged Cornish cliffs and the sparkling blue ocean filling my eyes and nourishing my soul, while I attempted to do the same for my body with a meal of tinned new potatoes, veggie sausages, broccoli and chilli mayo (Rubies in the Rubble – best mayonnaise in the world). Three other campervans, which must have been driving in convoy, pulled into the layby shortly after I had. All three were completely different: a vintage Volkswagen T1, a new Volkswagen T5 and a large Transit of indeterminable age.

I discovered, from chatting with the occupants, that they were a group of friends who lived in different areas of the southwest and had met up for the weekend in Cornwall to reconnect, hang out in their campervans and go surfing. Campervan owners often strike up conversations easily. We already have the ownership of a home on wheels as a common denominator and we are nosy buggers, especially those of us who have designed and fitted out our own van interiors. We like to have a look at other campervan designs and layouts, mostly to confirm whether our own chosen layout is superior (the competitive nature of humanity at its best), but also to steal ideas for an upgrade if it isn't.

When a campervan door is opened to an audience of other camperyan owners, you'll usually hear the following comments, or similar: 'Your top lockers are stunning luv, very well placed!' (top lockers being the cupboards above head height), or 'Three hobs!? You flashy bastard. Are you expecting to cook for the King or summat!?' (Warren has three hobs in his van . . . but only ever uses one: hob overkill), or 'It's brilliant how you've utilised the space with your corner kitchen, collapsible dining table, forty-two-inch plasma TV, slide-out hot tub and foldout authentic Swedish sauna!' (there are indeed some rather spectacular camp-ervans out there; however, mine is infinitely more modest).

The four of us in the sea view layby took turns to showcase our respective vans to each other, oohing and aahing at inventive cup-board placement, colour schemes, spice racks, foldout bed mech-anisms, layouts and expertise with joinery (or lack of expertise, in my case). It was finally my turn to show off my lovely little home. I was secretly hoping for a grand reaction; after all, I think it's brilliant. I opened the van side door with a flourish, like I was pulling a sheet off Michelangelo's David, and . . . nothing. They looked into the van, displaying varying expressions of vague bemusement and maybe even a flash of disgust, before one of them plucked up the courage to say, 'Err, it's, err . . . well, it's very blue.' How incredibly rude – it wasn't blue, it was sodding *teal*. He may as well have said that a dog was a cat, the tonally ignorant bastard. Still, no hard feelings. They were decidedly lovely people, and we can't all be as attuned as I am to the Dulux colour wheel of joy.

Lounging back on the large, single bed, my head gently propped up against the van window with a beautiful hand-crocheted cushion in all of my favourite shades of teal (an incredibly thoughtful Secret Santa gift from a work colleague; I still don't know who), I survey my tiny home. From my position on the bed, I have the best view out of the window and, if it's warm, out of the open side door (depending on where I'm parked, of course). Just in front of the side door, next to the foot of the bed, there is a small bookcase, something which I consider to be essential and a feature that I've always incorporated into my campervan builds over the years. The thing about books is that they remain accessible even when the internet signal doesn't (which is a frequent occurrence in Cornwall, seemingly dictated by which way the wind is blowing or how many seagulls are in the air at any given time).

Pride of place on my bookcase is an extensive collection of *Wild Guide* books (a series that details the best walks, castles, museums, forests, wild swimming spots, places to eat and places to stay for every area of the United Kingdom, and beyond – unnecessary weight which has a negative impact on the mechanical complexities of my van, if you ask Warren) and *Wild Swimming* books, including the very first guide to wild swimming by the author Kate Rew. This battered, well-worn, dandelion-yellow hardback book, with a stylised image of a pair of goggles embossed on the front cover, is undoubtedly what began the increasingly popular trend of outdoor dipping. It was a random gift many years ago, not for me, but for my best friend's stepdad. After we discovered it, tucked away in a dark corner on his bookcase, we 'borrowed' it on a long-term lend. It has been the source of many wonderful adventures, which is evident in the scrawling notes I've made in the book, the sun-bleached pages and the salt-rippled paper.

Books and stories are often the gateways to new experiences, new ways of thinking and new ways of being. Life experiences that have been bravely shared by others have, on many occasions, directly influenced the course of my life, in one way or another, such is the power that they have. New books seem to arrive in my life without apparent effort – lent to me by friends or found on the charity bookshelves in supermarkets. Once read, I then release them back into the world, either by passing them on to a friend who I think will engage with the story or by taking them to a charity shop. I make sure not to overspill from the bookcase, otherwise I end up with books shoved in inappropriate places, like in the cutlery drawer or behind the tinned new potatoes.

It takes time to write a book, to tie past and present into some semblance of coherence, to decide what to share and what to hold. It's a mindset, a way of being, which takes over all thought and attention, from the moment the morning sun shines through the sides of my campervan curtains to when I lay my head down to sleep – which is always, unfortunately, the exact time when inspiration, ideas and insights arrive.

Without a substantial advance, which no publisher would allocate to any new, unknown author, and without financial support from family or savings of any kind, the time that I spend writing is time that I am unable to earn. My van insurance, mobile phone bill, food, website domain and other essential living costs are covered by the income I receive from my part-time job working two days a week for the fabulous Seasalt (who also allow me to use a spare office, with sea views, for writing when I'm not working).

The small advance that I *did* receive was in and out of my bank account faster than you can say 'MOT' and was spent almost entirely on welding (I also bought another rucksack, continuing, as ever, my quest to find the perfect design, weight and colour combination). Unable to work full-time while writing, I no longer have any financial provision should any unplanned costs arise, like more welding, which will inevitably be required, or another part wearing out on my old van. Usually, if I wasn't writing, I'd work full-time for a few months in order to build up the money in my bank account, before having a few months off adventuring in some capacity or other. However, at this point in time, I have precisely £423 in my bank account.

I expect, judging by that small amount of money, that I would be considered poor by many and, unfortunately, rich by some. Yet I have everything I could possibly need and more. I determine my wealth by the free time that I have, my capacity for creativity and my well-being. Writing has allowed me to be creative, to put trauma on the page and change not only the nature of it, but my relationship with it; to recount the challenges I have overcome and the progress I have made. In terms of well-being, I am, at present, the happiest and most fulfilled I've been in a long time. What *is* clear is that, had I not been living in a van, with the subsequent reduction in financial outgoings, and had I instead been paying out for rent or a mortgage, I would not have been able to write a book. What I find incredibly distressing to comprehend is the amount of books, paintings, sculptures, life-changing innovations, revolutionary inventions, advances in technology, and so on, that surely exist within people who, rather than having the time to develop and explore their creativity, are forced instead to work every hour available. But perhaps that lack of time is not accidental and is, instead, by design . . . people who don't have the time to create also don't have the time to start a revolution.

In an economic model that relies on debt to function, money is King (or Queen, whichever way you look at it), and if you are working class, or poorer, the only choice that society allows for is between having more time or having more money. Unfortunately, these days, the cost to simply stay fed and have shelter requires more money than it's possible to make in a minimum wage role, which means that people in lower income jobs have very little time, and very little money: two states of being which have a huge detrimental effect on health and well-being. There are plenty of free things available to do and experience that enhance positive well-being, like hiking in nature, meditation, connecting with the community and wild swimming. Of course, all of these things require time, which is a currency more precious than any sheet of printed paper showing the face of someone who has all the time, and the money, in the world.

My love of swimming outdoors began early on in my life. Growing up near the Yorkshire Dales and in the heart of the countryside, days out at the river were commonplace. My fondest childhood memories are of long summer days spent playing in the clear, limestone-filtered waters, looking for crayfish and the speckled flash of a brown trout. It was safe at the river, a place of feminine energy; only the mums and children in our friendship groups would come. Fear was forgotten in these moments, allowing us to experience the true freedom and joy of childhood.

My last conventional home was full of art – prints, paintings, sculptures; every wall displayed at least one picture and every surface was anointed with knick-knacks that were a nod to some craft or other. In the van, with so little space, pictures on the wall do nothing but make it look cluttered and intrude on vital head-space. Art, in my opinion, can exist as a consumable resource – it doesn't have to be owned to be experienced. The only picture that I have on display in the van is a seventies oblong ceramic plate depicting a leaping tiger. Bought for me by my mum from an antiques shop, it's a piece that is completely out of place with the current decor of the van and is quite jarring compared to the soft florals and pastel shades. I like to think that the tiger displayed in this way lends it the impact of juxtaposition, but actually, it's because I impulsively stuck it on with extra strong double-sided sticky tape and now I can't get the sodding thing off.

Randomly, on the front of the dashboard of my van, welded on with sun-heated Blu Tack, I have a slightly faded and rusty badge displaying the face of Howard Moon, a character played by the comedian Julian Barratt from a show called *The Mighty Boosh*. This badge has been transferred from van to van over the years and is my lucky van charm, even though I try not to attach meaning to material things. In the same way that Terry Pratchett novels saw me through the darkest days of severe anxiety in my youth, *The Mighty Boosh*, with its nonsensical and hilarious humour, helped me deal with depression in my twenties. Howard is my favourite character from the show, and it has always been my ambition, and still is, to be in a jazz band with him.

With the reasonably extreme variations of temperature in the van, and the fact that I partake in emergency stops regularly (I'm sometimes a bit too keen approaching roundabouts, I'll admit), a goldfish as a pet wasn't really an option for me. And it's a bit cruel isn't it, keeping a fish in a small tank, so it would only be justifiable if the entire back of my van was literally just one big fish tank. Sometimes, the odd fly will stick around for a few days and we'll build up a rapport, well, on my side anyway, but they make a bid for freedom as soon as I open the door, most likely driven to madness by my inane chat. So instead of pets, I have a little van garden . . .

Situated on the shelf of the passenger side dashboard, my tiny van garden is in the perfect position to receive as much sunshine as possible. I have one succulent, in a pretty ceramic pot, a small fairy tower cactus and, randomly, two young apple trees, which a van probably isn't the ideal location for. I'd been eating one of the tastiest apples I'd ever had (I can't recall what variety it was, I wish I'd written it down) and, when I got to the core, the seeds had already sprouted, which was something I hadn't seen before. I decided that the little apple seeds were obviously keen on making a go of this life business, so I planted a few out in the wild and kept two to raise as my own. I have recently discovered that apple trees grown from seeds will produce a completely different, and often inferior, apple to the one that they came from. Which is frankly ridiculous, but I can't argue with evolution. No tasty apples for me off my little trees. The three pots that contain my four quiet, green companions are nestled among other treasures on my dashboard: shells from various beaches, a mermaid's purse, a medal acquired after walking the Yorkshire three peaks, rounded shards of frosted green sea glass and fragments of printed pottery. This is the only place in the van that I allow a few knick-knacks to reside.

During the process of getting rid of things and adapting to a life living with less, the way that I thought about 'things' changed dramatically. I no longer put sentimental value on stuff, and I tried to consciously disconnect any emotional attachments that I had to inanimate objects. I began to see them as anchors to past experiences or previous emotional states, which had a subtle, detrimental effect on my growth as a person and the rate at which I moved forward.

I found that an excess of 'things' not only took up physical space, but also seemed to inhabit space in my head, and I wanted that space for other, more fulfilling experiences. Of course, I am only human, and I will admit to having a certain level of attachment to particular items. There are some things that I would be genuinely upset about if my van caught on fire (I'd be pretty upset anyway if that happened because I'd be homeless and my dental retainer would melt, which my dentist wouldn't be happy about). Surprisingly, it all comes down to a pair of eighties trousers . . .

Placed tidily under the bed in the van are two, medium-sized plastic storage boxes. Contained within these boxes, like RuPauls walk in wardrobe, but far less glamorous and with minimum sequins (everyone, including me, should definitely wear more sparkle), is my identity. I'm not referring to a secret superhero outfit that I like to run around in on quiet nights or to an alternative birth certificate and passport, but rather, to the clothes that I own and wear. Colours, prints, brands, cuts and styles of clothing are a non-verbal message to the world around me communicating a multitude of information, from what my favourite colour is, what sex I am, my financial status, what music I might listen to, what social ideal I'm aligning myself with that day, what activity I'm taking part in and my grasp of colour coordination to my sense of style (or lack of it, especially if it's period week – hoodie, no bra, sweat pants, massive knickers). The clothes that I wear are how I want the world to see me and, also, how I see myself.

In my two boxes, alongside the hiking clothes, gym kit and multiple thermal vests, is a small, but beautiful collection of vintage clothes. This collection is probably the only thing I own which has any degree of sentimentality. Being vintage, most of the pieces are completely unique and irreplaceable. Some have been in my possession for twenty years or more. To me, they are a wearable exhibition – each garment a piece of art, a representation of cultural creativity, history, identity and self-expression. I'm particularly enamoured by the designs, prints and cuts created in the eighties, which I feel most accurately convey my personality: a mixture of both masculine and feminine qualities.

Other than the two boxes of clothes, there isn't much else that I own, these days, which I have any particular personal attachment to. I can't even begin to describe how freeing that feels and how much psychological space is released from simply letting go of those attachments.

A few years ago, I was the type of person who kept hold of everything. I had shoeboxes full of what can only be described as objects of affection: little knick-knacks, keyrings, paperweights, jewellery, plastic toys, postcards, all given to me by family, friends or previous lovers. Fundamentally, they were all objects which proved that I was lovable; they evidenced that someone, somewhere, had once liked me enough to buy me a token of their affection. Back then, I would fixate on the gift which I had been given and use it to inaccurately, and toxically, measure the strength or depth of love based on its thoughtfulness, it's monetary worth and how difficult it was to obtain. I once made a partner buy me four different necklaces (the poor bastard) and each one he bought, I hated more. In my head, each attempt at buying me a necklace evidenced how little he knew me, which I equated to thoughtlessness, and, to me (with my unhelpful poor mental health and low self-esteem), thoughtlessness meant a lack of love. I now know that real love has nothing at all to do with objects, gifts or perceived thoughtfulness, and is instead to do with acceptance and non-judgement. Accepting someone exactly as they are, having no expectations of them beyond their existence, is what I now consider to be real love.

It's impossible to measure love, just like you can't measure someone's true worth based on their financial or social status. Rather than material things, the object of my affection is now myself. If I am able to accept myself exactly as I am and without judgement, then not only does that cultivate self-love, but it opens up my capacity to love all beings exactly as they are.

Chapter Twenty-Seven
Humans Being Humans

'Ey up love, how you getting on in Cornwall? The weather is blumming shite up here, it's been pissing it down all week! I've been keeping busy though . . . I've fixed Wendy's knackered gate, painted Ian's fence, put some new flagging down for Earnest and I've been collecting Edith's prescription for the last few weeks as her hip is playing up summat chronic.' Minus the conspiracy theory updates ('Elvis is still alive and living as a preacher'; 'Alien disclosure will happen this year . . . no, I know I said that last year, and the year before, but it's *definitely* going to happen this year'; 'There's a race of beings living in the centre of the earth'; and so on), this is a typical conversation with my dad.

For the last few years, he has been living in social housing. His home is a lovely little flat in a whole street of residences specifically allocated for people over the age of sixty who tick the relevant boxes required by the council. Prior to the flat, he had been living permanently in a campervan, which he'd parked at the rear of my brother's little café (Dad has lived with me on and off for years; I was *so glad*, at that point, that my brother, having reconnected with my Dad – age, the passing of time and life experience allowing for an acceptance, if not total forgiveness – was finally having a turn at being responsible for him). My dad's campervan had been as basic as they come – there was no leisure battery, electrics or heater; all he'd had was a bed, some storage and a gas cooker. As a man with a serious heart condition, among other health issues, vanlife had not been working out for Dad. Despite advising him on several occasions to update his van and at least get a heater installed, he stubbornly ignored my advice and tried to stick it out, his argument being that he'd worked outdoors all his life, in all weathers, so he could manage just fine in the back of a cold, steel box in a frigid, northern winter. Turns out, he couldn't. His health rapidly declined, having already spent two winters in the van without a heater, and on his way into the third. I had to stage an intervention, put my foot down and overcome his Yorkshire stubbornness with my own, which is how he ended up in the little flat.

My dad helps all the people in the community where he lives: he fixes things that are broken, he takes people to hospital or to doctors' appointments who would otherwise struggle on public transport, he relandscapes neglected gardens for neighbours who don't have the health or mobility to do it for themselves, he replaces fences, paints railings, picks up litter and cuts the grass . . . the grass that the council should cut but doesn't. In short, he is the self-appointed maintenance manager for the street. And, of course, he may try to 'wake people up', as he calls it, by telling his neighbours that there's a secret alien base on the moon, that the pandemic was a staged depopulation event or that the royal family are really a race of lizard aliens, but they don't seem to mind. He does so much for everyone, giving things away to people who need it more than he does, buying shopping on occasions for neighbours who have run out of funds or for whom the benefits system has failed. He has always tried to be useful in some way – validation from others and to be appreciated is all he's ever wanted. I'm not a psychologist, but I suspect it may be because he doesn't love himself enough or because he didn't receive enough love as a child. Perhaps it was these issues, alongside the pressure to be seen as successful in the eyes of his peers and to provide for his family, that caused him to be violent when I was growing up.

My dad has been a monster. His actions, in the past, have caused immense suffering and pain, both physical and mental, the extent of which I think he still remains unaware. Yet he is not an evil man. If you ask any of his neighbours where he currently lives, or, indeed, any of the hitchhikers he has picked up over the years, or the numerous individuals he has talked out of suicide, or the people he has worked with, they will all say what a funny, generous and kind person he is. And they would be right, because he is.

From my experience, the majority of human beings are neither good nor bad. They are simply human. They sometimes say or do hurtful things, yet often the motivation behind that behaviour is fear of some description or a lack of love. The most important thing I learnt while I was a mental health support worker was to look at the bigger picture, to see beyond an action or an exchange of words and perceive the motivation behind it. When I was younger and drinking cider like I was in a desert and it was the only liquid available, I did and said things that I am ashamed of, like smashing an ex-partner's prize keyboard, launching another ex-partner's expensive fishing rods into the field behind my house, being physically abusive, starting fights, kicking, punching . . . and it was only when I learnt to look at the bigger picture that I realised my behaviour was motivated by fear and a lack of love (and the cider, obviously).

For a long time, when things were especially difficult for me, I blamed my dad, I blamed my mum, I blamed society in general and I blamed myself for how my life was and for how I felt. By allocating blame to everyone and anyone, including myself, all I was doing was evading responsibility and giving away any power that I had to change things, namely by changing myself. Placing blame doesn't change what has already occurred. The only thing it has the potential to do is to induce remorse in the individual who is being blamed, which may, or may not, influence their future behaviour. But from my experience, blame has no constructive place in the healing process.

Through counselling, I learnt to stop placing blame and to forgive myself for being, to put it bluntly, a massive dickhead in the past. If I couldn't forgive myself or show myself compassion, how could I ever hope to move forward and be happy in the future? It was only when I started to see my own worth and value that I no longer needed constant reassurance from the people around me that I was loved and liked. I was learning to love myself, to validate myself without requiring approval from others. Of course, it's a work in progress – change doesn't happen overnight, especially when it comes to core beliefs. I've conditioned myself for years to think that I'm broken, dysfunctional and generally crap, but every day that goes by is an opportunity for me to unlearn this belief and to reprogram myself with the facts: I am a human being of equal value to any other; I am good enough; I am amazing and unique; I am kind and considerate (most of the time); and I am beautiful. Try saying all that into a mirror without looking away . . . it's fucking hard.

In the same way that forgiveness of ourselves helps us to let go of who we were before so that we can be who we actually are right now, forgiveness of others also releases them from their past selves. I know that, by not processing my trauma regarding what happened with my dad, I was anchoring us both in the past. I was a victim of domestic abuse and he was the perpetrator. The fact is that I'm only a victim if I choose to be one, if I perpetuate that mentality by living in the past and perceiving myself in that way. Simply put, I am what I tell myself I am. My dad hasn't been violent for years; he is not the same person that he was twenty or thirty years ago. How could he be?

Every moment that goes by, every interaction or exchange that we have, every book that we read or film that we watch, every podcast that we listen to or artwork that we experience, every new town or place that we visit, changes us in some way. The process of writing this book will have changed me . . . and from now, to when it is published, I will be someone different. And though I may live in a van at the moment, who knows where I'll be in the future. Maybe I'll have reduced my belongings even more, perhaps to what would fit in a small waterproof bag so that I can happily reside, in a vastly uncomplicated manner, with a colony of seals on the Norfolk coast. I hope so. One thing I do know is that, while I have my health and mobility, I won't live in a stationary, conventional home. Not only would there be a temptation to fill it full of things I don't need that do nothing but anchor me, curtailing my creativity and progress, but in a non-moveable home I wouldn't be able to change the view out of my window whenever I choose, one of the many great advantages and privileges of living in a van.

It's the changes that occur from being open to *all* connections and interactions that I find particularly astounding. Up until my late teens, I was so wrapped up in my own problems, anxiety, depression, volatile relationships, substance abuse . . . that I was closed and inaccessible. At that point, I would never have opened a dialogue with a stranger, nor would I have been receptive if they'd tried to talk to me. Some of my behaviour will have stemmed from the simple shyness of being young, but I know that my reticence to reach out and connect with anyone was due to poor mental health. My attention was directed inside, instead of out.

Nowadays, I try to be open to all interactions, actively initiating conversations with everyone and anyone, from homeless addicts on the street, to CEOs of multimillion-pound companies (although I haven't met any of them yet, at least not that I know of). Without fail, regardless of how positive or negative the exchange may seem, there is always something valuable to be learnt, taught, shared or experienced.

The old man sitting in the café opposite me, occasionally catching my eye as I looked up from my laptop, was small and wiry, with a salt and pepper beard on his unshaven face, wild and unkempt. He wore a ladies' red coat and had by his side a ladies' brown leather handbag. I knew, without a doubt, that he was going to speak to me. I could see the intention in his eyes every time we exchanged a glace. A judgement immediately arrived in my head: for fuck's sake, I'm trying to soddin' write here, can't he see that, the silly old trout? I let the judgement that I'd made swirl around in my head and examined it for what it was . . . oh right, I'm feeling a bit stressed and scared because the deadline for the book is looming, and I'm also human, which means that I sometimes think mean things, and that's okay. Of course he isn't a silly old trout; he's a wonderful human being, the same as me.

I forgave myself for making the judgement about the old man and consciously decided that I would make an effort to have a conversation with him if he came over. I don't have much to give (being perpetually skint), but what I do have is my time. As predicted, he stood up and slowly zig-zagged his way over to my table (has anyone noticed that the older people get, the more they lose the ability to walk in a straight line?). His bright eyes bored into mine as he took up a standing position in front of me.

'What are you writing?' he asked directly, small talk being for the young who have time to waste. 'I'm writing a book,' I replied, smiling shyly. I always feel self-conscious when I tell people that I'm writing a book. I guess that's part of the ongoing battle with low self-esteem. He blinked slowly a couple of times, his eyes bright like a blackbird's, and tilted his head slightly to one side while he took in this new information. 'What's it about then, your book?' It was a difficult question to answer; what is my book about? Really? 'Well, it's about living in a van, my journey up to this point, healing trauma, overcoming adversity, connecting with people and nature, and finding a different way to live that has more meaning and space to thrive than the current capitalist-led societal model, err, yeah . . .' My words trailed off.

He blinked slowly at me a few more times before saying, in one long stream without pausing for breath, 'my cousin was in the concentration camps in the war, he lived in Poland, he was Polish, he survived the concentration camps but he couldn't walk as he'd lost both of his legs because of an infection that he contracted due to the living conditions of the camps, it was trench foot, it started as trench foot, you know, when feet are wet for a long time, but he ended up living in Australia, and I'd like to write his story one day, he was my cousin, you know.' He ran out of breath, and looked at me expectantly, waiting for my response with his bright, wide eyes. 'Thank you for sharing that with me. Your cousin overcame great adversity. You should write his story. Don't wait to write it, write it now. The things that we put off and say that we'll do "one day" never get done – start today! Just one sentence, one paragraph.'

He laughed, delighted, I think, at my passionate encouragement, then changed the subject abruptly and said, almost conspiratorially, 'I know a poem.' I responded with the only option available, 'I'd love to hear it, if you wouldn't mind?' He promptly, and without guise or embarrassment, began to speak. As he did so, the gentle hum of the café receded as those nearby turned to listen:

> Isn't it strange, that princes and kings,
> and ordinary people like you and me,
> are the builders of eternity,
> to each is given a bag of tools, and an hour of glass,
> and each must build, ere his time has flown,
> a stumbling block or a stepping stone.

'Gosh, that was beautiful! Thank you so much for sharing it!' I responded. He beamed, obviously pleased, thanked me for speaking with him and shuffled off back to his table to drink his nearly cold latte. After he had sat back down, I looked up the poem online and discovered that the original version was by an author called R. Lee Sharpe. The version that the old man (I found out that his name is Michael) recited had been slightly different, and that's the version that I wrote down – his interpretation of the work is art in its own right.

When he spoke the poem, I honestly nearly cried. I was overwhelmed that this wonderful human being had the courage and kindness to share with me words that had moved him, that had stayed with him from the first time he read them to that moment in the café. Such is the power, and privilege, of being open to every new connection, experience and opportunity that comes my way.

Chapter Twenty-Eight
Blue Relief

Unsteady, I pick my way across the sharp, uneven shingle beach beneath me and gasp as my bare feet enter the piercing cold sea. The discomfort of my feet vies for my attention alongside the aching cold, which seeps up to my legs like a natural anaesthetic. My breathing quickens as I steadily move in deeper, my submersed skin throbbing and stinging as the small, rolling waves rise up to lap at my waist.

Overwhelming sensation seizes my entire focus . . . my heartbeat becomes heavy and quick as it reacts to the temperature drop, my breathing suddenly brisk and erratic, aching numbness settles on the parts of my body that are submerged and the gritty feeling of cool salt water stings my bare skin. All thoughts scatter and my mind becomes still.

I pause here.

Consciously, I slow my breath and allow a moment for my body to acclimatise.

Wind whips my hair and bites at the skin that isn't submerged, protected by the water. It's an effort to drag my attention away from the urgency of the piercing, menthol cold, but I do, looking up to take in the landscape behind me. Towering, jagged-edged cliffs witness my baptism with the height and weight of millennia. Silent sentinels in pewter grey and dull silver guard the small shingle beach where I am. The turquoise waters that envelop me have spilled from the sky, purified by brush-soft clouds, filtered by the very bones of the landscape, before returning to the sea to repeat the cycle again.

A feeling of intense gratitude fills me, generating a sensation of inner warmth.

I prepare to immerse all that I am into the numbing, aching cold. Adrenaline rises and brings a smile of pure exhilaration, mixed with fear, as I close my eyes, snatch a quick breath and push my feet off the pebbled bottom. The whooshing, rushing sound of the water surrounds and overwhelms as it closes in over my head. Every pore of my skin tingles, like thousands of tiny needles pressing in.

I am weightless, rocked gently by the rhythmic melody of unbroken waves, held in the biting embrace of the cool, salt-rough water.

Opening my eyes under the water, I catch the silvery glint of tiny fish swimming beneath me. The tingling of my skin is subsiding now, to be replaced with bone-aching numbness. I kick my legs to generate some heat, venturing deeper into the clear depths, light fracturing around me. I revel in the power of my body as it propels me through the infinite ocean.

This moment belongs to me, shared with the silent cliffs, with the slate-grey sky, the lively wind and the turquoise crystalline sea. I am part of the landscape, connected to nature as one entity. Here, the sharp edges of my anxious mind, the jagged wounds and the brokenness are softened, soothed and made whole.

The water accepts me exactly as I am, without pretence, agenda or judgement. As I surrender to the water, and to the cold, I also surrender the judgements I have regarding myself – that I am not pretty enough, young enough, slim enough, wealthy or successful enough in the eyes of a society which puts value on these things. In the water, connected with nature, these ideologies become shallow, insubstantial and inconsequential. In that moment of clarity, I accept myself in the same way that I accept the turquoise ocean: like me, in this moment, it simply is.

Mindful of the low temperature and tuned into how my body feels, I conclude that it's time to get out. The shock of gravity after leaving the weightlessness of the sea equates to an ungainly clumsiness as I try to rush over to where I've left my backpack. Feet stumbling over the pebbles and rocks, I dry myself as quickly as possible. The rough, cotton towel dragged frantically over my wind-exposed skin feels raw and torturous, but the friction it generates warms me, alongside the spreading glow of returning blood flow to the colder parts of my body.

I throw on a soft, thick winter sweater the colour of the ocean that I have just been immersed in, along with some cosy, fleece-lined leopard print jogging bottoms. I am suffused with warmth, overflowing with gratitude and my heart is completely full.

My van is parked beyond the cliffs, up a steep, precarious track. I shoulder my rucksack and head up, taking in the rugged landscape as I climb, glowing from within. The wind is gusting and has a biting edge to it, bringing colour to my cheeks and nipping at my exposed fingers like a vengeful kitten. Returning to where my van is parked, I open the side door and step into the still, warm air within. Emptying my rucksack, I hang the damp towel on its usual drying rack, which is on the back of the front passenger chair. I pull out a flask of hot chocolate that I made before the swim and lay back to lounge on my soft, cosy bed. As the tingle of my skin slowly subsides, I settle into sleepy contentment, sip the sweet hot chocolate and watch the white breakers of distant waves curl and crash beyond the glass of my window. There's nowhere that I need to be and nothing that I need to do. My mind is free from worry and anxiety, allowing me the headspace to just simply be. I am so grateful for this moment, for the moments like this that have come before and for the moments that are still to come.

*   *   *

Everything is transient. However difficult my life was before, and however hard I found it to bear, it was only a matter of time before things changed, before I changed and before how I felt changed, such is the nature of life. In my darkest days, it was impossible to imagine that I would feel differently, that I could, and would, experience peace and happiness. That all I had to do was keep going, and eventually the darkness would lift and I would find myself, the true me, on the other side.

Creating more physical and mental space by existing with less doesn't require living alternatively or in a way which may be considered unconventional. It's simply about adopting a different way of thinking, actively choosing to search for meaning, value and purpose beyond the material. Rather than measuring happiness or success by what is owned, I've learnt to measure those concepts in different ways; the places I've visited, the people I've met and connected with, the mountains I've hiked, the art I have created, the art created by others that I've been moved by, the sunrises and sunsets I have witnessed, and the kindness I have both experienced and demonstrated.

Breaking free from the conditioning which teaches us that ownership of things makes us happy or is a measure of our success is one of the most liberating, transformative and positive changes that any person could make. And anyone can make that change. You don't have to live in a van, a caravan or a tent.

Owning moments, rather than things, begins by creating more space for these moments to inhabit. After my house was repossessed, it seemed that the less I owned and the more my financial outgoings were reduced, the more my mind became free. I was gradually unburdened from the stress, worry and struggle that I'd always thought was an integral part of life. It absolutely isn't, and it doesn't have to be. Reducing my financial outgoings meant that I was able to decrease the hours that I needed to work and could prioritise spending time in nature and with the people I love over working forty hours a week to own or pay for things that didn't nourish me in any meaningful way.

I had the capacity, finally, to focus on health and well-being, both mental and physical.

Time exists in an account that cannot be topped up, regardless of wealth or status. It is a finite resource available to all living creatures, and the amount that we have is not only completely unique to each of us, but also unknown. The pressures of making ends meet and living comfortably can sometimes feel like there is no choice in how our time is spent. From my experience, I can honestly say that there is more choice than I could have ever imagined.

Start small and think big . . . think wide-open landscapes, a clear mind, a living space free from clutter and a life free from the tyranny of debt. Anything is possible if we have the courage to change and the bravery to put something of ourselves out into the world.

Thank you for reading my journey so far.

I wish you all love, but, most importantly, I wish you all the freedom that you deserve.

Epilogue

Firstly, thank you for reading my story; certain aspects of it were difficult to write, and I expect that they may have also been difficult to read. Yet, as you navigated the words on the pages, just as I navigated the experiences of my life so far, I hope that you were left with a feeling of, well, hope, a sense of increased possibility and, for those of you who have shared similar experiences to myself, a feeling of comfort.

It's possible to transform the nature of trauma, adversity or suffering into whatever we choose to channel that energy into – this book is proof of that, which may have been written by me, but is comprised of the energy and humanity of all the people who have moved me towards this point.

I know that it may not be possible for everyone to get rid of all their material possessions, tell their bank or landlord to stick their rent/mortgage up their, erm, jumpers and drive off into the sunset in a campervan, but there are aspects of vanlife, and of my life, of living more lightly in the world, that can be applied to any life, with wonderful and positive results:

Stuff/things/clutter: I've never really understood the point of a decorative plate; if you can't eat your dinner off it (which, if it's hung vertically on a wall, would defy the laws of gravity and could get incredibly messy, especially if gravy is involved), then why bother with them in the first place? And display cabinets, what's that all about? A whole piece of furniture, which takes up loads of space and collects dust, designed purely to contain and showcase a load of miscellaneous knick-knacks that do nothing but take up space and collect dust. Don't get me wrong, material things have certainly provided me with comfort in the past, or distracted me from feelings that caused discomfort. And from my own experience, it's clear that a lot of the objects that we own have memories and emotions attached to them; they remind us of the people we love and the moments that we have shared together.

Moving from a house to a large caravan, then to a small caravan and, finally, to a campervan, transformed the relationship that I had with material things, as did the mindfulness counselling that I received. I learnt how to comfort myself, to sit with sometimes distressing thoughts and feelings, and to ease the busyness of my mind without running off to TK Maxx to change how I felt by buying something that I didn't need and that I'd likely never soddin' wear.

For years, my nanna collected paperweights of every size, colour and shape imaginable. I'm surprised that her display cabinet didn't go through the floorboards of her little terrace house, the word 'weight' in paperweight being of some importance when calculating the load-bearing capacity of cheap laminated MDF. When she moved into assisted living due to ill health, she gave me her paperweight collection, which I proudly displayed on my windowsill when I lived in a conventional house. When the house was repossessed and I moved into a caravan, I kept three of my favourite paperweights and took the rest to a charity shop. The time came when I made the decision to live full-time in a campervan and, by then, I was down to one paperweight: it was made of translucent blue resin and had a real flower with white petals tinged with pink hovered over by an actual bee (dead, of course, poor thing) preserved within. I didn't have any use for a paperweight in a campervan (to be honest, they're reasonably use-less anyway, even when employed for their intended purpose . . . it's not like you get strong westerlies blowing through the office on a regular basis) and yet I was loathe to relinquish it to the charity shop. It was a gift from my nan, and it brought her to my mind when I held it. But did I really need it, this physical manifestation of memory? This object which confirmed my identity, that I was someone's granddaughter, part of a family and loved? No, I don't think I did. My head holds the memories of the moments that I've shared with my nan, and the internet, via social media and digital storage, holds far more, in the form of photos and videos, than my mind ever could. And, after years of insecurity, I now know, with-out the need for physical evidence, that I am loved. I released the weight of the paperweight back into the world (in other words, I took it to the Sue Ryder charity shop) and I felt a little bit lighter as a result.

Arty inspirational things: Owning fewer things, for me, has meant that I have more headspace, increased living space in my van, more disposable income for adventures (on account of not buying all the things) and an increased capacity to connect, with the people around me, myself and my environment. This lifestyle choice can have positive results for anyone and everyone, regardless of whether you live in a house, a flat, a caravan, a boat, a campervan, a tent, a shepherd's hut or a shed. That's not to say that I don't appreciate art and objects of beauty; I absolutely do. I strongly believe that view-ing or interacting with art, in its many forms and formats, can be the spark that lights the fire for further creativity and positive change, however that may manifest. The handy thing about art, interesting artefacts and beautiful objects is that there are amazing spaces spe-cifically dedicated to displaying them, like exhibition halls, galler-ies and museums. Accessing these spaces (many of which are free to enjoy) may minimise the number of objects bought, stored or displayed at home, and will also get you out of the house (or van, or tent, or shed, and so on) and into a community area where the experience of viewing or engaging with art is shared.

The concept of home: The vast array of structures, machines and buildings that I have called home over the years – from stone houses, plastic caravans and metal campervans, right through to canvas tents – has taught me, alongside the words of my friend Andrew Varley, that home doesn't have to be a place, a physical property or premises, it can be so much more. True home can be a feeling, a way of being, the groundedness and steadfast assurance that comes with fully accepting ourselves and others – and indeed life – exactly as we are. Home is something that we all carry within us; wherever we are in the world, we are always home.

Soft fascination: Throughout this book, I've discussed connecting with nature and the positive effect that being outdoors can have on our well-being. In everyday life, we are constantly bombarded with stimulation, from glaring shop signage, continuously beeping smartphones, flickering TV screens, views that are crowded with buildings of every shape and size, and cars that fill the roads with their frantic energy. All of this requires our direct attention; in fact, it demands it, whether we want to give it or not, which can have a negative effect on our energy levels and mental clarity. 'Voluntary and passive attention' are concepts devised by the philosopher, historian and psychologist William James. Rachel and Stephen Kaplan, professors of psychology, who specialised in environmental psychology, referred to passive attention as 'soft fascination'. Soft fascination is a state of being, a way of paying less direct attention, that soothes the mind and is often achieved by spending time in a natural environment. Sitting on a soft sandy beach, watching gentle waves rolling in from the sea, presided over by slow-moving, ponderous clouds or walking through woodland, taking in the various hues of green in the breeze-caressed canopy above is a lot less demanding of our attention than, say, going to IKEA on a Saturday afternoon.

The sea is a swimming pool (but please follow RNLI safety guidelines and be aware of tidal patterns at all times): And it truly is, well, when the various water companies aren't pumping sewage into it. The world is also our garden, which works really well as we can enjoy delightful flora and fauna without having to piss about watering or feeding it (unless you have an actual garden, in which case you'd better pop out and check on the petunias). What I'm trying to say is, I view my van home as a place to sleep, cook, eat, store clothes and reset; for anything else beyond that, there's an entire world to access. Reducing my material things has meant that the space I take up with my existence is minimal, which enabled me to downsize my 'house', as it were, and reduce the expenditure required to run a home. This upsized my disposable income, allowing me to work less, but experience so much more. I do most of my actual 'living' – whether that's hiking, swimming, yoga, socialising, sports and fitness, or attending art classes, craft workshops, exhibitions and museums – outside of my home. As a result of this, I've found that I naturally interact more with others, accessing and being part of various communities, from the yoga studio crew to the staff and regulars at the church café where I sometimes hang out. Being part of something beyond myself increases my feelings of well-being and connectedness and affirms that I, too, deserve a place in this world. Downsizing isn't always easy, whether it's moving from a house into a campervan, or moving from a bigger place to a smaller one, but it is doable, and the benefits can be life-changing.

Money for moments: We all need cash, that's a fact of life – or at least a fact of the society and age that we currently live in. And let's face it, most jobs do not bring us incandescent joy – they are a means to an end or, as I like to say, a way of earning money so that we can experience more wonderful moments. However, no job and no amount of money is ever worth becoming ill for. I remember working in a role that caused me so much anxiety I would sometimes be physically sick on a Sunday night before my return to work on Monday (it was definitely the job and not the sherry that made me ill, or perhaps the job was the reason I drank the sherry; either way, it wasn't fun). In my opinion, we should earn money so that we can live a life, not live solely to earn money. When my outgoings were vastly reduced by ceasing to buy stuff that I didn't need and by moving into a campervan full-time, I suddenly had more choice regarding what I did to earn money and how often I did it. With a better work/life balance, I found that I was able to deal with stress that may have arisen at work much more effectively and with more resilience: if I'm only working three days a week, for example, I can handle Janet from Accounts flipping her lid because someone licked all the icing sugar off the party rings and put them back in the staff biscuit tin (it wasn't me, by the way, honest). Leaving an employment role that causes distress or illness is a direct act of self-love, however well-paid or prestigious the role may be. Health, happiness and self-worth, for me, come before anything else. I am proof that it's possible to be happy living with very little in a small box, even if that box does have wheels on it. And there are always plenty more fish in the sea, or certainly plenty more jobs on Indeed.

Give to receive: And I don't mean presents, in the traditional sense, but gifts of yourself. From my experience, the more you give to the world, the more it gives back, even when doing so can be sometimes terrifying. When I sent the article to the *Guardian* detailing my life living in a van, I was scared. I feared rejection. I told myself I wasn't good enough or important enough to be published by anyone, in any capacity, ever, that I'd be laughed at and ridiculed by the people in the *Guardian* office who were unfortunate enough to read it. But, as advised by my friend Eleanor ('it's fucking brilliant; fuck it, just send it lass!'), I sent it anyway. What did I have to lose? Absolutely nothing. Yes, I felt incredibly vulnerable and frightened of judgement, and of failure, but I'd been through worse (frankly nothing can be as bad as a four-bottle red wine hangover). And, unbelievably, they liked it so much that they published it. I'd faced my fears and I'd had the courage to put something of myself out into the world. As a result, the world came back to me and said, in a voice very similar to that of the literary agent Simon Trewin, 'Ey up duck, do you fancy writing a book?' (he does do a rather impressive rendition of the Yorkshire accent).

My advice to you is to be brave, be bold, be open and don't be afraid to be vulnerable. It takes more strength to embrace vulnerability than it does to deny it. Paint that picture, write that book, compose that music, send that email, make that call, book those flights, smile at the guy in the train station ticket office, start a conversation with the stranger sitting next to you on the bus – who knows what wonderful things, connections and experiences it may lead to . . . Opportunity is like a river that you are standing on the edge of: occasionally it will rise up of its own accord and sweep you into its current without you having to do a thing, but, more often than not, you'll have to brave the waters, face the fear and jump in, putting yourself in the flow and trusting that where you end up is where you are meant to be.

Acknowledgements

Eleanor Barrett – thank you for being my champion and for showing me that anything is possible; you were right lass, it really is!

Aida Edemariam – thank you for publishing my article in the *Guardian*, which began the wonderful, and surreal, journey of writing this book.

Simon Trewin – if Superman was a literary agent . . . Thank you for making me laugh and for continually astounding me with your profound creativity, for being passionate about my story, for your unwavering support and for your generous gift of a leisure battery when mine lit its last twelve-volt light.

Nicky Ross – Editorial Director and mentor, thank you for your compassion, for taking a chance, for your trust in me, for your guidance and for your wonderful feedback.

Julia Kellaway – editor and amazing human being, thank you for loving this book, for picking it up, like a piece of sea glass on the beach of my mind, and setting it in the polished silver of your immeasurable talent.

Becca Mundy – Publicity Director, wild swimmer, campervan adventurer and all-round awesome human, thank you for pizza and 'meetings' on the beach (best office ever!), and for moving my words forward with your innovation and artistry.

Dawn Mason – Publicity Agent.

Louie Gordon – Publicity Agent.

Mark Smith (and Tommy and Basil, the little doggos).

Philip Freeman – drive 'em on young 'un!

Julie Bradman – thank you for being my mum, for getting on a plane to Guernsey to help cure me of my fear of flying (even though you're more scared than me!), for always being there when I need you and for still loving me during the times when I was hard to love.

Gareth Bradman – thank you for being my family, even during the hard times . . . arguing is just another way of showing love, everyone knows that!

Bryn Price – thank you for your friendship, you are a wonderful human being of many talents (and good hair). Putting up with me for nearly twenty years is surely your most demanding creative challenge yet, long may it continue!

Gordon Wilkinson – expert cabinetmaker, carpenter, joiner, campervan fettler and doom metal drummer, thank you for helping me turn a van into a true home.

Alex Hutchinson (the author Penny Thorpe) – thank you for taking the time to read the first incarnation of this book, all those years ago, the letter you wrote to me was, and is, pivotal in building my confidence and the belief that I have in myself.

Diesel Dave, Simon and Rob – thank you for keeping my many knackered vans on the road for all these years. If you're reading this, can I book in for next Tuesday? I think it's safe to assume that my van will need something fixing/welding/replacing by then.

Alice Cooke – thank you so much for getting up ridiculously early to photograph me, with your amazing talent, at Mevagissey Harbour and for trusting me not to drive us into the sea. I'll always remember the dolphins that we saw that morning, although they were overshadowed by the fat ginger tom cat waiting for his freshly caught fish breakfast.

Andrew Varley

Scott Leach

Acknowledgements

Bobby Weaver
Russell Ashcroft
Courtney Prynne
Dave Giffould
Dave Greaves
Richard Jones
Karl Stoddart
Michelle Gardiner
Lorraine Campbell
Dusty Rhodes
Carole Griffiths
Brian Hindmarch
Matthew Coffey
Rhiannon Coffey

Everyone at the Wave House Cafe in Newquay (including Michael . . . thank you for the rings, poems, stories and cigarettes).

The Windhill Green and Shipley District Nursing Teams.

Seasalt Cornwall, and all the Falmouth shop Seasalt crew – especially Benjamin-Alexander Morris.

Lastly, thank you to everyone who has supported me and gifted me with their friendship, their time, a conversation, an exchange or even just a smile.

Resources

If you are experiencing a mental health crisis which you need urgent support for, don't hesitate to reach out. A 24/7 service, local to your area in the UK, can be found on www.nhs.uk

If you need to talk to someone . . .

ARCH (Abortion Recovery Care and Helpline)
Helping women, men, families and relationships.
0345 603 8501
info@archtrust.org.uk

CALM (Campaign Against Living Miserably)
Suicide support helpline: 0800 58 58 58 (lines open 5pm–midnight every day)
www.thecalmzone.net

Galop
National helpline for LGBT+ victims and survivors of abuse and violence: 0800 999 5428
www.galop.org.uk

MIND
Mental health information and support.
Infoline: 0300 123 3393
www.mind.org.uk

Papyrus
Prevention of young suicide.
Helpline: 0800 068 4141 or text 07860 039967 (24/7 service)
www.papyrus-uk.org

Refuge
For women and children. Against domestic violence.
National domestic abuse helpline: 0808 2000 247 (24/7 service)
www.nationaldahelpline.org.uk

Respect
Helpline for male victims of domestic abuse.
Domestic abuse helpline for men: 0808 801 0327
mensadviceline.org.uk

Samaritans
Call: 116 123 (24/7 service)
Email: jo@samaritans.org
www.samaritans.org

SOS (Silence of Suicide)
Suicide support helpline: 0808 115 1505 (8pm–midnight week-
nights; 4pm–midnight weekends)
sossilenceofsuicide.org

The Mix
Free information and support for under-25s in the UK.
0808 808 4994
www.themix.org.uk

Other support resources

Bereavement: www.cruse.org.uk

Children: www.childline.org.uk

Domestic violence: www.womensaid.org.uk

Financial support: www.turn2us.org.uk, www.citizensadvice. org.uk

Mental health: www.rethink.org, www.giveusashout.org, www.youngminds.org.uk

If you'd like to join a community that gets out and about . . .

Ramblers
Nationwide hiking and walking groups suitable for every fitness level.
www.ramblers.org.uk

The Bluetits Chill Swimmers
Nationwide groups for wild swimming and cold-water bathing.
www.thebluetits.com

In most areas of the UK, and beyond, by searching online or looking on social media platforms, you'll find walking, hiking and swimming groups local to your area. Here are a few that I would recommend, located in my two home counties of Cornwall and Yorkshire:

Cornish Ramblings
A fantastic and friendly community which aims to connect people both with nature and with each other.
www.cornishramblings.co.uk

The Dales Dipper
Les offers fun and comprehensive guided wild-swimming tours of both the Yorkshire Dales and the Lake District.
www.thedalesdipper.co.uk

Socials . . .

If you'd like to continue following my journey, find me on Instagram: @wildwomanintheblue

For further campervan conversion inspiration and ideas, my favourite Instagram accounts are: @eyesopen_vanlife_workshop, @nomads_creations, @vango_fitouts_uk, @croziercampers, @vanlifeconversionsuk, @scandivans.uk, @_camper_camper_, @chcamperconversions, @jorvikvanconversions, @northern_conversions, @method.vans, @trekkvans, @timberandstitchvans, @vanlifebuilds

For wild swimming inspiration, check out the following Instagram accounts: @thedalesdipper, @weswimwild, @wildswimmingcornwall, @theoutdoorswimmingsociety, @seaswimcornwall

books to help you live a good life

Join the conversation and tell
us how you live a #goodlife

 @yellowkitebooks

 YellowKiteBooks

 Yellow Kite Books

 YellowKiteBooks